PRIMITIVE MINDS

PRIMITIVE MINDS

Evolution and
Spiritual Experience in the Victorian Novel

Anna Neill

THE OHIO STATE UNIVERSITY PRESS • COLUMBUS

Library of Congress Cataloging-in-Publication Data
Neill, Anna, 1965–
Primitive minds : evolution and spiritual experience in the Victorian novel / Anna Neill.
p. cm.
Includes bibliographical references and index.
ISBN 978-0-8142-1225-7 (cloth : alk. paper) — ISBN 978-0-8142-9327-0 (cd)
1. English fiction—19th century—History and criticism. 2. English literature—19th century—History and criticism. 3. Spiritualism in literature. 4. Psychology in literature. 5. Psychology and literature. 6. Realism in literature. 7. Literature and science. I. Title.
PR878.P75N45 2013
823'.809353—dc23
2013008650

Cover design by Laurence J. Nozik
Text design by Juliet Williams
Type set in Adobe Garamond Pro

∞ The paper used in this publication meets the minimum requirements of the American National Standard for Information Sciences—Permanence of Paper for Printed Library Materials. ANSI Z39.48–1992.

9 8 7 6 5 4 3 2 1

For Kirk and Connor

ONTENTS

ACKNOWLEDGMENTS

I began writing this book nearly a decade ago when I was new to the fields of nineteenth-century literature and evolutionary science. For that reason, I am deeply indebted to the Victorianist friends and colleagues who encouraged and guided me and who read (sometimes multiple) drafts of portions of the manuscript. I owe a great deal especially to Dorice Elliott, Talia Schaffer, and Pamela Thurschwell. Other readers and advisors who helped me enormously include Sebastian Black, Byron Caminero-Santangelo, Marta Caminero-Santangelo, Joseph Carroll, Santanu Das, Vicky Eden, Jocelyn Harris, Linda Hughes, Michael Neill, Phil Wedge, and anonymous reviewers. The students in my 2008 graduate seminar, "Evolution and the Victorian Novel," responded generously to my prodding about some of the issues discussed here and gave me much to ponder. The English Departments at the University of Otago and University College London, and the Department of Humanities and Western Civilization at the University of Kansas, all kindly hosted me as a speaker on the book's topic and gave me wonderful feedback. I am also grateful to Dawn McGinnis at the Clendening History of Medicine Library at the University of Kansas Medical Center for her considerable help and support in the early phases of the project.

Portions of several chapters of this book have already appeared in print, and I would like to thank Cambridge University Press and Johns Hopkins University Press for their permission to reproduce the material here:

> Chapter 2: "Evolution and Epilepsy in *Bleak House.*" Reprinted with permission from *SEL Studies in English Literature 1500–1900* 51, no. 4 (Autumn 2011).
>
> Chapter 3: Copyright © 2008 by the Johns Hopkins University Press. This article, "The Primitive Mind of *Silas Marner,*" first appeared in *ELH* 75.4 (2008), 939–62. Reprinted with permission by the Johns Hopkins University Press.
>
> Chapter 4: "The Savage Genius of Sherlock Holmes," first published in *Victorian Literature and Culture* 37, no. 2 (2009).

The project was supported by the University of Kansas General Research Fund awards 2301445, 2301247, and 2301023. The Hall Center for the Humanities at KU generously assisted me with grant proposals related to the project. I am also grateful to Joanne Wilkes and the University of Auckland English Department for hosting me as an Honorary Research Fellow during the final writing stages. During that time, too, I was privileged and honored to be working in the private study of the late Dame Judith Binney.

I also owe tremendous thanks to Sandy Crooms and the other editorial, production, and marketing staff at The Ohio State University Press, especially Maggie Diehl, Juliet Williams, and Laurie Avery.

Finally, I owe perhaps the greatest debt to my family, especially my son, Connor, and to the dear friends in Lawrence and elsewhere who anchored me during the difficult years that this book tries indirectly to describe.

EVOLUTION AND THE DREAMY MIND

> Ancient traditions, tested by severe processes of modern investigation, commonly enough fade away into mere dreams: but it is singular how often the dream turns out to have been a half-waking one, presaging a reality. Ovid foreshadowed the discoveries of the geologist: the Atlantis was an imagination, but Columbus found a western world: and though the quaint forms of Centaurs and Satyrs have an existence only in the realms of art, creatures approaching man more nearly than they in essential structure, and yet as thoroughly brutal as the goat's or horse's half of the mythical compound, are now not only known, but notorious.
>
> —Thomas Henry Huxley, *Evidence as to Man's Place in Nature* 9

It is curious that Thomas Huxley begins his essay "On the Natural History of Man-like Apes" (1863) with a reference to the prophetic content of waking dreams. Dream, prophecy, and artistic imagination are, on the face of it, anathema to the rigor of nascent professional science that Huxley represents in mid-nineteenth-century Britain. Creation stories and magical teleologies are precisely what the theory of natural selection ejects from natural history, and Huxley had defended the theory on Darwin's behalf in 1860. Yet in this rather surprising passage, Huxley rhetorically folds the history of science into the projections of dreamy or mystical vision. In his description, the "mere dreams" of religion and art that should vanish under the pressure of Darwinian evolution are not discarded as the detritus of a pre-modern past but instead mutate into prophetic intuition. The "half-waking" state in which prevision occurs reveals a primordial power of awareness whose discoveries empirical knowledge will subsequently confirm.

Huxley links evolutionary science with the stuff of dream as a preface to his record of travelers' descriptions of chimpanzees, gibbons, and orangutans. In other nineteenth-century British applications of evolutionary theory, how-ever, dreamy visions become a central object of medical investigation or, alter-natively, a vehicle of explanation that may compete or even converge with scientific inquiry. For Victorian psychology, the dreamy mind offered a rich source of information about the history and nature of unconscious mental processes, nervous organization and the brain, and about human intellectual development. In imaginative literature, the physiology of dreamy states—including the study of those nervous arrangements that produce clairvoy-ance, expanded reminiscence, double-consciousness, or simply a brief shift of awareness such as déjà vu—influences character and events often as pow-erfully as conscious motives or uncontrollable passions do. In realist fiction especially, a character's or narrator's dreamy awareness often provides insight into human nature, social bonds, and heredity, intuiting connections that careful, clinical observation and documentation cannot capture, or at least not as quickly.

Primitive Minds explores how dreamy, usually spiritual, experience inter-sects with the findings of evolutionary science in the Victorian realist novel—a form that rose largely as an expression of secular culture and scientific method.[1] In combination with its patient accumulation of observable facts about the physical and social worlds it describes, the novel also rests its claim to modernity on the creation of a narrative first-person or omniscient, cen-tered consciousness, whose finely tuned responses to environment and broad observational talents make it a suitable instrument for delivering such facts to the reader. This conception of literary responsibility to the evidence of the senses, to the depiction of contemporary events, and to concrete social experience is very remote from Sir Philip Sidney's idea of the poet as one who converts the brazen world of reality into a delightful, golden imitation of it. Yet it involves a conversion process nonetheless. In its endeavor to depict "things as they are," realist narrative consciousness transforms what N. Katherine Hayles calls "the inherently unknowable and unreachable flux" of a reality "out there" into the constructed concepts that constitute our human world.[2] However limited its direct communication of the real, this narrative awareness can, in György Lukács's formulation, open a "multitude of doors" or perspectives that together bridge the gap between individual experience and the otherwise invisible social totality.[3] This transformative dimension of realism reminds us that its narrative mode does not claim to be transparent. Rather, realism selects among substantial objects and then demands we make sense of such objects and their relation to one another.[4] *Primitive Minds* asks what happens when the world-organizing narrative mind within the realist text malfunctions, even slightly.

If realism negotiates between mind work and facts in the world, then, as Jason Tougaw argues, it has clear affinities with mental science. In the form of the case study, he shows, subjective human story converges with the objective medical diagnosis, to produce an interpretation of experience that comes at once from inside and outside the mind.[5] The discerning mind must itself be scrutinized for aberrancies and distortions of the world it tries to reveal. This introduces a medical component to the phenomenon of self-abnegation that George Levine recognizes in realism. Realist novels, in Levine's account, insist upon the annihilation of self in the interests of producing objective knowledge. At the same time, this self-erasure leaves an ethical residue in the form of a constraint upon the very situatedness that it recognizes and resists.[6] Levine posits an abstract, self-conscious, once-removed mind, remote from the nervous tissue that houses it.

However, the artful fluctuations between situated perspective and objective knowledge that underpin realist representation in Levine's analysis may be destabilized through the flesh-and-blood environment of the body. Under certain nervous conditions, boundaries between self and world risk dissolving as either the immediate surroundings become enormously remote from mental experience and surrender to its dreamy creations or else as the mind feels itself merging with a world whose dimensions and details may become fantastic. These usually mystical experiences are not simply objectified by the force of rational, diagnostic voices in the text, for they involve forms of awareness operating beneath either the threshold of the unified self or reasoning thought.[7] While they are so anchored in the body that they indicate pathological mental events or at least temporary cerebral malfunction, these experiences nevertheless expand awareness beyond the reach of ordinary sense perception, linking events and images across space and time or seeing into the minds of others. Nineteenth-century physiological psychology frequently identifies events that compromise the highest operations of the human mind in this way with an evolutionarily lower state. Endeavoring to combine the visionary potential of the mind with scientific knowledge about it, realist narrative fiction exploits the capacious dimensions of dreamy awareness while preserving allegiance to the new discoveries about human nature made by evolutionist mental science.

By focusing on a form that foregrounds the mediation of knowledge by the mind and its aberrancies, *Primitive Minds* thus continues the scholarly investigation of the epistemological unit of the fact that Mary Poovey calls for in *The History of the Modern Fact*.[8] Victorian realist novels remind us that the counterpart of the modern fact is what Thomas Nagel christened the "view from nowhere," in which subjective awareness is modified by general concepts that enable a more objective grasp of our universe.[9] As Lorraine Daston has shown, a-perspectival objectivity entered the natural sciences by way of eighteenth-century moral philosophy, in which the figure of the "man in general" or Adam Smith's "impartial spectator" modeled an ideal observer, detached from his own natural self-interest.[10] The impartial spectator also becomes the guarantor of narrative truth in realist fiction: the moment-by-moment flow of experience recorded by eighteenth-century epistolary heroines, or the flux of feeling that guides the sentimental raconteur, surrenders to the larger view of detached, omniscient narrators and the confident authority of free indirect discourse. That spectator is also implied in the challenge to individual perspective: the element of suspense in realist novels encourages a "skeptical pause" in which readers examine the beliefs that lie behind their expectations, as Caroline Levine has argued; or, as Elizabeth Deeds Ermath has shown, they allow multiple perspectives to converge, abstracting or rationalizing consciousness and creating spatial and temporal continuity among those viewpoints.[11] Yet these suspensions of individual interest or perspective do not preclude a different kind of self-loss, in which interior landscapes overwhelm or merge with external objects. Such events are rehearsed in narrative fiction as spiritualizations of objective fact—disturbances in perception like the intrusion of past, future, or physically remote events or personalities onto present and immediate circumstances. Spectral intrusions of this kind onto the social and natural landscape do not so much undo these facts about the world as explore their unexpected and tremulous dimensions.

Nineteenth-century medical investigations of dreamy or altered consciousness embrace everyday changes in conscious awareness as well as more radical distortions of perspective associated with changes in nervous organization. These studies, framed by evolutionist accounts of mental development, document experiences of heightened awareness, of the mind fusing with a greater universe, of direct communication with God, or simply of the uncanny or inexplicably familiar, endeavoring to link such episodes with specific, retrogressive events in the brain and nervous system. Correspond-ingly, in realist novels of the period, narrative distortions of the mind-world relationship point to the influence of these new investigations of the physical basis of mind. In the novels, however, such distortions also unlock percep-tions of the "real" beyond the lens of ordinary human consciousness, disturb-ing the perceived arrangement of objects and events in space and time. In this respect, they disturb the "cultivated detachment" that Amanda Anderson sees as an ambivalent ideal in the Victorian novel, not so much by empha-sizing situatedness or organicism, as in their attention to the involuntary or reflex activity that produces an excessively subjective or dreamy experience of the world.[12] The dreamy mind opens a space in the realist narrative fab-ric for the supernatural, that is, for apparitions, clairvoyance, prevision, and ecstatic communication with the dead or the divine. These spiritual episodes are not merely objects of scientific curiosity in the novels, for they form the very perceptual basis by which these narratives are able to discern significant connections among characters, objects, and everyday human events.

This is the place to explain that by "dreamy," I do not mean the state associated with ordinary night sleep. Although Victorian neurologists and psychologists sometimes commented on night dreaming alongside other forms of reduced consciousness, the "dreamy state," a term coined by the neurologist John Hughlings Jackson to describe the intellectual symptoms of epileptic and postepileptic episodes, refers to exotic phenomena produced in nervous disintegration that range from the expanded reminiscence of déjà vu to double consciousness, the sense of a former life, or even ghost sightings. Victorian psychologists increasingly identified abnormal nervous arrangements at the origin of unusual mental events and spiritual experi-ences, including artificial and spontaneous hypnotism, telepathy, and second sight; the suspended animation of cataleptic states; and spiritualist phenom-ena. They recognized these mental wonders both as mundane physiological events and as evidence of the mind's extraordinary recessed powers. Scruti-nized scientifically, these strange and often marvelous psychical productions could be exposed as nervous epiphenomena and yet, on the other hand, highlight the unfathomable gifts of the mind, thereby reintroducing spiritual questions to empirical investigation.[13]

Although I assign the term "dreamy" to describe this range of spiritual experiences, the title of this book, *Primitive Minds*, evokes the evolutionary dimension to Victorian studies of mind. "Primitive," in this context does not necessarily refer to non-European cultures or to supposed biological differ-ences among "races," although these meanings did also belong to texts using racial science and criminal anthropology such as those I discuss in chapters

1 and 4. Principally, it suggests both an earlier stage in the history of species (whereby certain neuro-pathological conditions resemble the nervous arrangements of other animals) and a developmentally lower level of organization in the individual nervous system to which a complex organism might, often temporarily, return. Understanding nervous disorders in evolutionary terms also meant focusing on the interaction between mind and environment, again both to understand what shapes the deep history of the species and to trace the degree to which mental events respond to and represent external realities—itself a factor in individual development. As episodes of "nervous dissolution," dreamy states represent "lower" forms of mind. Yet, for some investigators of mesmerism and spiritualism, they also offered therapeutic potential or suggested the future reach of the human mind beyond its narrow dependence on ordinary sense perception.

In his 1874 presidential address to the British Association for the Advancement of Science, John Tyndall represented the thirst for scientific knowledge as a symptom of the "unquenchable claims of [man's] moral and emotional nature."[14] Elsewhere, he described the religious opponents of evolutionary science as "squatters" in the territory of true investigation.[15] In the 1874 address, however, he struck a different tone, suggesting that the pursuit of knowledge seeks fulfillment as much through Shakespeare or Carlyle as through Newton or Darwin and as much in open-minded theology as in science itself: all intelligent human beings struggle for the "bettering of man's estate."[16] Proposing that the pursuit of moral and spiritual truths complements science, Tyndall traces both forms of inquiry to the "yearnings" of human thought, as it strives for the satisfying conceptions that it can never quite fix or attain.[17] These longings belong to both physical and moral dimensions of human nature; they suggest that scientific investigation may be stimulated by open, nondogmatic, and yet spiritually guided modes of analysis. It may even be faith-driven questions that demand to know how mere molecular relationships can produce the marvelously diverse and complex phenomena of consciousness.[18]

Emphasizing exchanges among science, theology, and literature as a force of inquiry, Tyndall not only recruits faith and literary imagination into the service of advancing science; he also locates such inquiry in the intellectual progress of the human species. Prompted by spiritually driven and lettered exploration of the moral and emotional states that produce human action, science promises to elevate the human intellect and "raise life to a higher level."[19] Just as "the promise and the potency of all terrestrial life"[20] can be traced to matter, human intellect has emerged out of the lower states of feeling and narrow constraints of superstition, unfolding into the freedom of scientific thought. Here, he echoes Huxley's observation in "On the Relations of Man to the Lower Animals" that "the mental progress of the race" can be followed through discoveries illuminating the physical history humans share with other living creatures.[21] Moreover, Tyndall and Huxley both second Darwin's praise in *The Descent of Man* (1871) for the naturalist who can recognize the marvels of natural selection and other forces of heredity that have produced modern intellectual and moral man.[22] For Darwin, examining the moral sense from the perspective of natural history means seeing how human social virtues and the moral acuity that supports them developed: Social organization led to the development of a moral sense while sympathy encouraged the growth of the mental faculties through reflection.[23] Tyndall concurs with Darwin and Huxley that evolutionary science not only discovers the histories of human mental development; it also, along with moral and spiritual growth, provides evidence of such development.

Yet there are numerous Victorian literary accounts of spiritual experience that suggest not species progress but rather the evisceration of the very entities—self, other, space, and time—around which our perception of reality is organized and whose existence is evidence of the complex achievements of consciousness. Alfred Tennyson, who suffered from epileptic seizures, described a state in which "individuality . . . seemed to dissolve and fade away into boundless being."[24] The psychologist and asylum physician James Crichton-Brown identified other accounts of nonpathological and near-universal dreamy phenomena by, especially, Victorian literati: Walter Scott, he notes, describes in *Guy Mannering* the "mysterious, ill-defined consciousness" that constitutes déjà vu;[25] Oliver Wendell Holmes reports accounts of a "conviction [that] flashes through us" of having experienced a precise set of circumstances before, which in some cases produces a feeling of being "like a ghost";[26] and in *A Pair of Blue Eyes*, Thomas Hardy recognizes "those strange sensations we sometimes have, that our life for the moment exists in duplicate, that we have lived through that moment before or shall again."[27] The struggle to find words for sensations that are mysterious, strange, or simply "like" something else more easily described also troubles John Addington Symonds, who is barely able to express the feeling of self-loss that accompanied his sudden trancelike moods:

> Irresistibly [they] took possession of my mind and will, lasted what seemed
> like an eternity and disappeared in a series of rapid sensations which resem-

bled the awakening from anaesthetic influence. One reason why I disliked this kind of trance was that I could not describe it to myself. I cannot even now find words to render it intelligible, though it is probable that many readers of these pages will recognize the state in question. It consisted of a gradual but swiftly progressive obliteration of space, time, sensation and the multitudinous factors of experience which seemed to qualify what we are pleased to call ourself.[28]

The spiritual significance attached to this kind of experience varies enormously. Tennyson's seizures enabled an ecstatic appreciation of the "true life," while Symonds's trances elicit an "awful . . . initiation into the mysteries of skepticism."[29] Yet like Scott's account of illusory reminiscence or Hardy's double consciousness, they represent an altered experience in which awareness is no longer anchored in a bounded self. Such self-loss, or the sense of self dissolving into some greater entity or force, is inevitably charged with transcendental feeling.

Recent investigations of the neural substrate of religiosity have observed the heritability of powerful religious temperament.[30] Other studies have sought to identify specific mechanisms in the brain that trigger what we broadly describe as spiritual experiences: awareness of the presence of God, attaching deep significance to events and objects, magical ideation, a sense of timelessness or distorted space, religious ecstasy, depersonalization, or derealization. Temperolimbic instability or atrophy, associated with epilepsy, explains these unusual or hyperreligious experiences.[31] In the 1940s and 1950s, the neurologist Wilder Penfield was able to artificially stimulate dreamy episodes in epileptic patients, by stimulating areas in the brain that are now recognized to be associated with such states: the lateral temporal neocortex, the anterior hippocampus, and the amygdala. These episodes were characterized by altered relationships to the environment that carried religious significance.[32] V. S. Ramachandran points out that the discovering the existence of a "God module" in the brain, of a tendency to belief that can be investigated experimentally, has no bearing on the question of whether God actually exists.[33] Nevertheless, investigations of the neural circuitry behind spiritual experience discover God in the brain with as much anatomical precision as Descartes located the rational soul in the pineal gland.

The following chapters explore both neuropsychological and literary representations of dreamy disturbances of consciousness in the Victorian period that offer an evolutionist, physical explanation of spiritual experience. Yet by concentrating on the spiritual dimensions of the "neuro-narrative," I show

how the novels resist easy distinctions between evolutionary-materialist and spiritual explanations for the human mind and its relationship to the world it mediates. I examine both scientific and literary texts that recognize in spirituality and its cognate emotional and mental states neither the outcome of nor the trigger for greater intellectual accomplishment but rather a more rudimentary stage of mental development, while the higher faculties such as reason and will are suspended. Borrowing William James's distinction between the "dull habit" of learned or "secondhand" religious life and the "acute fever" of original religious experience, I focus on British medical and literary representations of clairvoyance, prevision, spirit communication, or ecstatic communion with a divine being and their expression in the physiological states of hypochondriasis, epilepsy, catalepsy, hypnotic trance, and reverie which temporarily suspends the brain's higher, conscious activity.[34] The marvelous events associated with dreamy mental states pointed to the nervous pathologies of lower nervous arrangements, but they also revealed latent mental powers as forgotten elements of the physical history of the species.

Marilynne Robinson has recently stressed how the culture of scientific positivism dismisses subjective experience as an illusion that must be reduced to the physical or psychological coordinates that produced it.[35] This project of explaining the self in objective terms, she objects, originates in modernity's polemic against religion. Nineteenth-century medical science, which oversees the emergence of what we consider "respectable" fields like neurology, as well as of so-called pseudo-sciences like phrenology, was a major historical player in the process of physicalizing and demystifying inwardness, because it did much to identify mystical and religious experience as the product of faulty cerebral organization and nervous disorder. Yet in the process of accounting objectively for spiritualized subjective states and the neurally triggered disintegrations of self that underlie them, Victorian investigations of the mind also recognized the rich meanings and considerable human potential that such disorders could engender.

Foregrounding pathological forms of dreaminess, the novels I discuss here all recognize nervous malfunction as simultaneously a sign of organismic retreat to a more primitive mental state and as the occasion for transcending everyday forms of perception. While it sometimes enacts the transcendence of detached omniscience, an otherworldly narrative vision may also be as profoundly embodied as the impassioned narrative voice of sentimental fiction. Whether first-person or "impartial" third-person narrators, these voices often mimic the symptoms of the nervous characters they represent, generating spectral figures, drifting into reverie, falling into trance states that infuse ordinary surroundings with spiritual significance or that freeze the mind's engagement with the external world. Both the disordered and at least temporarily primitive nervous states that these voices represent and the spiritual experiences that they communicate are, I propose, integral to the capacious vision of Victorian narrative realism. In this way, the novel performs what James faults medical materialism for ignoring, namely, the preservation of "spiritual authority" and "judgment" irrespective of the "organic causation" that lies behind it.[36]

By "spiritual" events, I mean those states investigated by medical scientists that range from ecstatic communion with a divine being, to occult communication with the dead and exotic mental phenomena such as clairvoyance, expanded reminiscence, double-consciousness, cataleptic trance, or even simply a brief shift of awareness that seems to invoke another reality. This is, I admit, a somewhat elongated definition. "Spiritualism," strictly speaking, refers to the popular belief beginning (in Britain) in the 1850s in a parallel world of the dead and the capacity of certain sensitive individuals to communicate with it. Victorian reports of rapping, table-turning, levitation, automatic writing, the release of ectoplasm as the spirits took material form were the subjects of wide skepticism as well as a source of conversion, even among scientific figures like Alfred Russell Wallace (who was a prominent advocate of spiritualism as well as Darwin's rival in the discovery of natural selection). Spiritualism was associated with notorious figures, such as the medium Daniel Home, who was said to be able to handle red-hot coals during séance sessions and achieve full-body levitation while in a trance state. Or Florence Cook, who was supposed to have conjured up full form materializations in the form of her spirit contact Katie King. Such phenomena were sometimes exposed as fraudulent, but they also generated inquiry into the nervous susceptibility of both trance mediums and their audiences and thus into the natural origins of apparently supernatural forms of communication. These medical investigations of spiritualist phenomena built on studies of trance states from earlier decades, including investigations of the clairvoyant perception achieved in mesmeric séances in the 1830s and 1840s, of the marvelous power of religious feeling to cataleptically suspend normal organismic response to the environment, and of the power of the unconscious to produce intellectual marvels or religious revelations outside the ordinary demands of consciousness. In each case, lower cerebral events permit spiritual ideas to take hold of the mind. Yet studies of the objective, physical circumstances in which spiritual events occur emphasized the marvelous potential of that buried, "lower" mind even as they identified it as the seat of nervous pathology or malfunction.

Some of this territory has already been plotted in studies of Victorian psychology and the novel. The work of, in particular, Jenny Bourne Taylor, Sally Shuttleworth, Jane Wood, and Athena Vrettos has taught us how Victorian novelists investigated the organic, and increasingly the neurological, origins of altered awareness, yet also where nervous voices in imaginative literature challenged the medical reduction of spiritual experience to neurosis.[37] Especially relevant to my argument, Taylor has also shown how the structure of Victorian novels dramatizes studies of the unconscious, thus "extending and exploring the limits of realism."[38] These expressions of the unconscious and its suppressed forms of knowledge can resist dominant or "conscious" articulations of identity or authority. The novels I explore recognize this alternative, even subversive voice of the unconscious (or, more exactly in this study, of altered consciousness) but they also *merge* the newly authorized sciences of evolutionary biology and physiological psychology with mystical interpretations of unusual mental experience. In imaginative narratives, the dreamy mind itself becomes the vehicle for the expanded, exquisite, even precise awareness to which the new sciences aspire. Dreamy representations are therefore less subversive or counterfactual ways of seeing than they are what Laura Otis describes as "ganglia in a network of organic and technological communications devices";[39] they are intimate with the modern epistemology that liberates awareness from direct sense perception, even as they revisit what the psychiatrist Henry Maudsley described as "intellect in its infancy."[40]

We now know that the Victorian fascination with exotic mental events and the occult did not oppose authorized medical science but rather became integral to the ways that knowledge was remapped in the nineteenth century—through laboratory experiment, new communications technology, and transfers of energy among physical systems. Thanks to Alison Winter, mesmerism is no longer seen as fringe or popular science; instead, she shows, it helped shape mainstream physiology.[41] Nor can Victorian science be understood crudely to reject all spiritualized accounts of natural phenomena. Even as the late nineteenth-century fashion to biologize cultural differences and destinies appeared to squeeze God out of the human story, Roger Luckhurst has stressed, "the emergence of a scientific culture . . . produced other, less predictable effects." These spandrel-like "strange, unforeseen knowledges" included investigations of telepathy and the spiritual afterlife supported by the new discipline of psychical research.[42] Although the study of altered states and psychic phenomena became a contested site for scientific authority, such research itself was intimate with the most up-to-date developments in science and technology.[43]

This discovery that relationships between the authorized and so-called pseudo-science of the psyche in the nineteenth century are complex and overlapping in turn challenges simple distinctions between evolutionary and metaphysical accounts of the mind. The persistence of dreamy, often mystical phenomena in evolutionist psychology and in evolution-inspired, realist literary investigations of the psyche challenges the cartoonish depiction of Victorian faith at war with Darwinian materialism that drives the evolution debate of our own cultural moment. Although the continuities between scientific naturalism and Protestant theology following the publication of Darwin's major works were established some time ago, the compatibility between spiritual experience (in states ranging from voluminous perception to religious ecstasy) and the deep history of human development is yet to be fully unpacked.[44] Recently, Janis McLarren Caldwell has shown how pre-Darwinian exchanges between medical and imaginative literature combine supernatural and scientific representations of the body. For Caldwell, however, the dualistic, natural theology of Romantic medicine terminates in Darwin's "unitextual or naturalistic explanation of life."[45] Yet Victorian novels, responding to a variety of evolution theories before and after Darwin, allow spiritualist, superstitious, pagan, or other premodern forms of belief to hover over the naturalist depiction of life in the form of aberrant, or "lower" mental events that reveal life's normally imperceptible dimensions and possibilities. The nervous disarray that underlies not only the obscure motives and self-misreadings of characters but also the peculiar, dreamy quality of narrative voice in realist novels across the period gives a spiritual dimension to stories that otherwise seem to describe the social and psychological toll of life in a scientific and secular world. They illuminate and enlarge the rejuvenating promise of the primitive mind, even as they recognize that mind as the production of a disordered or diseased brain.

In so doing, these narratives evoke Victorian understandings of the *evolution* of mind, not simply its correlation with physical events in the brain. Victorian evolutionism, or the "transmutation" or "transformation" of species, combines a number of biological concepts including common descent, heritable acquired characteristics, increasing organic complexity over time, and gradualism, as well as the theory of natural selection developed by Darwin and (independently) Alfred Russell Wallace. Although different combinations of these principles represent different emphases in evolutionary thought, they are not fixed in opposition to one another, as, for example, both the continuation of use/disuse as a possible evolutionary mechanism and an occasional residual notion of inherent evolutionary progress in Darwin's account of species history illustrate.[46] Indeed, even the Victorian scientific opponents of evolution like Georges Cuvier, the younger Charles Lyell, and Richard Owen, who did not accept species transmutation, developed, respectively, the concepts of catastrophism (which identified extinction as the cause of organic succession), gradualism (slow geological transformation over vast periods of time), and homology (the same organ with varying functions in different animals) that remain integral to evolutionary terminology and debate.[47] In psychology, the principle that organic changes did not follow preestablished, archetypal patterns but instead fanned out in response to changing conditions in the environment produced a new hierarchical understanding of the mind, whose status on the ladder of life reflected its degree of nervous complexity rather than its proximity to God.[48] In this context, nervous pathologies could be recognized as expressions of earlier mental or even premental incarnations, as when the organism reverts to unconscious or reflex behavior. The concept of the primitive mind therefore captures not just the new psychology's investigation of the physical origin of mental events but also the evolutionary history within which peculiar mental experiences can be seen in fullest explanatory relief.

My emphasis on the way Victorian psychology frames spiritual experience with human evolutionary history also precludes any direct focus on Freud's account of the unconscious, which in other ways might seem relevant to this study. The fin-de-siècle texts discussed in chapters 4 and 5 of course overlap with Freud's early publications on the subject, including the studies on hysteria with Joseph Breuer (1895), *The Interpretation of Dreams* (1899), and the essays on sexuality (1905).[49] Freud's debt to Jean-Martin Charcot's study of the pathophysiology of nervous illnesses also positions him within the historical scope of this book. Moreover, because he was at once resolutely materialist in his approach to questions of belief and yet both profoundly superstitious and reluctant to engage with occult phenomena in his own practice or research, he reveals a bifurcated attitude to spiritualism characteristic of many of the mental scientists who preceded him.[50] In the early 1920s, he wrote several papers on forecasting dreams and on telepathy, arguing that the former contained infantile wishes projected onto the future, but that there might be evidence for the existence of the latter.[51] Yet in other ways, Freud represents an end to the particular configuration of neurological, evolutionist, and spiritual accounts of mental experience that formed the psychological landscape of Victorian realist novels. His work focused on the unconscious as a *universal* scene of malfunction. As Robinson argues, this "universal yet radically interior dynamic of self" made that unconscious a site of unequivocally post-metaphysical inquiry.[52] In both the medical studies and novels I read here, states of reduced consciousness are

primitive sites of abnormal nervous disarray and often of expanded awareness and untapped human potential. In the realist novel especially, altered
consciousness becomes the meeting place of two seemingly irreconcilable
ways of seeing. Evolutionary science and spiritualism—two of the great Victorian "discoveries"—offer competing claims on the dreamy mind but also,
cooperatively, map its considerable reach.

I. CORPOREAL SPIRIT:
THE EVOLUTION AND DISSOLUTION OF MIND

Victorian investigation of "God in the brain" updated the question of the
material soul that preoccupied associationist psychology.[53] In keeping with
a philosophical tradition that looked back to David Hartley's theory of the
nervous transmission of ideas, and beyond that to John Locke's substitution
of sensation and reflection for an innate content in consciousness, Thomas
Huxley claimed in 1866 that all mental activity is the product of physical
laws: "even while the cerebral hemispheres are entire, and in full possession
of their powers, the brain gives rise to actions that are as completely reflex as
those of the spinal cord."[54] No longer the host of a divinely inspired capacity
for reason that privileges human beings above all other living things, mind
in Huxley's formulation becomes merely the epiphenomenon of the nervous
system.

Such stark materialism was far from uncontroversial, even among the
scientifically minded in the mid-nineteenth century. The "discourse of the
soul," Rick Rylance has shown, remained the primary philosophical influence on Victorian medical practice, maintaining reformist confidence in
the power of the higher, God-given faculties to dominate the lower, animal impulses. Although it did not take firm root in the medical establish-
ment, phrenology—a powerfully materialist approach to personality from
the first half of the century that mapped a hierarchy of mental faculties
onto the brain—insisted that the human mind could transcend its fundamental physical origins.[55] Even Huxley himself proposed in *Evolution and
Ethics* that "intelligence and will . . . may modify the conditions of existence."[56] Moreover, cerebralist approaches to the mind were not necessarily
irreligious. The new physiologically based psychology often either incorporated Protestant concepts of the soul or reconfigured these concepts within a
natural framework that united soul and body.[57] Although it faced a considerable challenge in studies of the physical world that denied the special status
of human beings, natural theology maintained a foothold in the physical

sciences because the latter could be said to reveal, in the physiologist William Carpenter's words, "the wisdom and beneficence of the Divine Author of the universe."[58]

Still, it cannot be denied that the privileged status of human beings in the Christian universe was enormously strained by nineteenth century mental science and its debt to evolutionary theory. Evolutionary biology transformed the mechanical human body, which for all but the most committed eighteenth-century materialists housed an animating or rational soul, into a dynamic organization characterized, like all living things, by the organization, integration and mutual adjustment of parts, and their development or shifting function over time.[59] Already, at the turn of the century, Erasmus Darwin had captured this deep history of the mind and its relationship to individual growth in his effort to explain "[h]ow the first embryonfibre, sphere or cube / Lives in new forms" and "[l]eads the long nerve" or "expands the impatient sense."[60] Darwin's emphasis on the embodied mind positioned those animal motions that emerge as mental events in the brain within a principle of common descent. "The Great Creator," he proposed, "has infinitely diversified the work of his hands, but has at the same time stamped a certain similitude on the features of nature that demonstrates to us that *the whole is one family of one parent.*"[61] With such understanding, he proposed, medical knowledge should draw on the macro-history of animal movements that determine all emotional and intellectual activity as well as all "production, growth, diseases and decay of the animal system."[62] Robert Chambers's enormously popular, anonymously published *Vestiges of the History of Creation* (1844) similarly argued, albeit within a natural-theistic vision of God's evolutionary "plan," that lower animals demonstrate rudimentary faculties of reason and that despite our greater development, we are "bound up . . . by an identity in the character of our organization with the lower animals."[63] In this respect, he anticipated Charles Darwin's assertion in *The Descent of Man* (1871) that the distinctly human talents of abstraction and self-consciousness have "evolved through the development and combination of the simpler ones" and that human minds are therefore distinguishable from those of other animals only by their level of complexity.[64]

Victorian novelists, as consumers of, contributors to, and in some cases, editors of serial publications, were immersed in the cultural issues surrounding evolutionary biology and mental health that concerned the middle-class reading public.[65] The careers of several prominent intellectuals also highlight intimacies between science and literature in the period: George Henry Lewes, of course, was a physiologist as well as a philosopher and literary critic and, along with George Eliot, belonged to the same salon as Herbert

Spencer and Huxley; Alexander Bain, the founder of *Mind*, the "first English journal devoted to Psychology,"[66] which is sometimes thought to mark its strict disciplinary beginnings, also held the title, among others, of professor of literature;[67] Charles Darwin famously mourned the disappearance of poetry from his reading life.[68] C. P. Snow's mid-twentieth-century lament at the impoverishment of intellectual life by divisions between the "two cultures" of science and the humanities would have resonated for the participants in what Luckhurst calls the "uneven process" of science's professionalization before the end of the century.[69]

These porous intellectual boundaries between imaginative culture and evolutionary science allowed literary figures to express concern about what seemed like biological determinism in the new physiologically based psychology. Charlotte Brontë, scientifically literate and phrenologically inclined, was nonetheless enormously disturbed by her friend Harriet Martineau's claim in *Laws of Man's Nature and Development* (1851) that material conditions proved "the origin of all religion, all philosophies, all opinions, all virtues, all spiritual conditions and influences."[70] G. H. Lewes and George Eliot were sympathetic to investigations of the physiological and evolutionary origins of intellectual and spiritual events, yet nonetheless refused to see intelligence and will as merely the calculable effects of a set of physical causes or as an expression of "molecular changes" in the efferent nerves.[71] Eliot insisted on a volitional self, even if it were formed out of the external and internal contingencies of circumstance—a self, she claimed, that in turn exercises influence over the conditions of thought.[72] Lewes, while recognizing that objectively, mental phenomena arise out of organic events, stressed that mind develops subjectively as individuals adjust to their social environments. Such interaction, he proposed, was stored as experience and released in the form of choice, enabling those individuals to respond in a variety of ways to external pressures.[73]

The endeavors of mental science to restore soul to matter through evolutionary theory (or more specifically a theory of transmutation based in the relationship between an organism and its environment) depended on linking the development of species to the growth of the individual. In "The Development Hypothesis" (1852), Spencer pointed to individual development, or the emergence of complex organisms from simple embryonic beginnings, to demonstrate the evolution of species through successive modifications, stressing there is no evidence whatsoever for special creation. Because we can witness the process of modification under the pressure of environmental influences or through the exercise of particular organs or faculties at the expense of others in growing organisms, it is easy to fathom how, over the course of millions of years and under the influence of changing varieties of condition, such modifications would eventually produce a mammal from what began as a protozoon.[74]

By the end of the1860s, the new mental science had gained institutional footing, and metaphysical inquiry into the powers of static mental faculties had begun to lose ground to an organic understanding of consciousness as the product of multiple interactive events.[75] This new approach openly used evolutionary principles of development to represent the brain and nervous system. In his second edition of *The Emotions and the Will* (1865), Bain acknowledged developmentalism as an important supplement to his earlier account of the physical character of emotions, which should be traced through the study of lower animals, savages, and children.[76] In this considerably revised edition, he also uses Spencer's language of "adjustment and adaptation" as he describes the reaction of the nervous system to pain and shock.[77] In a review of Charles Darwin's *Expression of the Emotions in Man and Animals* (1872), Bain announced his intentions to revise *The Emotions and the Will* once again so as to further accommodate evolutionary principles.[78] The third edition in 1888 then included a chapter on "Evolution as applied to mind."

Yet it was Lamarckism, rather than Darwinism, that tooled Victorian mental science with an explanation of species change over time and provided the evolutionary model that would dominate nineteenth-century physiological psychology, more powerfully in many ways than the theory of natural selection.[79] Jean-Baptiste Lamarck's theory of the inheritance of acquired characteristics stressed the actions of individual organisms in the emergence of new, heritable traits, and it emphasized animal preferences rather than blind selection as the mechanism of evolutionary change. Lamarck proposed that, by developing habits of use and disuse, individual organisms acquired physical modifications that they then passed down to their offspring—a model for descent with modification as well as for increasing complexity in all life forms.[80] In the context of the new psychology, "evolution" refers to both to progressive phylogeny and to development in the individual brain. These levels of development merge, not only in Ernst Haeckel's proposition that "ontogeny recapitulates phylogeny"[81] but also in Lamarck's account of the influence of habit and the heritability of modified characteristics. Evolution in the individual organism is an event in the evolution of the species; each organism arrives at increasingly complex cerebral arrangements and communicates these to subsequent generations, suggesting that the mind, like the neck of the giraffe in Lamarck's best-known example, becomes strengthened and enlarged, so as to make the most of its environment.

Lamarck describes such changes as evidence of "that remarkable progression that [animals] exhibit in the complexity of their organization, as well as in the number and development of their functions."[82]

Darwin himself proposed in *The Descent of Man* (1871) that, in the development of human mental powers, natural selection worked in combination with the inherited effects of habit. Overall, Darwin's theory of selection had limited influence on the physical study of mind before James reintroduced the concept of selection to inherited mental characteristics.[83] To some extent this may have been because natural selection erased the natural-theological possibility of design at a distance.[84] Yet the agnostic Lewes, who supported other aspects of Darwinian evolution, did not endorse natural selection. Although Lewes emphasized interactions between organism and social milieu over the associationist processes that Bain and Spencer continued to stress, Darwin's exclusive focus on the external conditions of the struggle for existence, he objected, ignored the organic laws that produce modifications of structure in an individual: "the best-fitted individual survives because of that modification of structure that has given it its superiority."[85] Both Darwin and Spencer recognized the difficulty of accounting for useful inherited variations triggered by specific external pressures. Lewes responded that the "struggle of the tissues and organs enables the adaptation of an organism to its external conditions," thus ripening it for selection, and that some of these effects are "produced by very complex and obscure causes in operation during ancestral development."[86]

For novelists, the idea that an organism's interactions with its environment generate ever-increasing complexity was enormously compelling. Beginning with Defoe and Richardson, psychological realism had explored the development of the interior self and moral feeling in relationship to the exigencies of the external environment. Once such interactions between mind and milieu are framed in evolutionary terms, realist concerns with moment-to-moment experience, the nonheroic dimensions of (usually) ordinary lives, and the objective representation of human behavior become concentrated on at once the development of the individual mind and the deep history of human cerebration. Focused through the lens of mental science, Lamarckism provided realist fiction with the philosophical background to describe not just how characters are transformed by circumstance but also how such transformations represent increasingly complex negotiations between a thinking being and its environment with implications for future generations. In Eliot's novels especially, nuanced shifts in feeling record individual response to circumstance, while these in turn register as minute episodes in greater human stories.

Yet while the trope of increasing complexity seems to influence both characterization and narrative form in realist fiction, the novels I investigate in this book also recognize psychological and neurological studies of a reverse evolutionary movement. Even the very teleologically inclined Spencer questioned the notion of inevitable, unidirectional progress. For him, mental faculties, like all other organic phenomena, are the product of accumulated modifications triggered by interactions between an organism and its environment. Such nervous modifications allow for increasing heterogeneity of form and progressive differentiation of function. This tendency of life (including social life) to move in the direction of complexity, however, is balanced by the principle of *dissolution,* or "a destructive change as opposed to a constructive change—a change by which the definite is gradually rendered indefinite, the coherent slowly becomes incoherent, and the heterogeneous eventually lapses into comparative homogeneity."[87] Spencer's account of the nervous substratum and the organizational structure that determines complex events of consciousness along with his theory of dissolution indirectly exercised considerable influence over later-century neurophysiology.[88]

In particular, John Hughlings Jackson, whose medical essays together contain over 60 references to Spencer's *Principles,* adapted the latter's representations of evolution and dissolution in the physical laws of mind for his neurological studies of epilepsy, including of those dreamy symptoms belonging to what we now know as "complex partial epilepsy."[89] For Jackson, evolution represents movement toward increasingly voluntary activity, while dissolution occurs when the highest, most voluntary centers revert to the simplest and most automatic. In seizure, he proposed, the evolutionary nervous movement from the automatic to the increasingly voluntary is reversed: Dissolution is a " 'taking to pieces' in order from the least organized, most complex and most voluntary, towards the most organized, the most simple and most automatic."[90] The excessive discharge of nervous energy that causes a seizure provokes a loss of voluntary movement and an increase in involuntary or automatic activity, which could be expressed as dreamy or voluminous experience.

Jackson's account of nervous evolution and dissolution had a theoretical successor of sorts in degenerationism. In *Degeneration: A Chapter in Darwinism* (1880), E. Ray Lankester proposed that organisms might adapt to "*less* varied and *less* complex conditions of life," leading to a suppression of form, in some cases bringing an animal to a "*lower* condition, that is fitted to less complex action and reaction in regard to its surroundings" than its ancestors.[91] By the end of the century, questions about the structure of the brain, its production of mystical experience, and the role of the mind in human evolution combined in a powerful narrative of degeneration that identified dreamy or spiritual episodes as a sign of heritable physical decline. Even Henry Maudsley, an asylum physician and editor of the respectable *Journal of Mental Science,* positioned the heritable characteristics of mental illness—many of which could be seen in the symptoms of overactive imagination and hallucination or ecstatic "illumination'—in a degenerative stage in human history.[92] Max Nordau devoted a chapter of his widely read *Degeneration* to the psychology of mysticism, arguing that the mystic's exhausted and "capricious" mind fails to exercise strength of will against an "unrestricted play of associations."[93] The impressions that the nerves communicate to consciousness thus run riot, creating false ideas and judgments of the objective world, which it fills with "ambiguous, formless shadows."[94]

The novels explored in this book assign narrative force to these phantasms, reinvesting the mind with soul at the very point that it seems most physiologically "readable" as an aberrant nervous organization. Identifiable nervous diseases like catalepsy or epilepsy, or the nonpathological dreamy states of reverie or rapture, do not so much explain away their "symptoms"—prophetic vision and trance phenomena including telepathy, clairvoyance, and encounters with the dead or divine—as they provide opportunities for spiritual experience to animate otherwise imperceptible aspects of reality. Evolutionist accounts of the mind, drawn from Lamarck-inspired developmentalism but expanded to account for regressive tendencies in organic life, underpin these narrative studies of nervous insight. Even where, for Doyle and Hardy, Darwinian principles of inheritance determine traits and destinies, episodes of suddenly expanded awareness represent the nervous evolution and dissolution that patterns human responses to the environment. Describing the relationship between second sight and omniscient narration in Eliot's novels, Nicholas Royle reminds us how realist and preternatural sensitivities are linked in *Middlemarch,* where "a keen vision and feeling of all ordinary human life . . . would be like hearing the grass grow and the squirrel's heart beat."[95] Here, Eliot paraphrases Huxley, who illustrated the common physical basis of all life and its marvelously complex but imperceptible configurations by remarking that "the wonderful noonday silence of a tropical forest is, after all, due only to the dullness of our hearing; and could our ears catch the murmur of these tiny Maelstroms, as they whirl in the innumerable myriads of living cells which constitute each tree, we should be stunned, as with the roar of a great city."[96] Evolutionist accounts of the retreating movement as well as the increasing complexities of human nervous organization are what enable such peculiar conflations of science and soul in Victorian realist fiction.

II. WILL, AUTOMATISM, AND SPIRITUAL EXPERIENCE

Although, Huxley argued, the grandeur of human intellectual achievement is illuminated, not reduced, by the evidence of descent from lower animals, yet neither our pursuit of the moral life nor our experience of God is categorically removed from the "selfish passions and fierce appetites" that represent our baser nature as well as the behavioral characteristics of other, lower animals.[97] Victorian investigations of the physiological origins of such phenomena as conversion experience, prevision, and ecstatic somnambulism implicitly rejected distinctions between the higher, soul-sustaining powers of reason, faith, and will and the lower, life-sustaining faculties of sensation and desire. Evolutionary theory's demotion of the will, especially, from an innate, God-given faculty to a developed trait implied that subvolitional or automatic events in the mind-brain need be no less spiritually significant than higher events. In *The Physiology of Mind* (1876), Maudsley suggested that "it would belie observation less to place an ideal entity behind an innate, instinctive impulse of the animal than behind the gradually fashioned will of man."[98] In *Natural Causes and Supernatural Seemings* (1886), he observed that nature does not work "by means of complete minds only,"[99] and that human thought and faith, although regulated by "the common consent of mankind" may emerge from the illusions that accompany defective character.[100] Maudsley emphasized the influence of the incapacitated mind on the development of religious institutions. Yet in *Varieties of Religious Experience,* William James quoted Maudsley's claim in order to show that even the most aggressively positivist interpretation of religious experience must look forward to the net spiritual outcome of revelation and conversion rather than skeptically backward at the natural origins of such events: hysteric fit, poor digestion, overtaxed nerves, or (in epilepsy) a discharging lesion in the occipital cortex may be at the root of supernatural experience, but this should not compromise their spiritual value any more than the neurotic scientist should have his findings dismissed as the epiphenomena of nervous strain.[101]

Some mental physiology did preserve the higher agency of the will as a metaphysical phenomenon independent, or at least semi-independent, of the sensorimotor system. Phrenology, which localized mental faculties in discrete regions of the brain, also proposed that, by deliberate cultivation of the more civilized faculties at the expense of the baser ones, any individual could choreograph his or her own moral improvement.[102] This assumed, of course, that such power of cultivation transcended that of the individual faculties themselves. Despite Carpenter's skepticism about any theory of localization as the basis of psychic phenomena,[103] his account of the will echoed phrenology's model of self-advancement, allowing that any state of consciousness can be subjected to moral judgment and then may be modified by a freedom or power that we have to act in accordance with such judgment (*Principles* 3, 76). This self-determining power, he claimed, can "within certain limits" (5) enable us to shape external circumstances to our own ends. The will restrains the automatic impulses to bodily and mental movement by an effort of attention that in turn increases the nervous tension in a particular region of the cortex concerned with ideation (384). Such mental exercise, with its influence over thought and action, cannot be explained by the physical topography of the brain or reduced to the exchanges between sensory input and cerebral activity that produce ideation. As Carpenter put it,

> To whatever extent . . . we may be ready to admit the dependence of our mental operations upon the organization and functional activity of our nervous system, we cannot but feel that there is *something beyond and above* all this, to which, in the fully developed and self-regulating intellect, that activity is subordinated. (7)

Although Carpenter located the will in a physical environment by observing that individual and social habits played a large role in its formation (423), he stressed its independence from the internal and involuntary movements of the body and proposed that mental health could be measured in the ratio between voluntary and involuntary mental events.[104] He traced the supposed facts of spiritualism, including eye-witness accounts of marvels like materialization or levitation and personal testimonies from Methodist revivalists and camp-meeting participants, to the psychological phenomena of expectancy or suggestion. These "miracles" were produced by automatic cerebral movements responding to a dominant idea.[105] Such emancipation of the mind from the disciplinary activity of the will, he stressed, suggested that converts to spiritualism were close relatives of madmen:

> In all ages, the possession of men's minds by dominant ideas has been most complete when these ideas have been religious aberrations. The origin of such aberrations has uniformly lain in the preference given to the feelings over the judgment [and] the inordinate indulgence of emotional excitement without adequate control on the part of the will. . . . [Such people] are no more to be argued with than insane patients."[106]

In identifying religious transport with insanity, Carpenter drew upon earlier medical literature on nervous pathology and spiritualism. J. D. Esquirol's enormously influential *Mental Maladies* (1817) had identified religious melancholic, ecstatic, and demoniacal possession as conditions triggered by nervous habit, easily excited imagination, and pusillanimous disposition;[107] while James Cowles Prichard proposed in *A Treatise on Insanity* (1835) that the ecstatic affections—expressed in dreaming, somnambulism, delusion, trance, and ecstasy—were suspensions of the external sense that should be linked to pathological mental disorders.[108] Carpenter's confidence in the legislative power of the will also echoed reformist approaches to the treatment of mental illness. In 1843, John Barlow, an associate of the asylum reformist John Conolly, had argued that madness could not be recognized in delusions, per se, but rather in "the want of power or resolution to examine them."[109] Barlow, like Conolly, advocated moral management and cultivation of the will in the insane rather than punishment.

Yet the idea that a robust and independent will could keep lower and lazier regions of the mind from overwhelming the higher and causing physical and mental disease had limited traction in the second half of the century. Physiological investigations into unconscious mental reflexes and latent cognitive processes tended to emphasize the automatic events that remain inaccessible to consciousness. Dreams, trances, somnambulism, and double-consciousness were all, as William Hamilton explained, exotic productions of the brain's "obscure recesses,"[110] and these, far from being restrained by the exercise of the higher faculties, demonstrate the limits of self-disciplining thought. Although the disruption of ordinary consciousness by these recessed powers may indicate deranged activity in the nervous system, they also afford us glimpses into regions of the mind unfettered by ordinary nervous constraints.

This interest in mental automata owed much to Thomas Laycock's 1844 essay on "The Reflex Function of the Brain," which applied Marshall Hall's study of reflex activity to mental phenomena. Reflex motor phenomena, Hall had shown, are independent of sensation, perception, volition, or consciousness. Laycock proposed that encephalic ganglia were also subject to the laws of reflex action, suggesting that multiple involuntary nervous events occur in the cerebrum, accounting for unconscious mental activity. "If the brain be indeed the organ of ideas, and the cerebellum of combined movements, the inference is manifest that they are both excitors of reflex actions."[111] This "automatic action of the cerebrum" represented the same principle that Carpenter named "unconscious cerebration" to describe intellectual activity that takes place outside ordinary waking awareness as an effect of "reflex action in the cerebrum" (*Principles,* 515).[112] Carpenter attributed the phenomena of spiritualism and mesmerism (where genuine and unstaged) to unconscious ideo-motor activity and events stored in the memory that do not penetrate consciousness. Citing Hamilton's account of "latent mental modification," he argues that the mind may engage in considerable intellectual undertakings without conscious awareness (516). This principle of reflex shaped numerous studies of mental automata, including elder John Addington Symonds's analysis of the transformation of will into habit, the physician Daniel Hack Tuke's study of sleepwalking and hypnotism, Maudsley's account of higher-order nervous events in consciousness, and Jackson's representations of the evolution of consciousness and the neuropathology of epilepsy.[113]

Such investigations, focused on the will-in-abeyance, endeavored to explain dreamy phenomena such as religious trance, clairvoyance, lucid vision, and double consciousness in terms of naturally occurring, recessed powers belonging to lower or more primitive activity in the brain. Carpenter positioned the normal process of unconscious cerebration—that is, the accumulated memories of minute experiences outside consciousness that congregate to form intuitions—within the history of the evolving human brain, whose size, complex structure, and progressive additions he compared with other vertebrate animals including monkeys and anthropoid apes (*Principles,* 116). In human cerebro-spinal organization, sensations and ideas that penetrate the highest, conscious regions of mental activity influence the will to produce or suppress motor activity; those that do not reach high enough will generate only reflex activity (123–25). These lower cerebral events allow spiritual ideas to take hold of the mind, working through the reflex functions and bypassing the corrective activity of the will. In a "historical and scientific" account of mesmerism, he recommended early scientific training to encourage habits of accurate observation and to check the influence of dominant or prepossessing ideas. Such ideas are "most tyrannous and most likely to spread," he noted, "when connected with religious enthusiasm."[114] Demoniacal possession, ecstatic revelations of Christian visionaries, Methodist revivals, and spiritualist encounters with the departed may all be traced to the force of a dominant idea and the heightened nervous state attending expectation. The ecstatic or somnambulist subject is a "conscious automaton" at once freed from the influence of the will that directs it in the waking state and at the same time preternaturally alert to suggestions conveyed through the senses, which are locked up in normal dreaming sleep. It may thus be made to "think, feel, say or do anything that its director wills it to think, feel, say or do," while its whole power is concentrated on the state of the present moment.[115] Hence, in this state in which its higher activity of the will is suspended, the mesmerized subject may be capable of extraordinary acts of perception or displays of physical strength.

The coincidence of powerful ideas and reflex nervous activity overwhelming higher conscious activity appears in other accounts of spiritual automata. In his essay on habit, Symonds included a section on table-turning, which identified "secondarily automatic" activity of the séance participants—partly prompted by idea or suggestion and partly reflex—as the cause of the apparent wonderful movement of the table.[116] Maudsley similarly interpreted hallucinations, religious excitement, and belief in miracles as the effect of undisciplined ideas on the lower sensorimotor system, which then generates powerful sensory experiences automatically, or without the intervention of consciousness. Such phenomena are therefore related to those of somnambulism and the automata of epilepsy as well as to the instinctive behavior usually associated with lower animals.[117] This nervous susceptibility, he argued, represented degeneration both at the level of cerebrospinal nervous coordination in an individual whose life should properly "represent[] a progressive development of the nervous system"[118] and in the evidence that nervous weakness was a feature of "bad descent."[119] Tuke identified "inhibition of certain cerebral centers . . . along with normal or increased ability of ideas," as the physical representation of what is experienced psychically as dreaminess.[120] He also suggested that Jackson's principle of dissolution should be applied not only to pathological conditions like epilepsy but also to temporary suspensions of conscious activity like dreaming and sleepwalking along with the ecstatic experiences or hallucinations that often accompany both spontaneous and artificial somnambulism.[121]

However, not all scientific accounts of the physical basis for mysticism and spriritualism objectified them as symptoms of disease or degeneration, and the therapeutic approach to dreamy experience included investigation into the buried talents that such experience might reveal. John Elliotson's efforts to introduce mesmerism into mainstream medical science in the 1840s included publication of lengthy accounts of séance room marvels and suggested that latent mental powers could be tapped to discover the body's own healing methods and provide a natural anesthesia in surgical operations. In the same decade, James Braid developed hypnotism as a therapeutic technique in the treatment of nervous disorders after studying the religious exercises of Hindu mystics and documenting the remarkable instances of exalted perception that took place in these states.[122] Subsequently, in France, hypnosis became a favored technique for the treatment of hysterics under the influence of Jean-Martin Charcot at the Salpêtrière Hospital in Paris and for suggestive therapeutics developed by the Nancy School in the 1860s. Although it did not acquire the foothold in medical practice in Britain that it did in France, this form of therapy was the subject of articles, reports, and correspondence in *Brain,* the *Journal of Mental Science,* and the *British Medical Journal,* as well as book-length studies by Tuke and Albert Moll (whose *Hypnotism* went through several editions in Britain in the 1890s).[123]

By the end of the century too, the potential of nervous automata to reveal latent powers of mind provided overlap between psychology and psychical research. James, who also located the origin of spiritual events in cerebrospinal physiology, stressed in his lecture on religion and neurology (1902), that the "genius" of highly religious individuals and spiritual leaders is often expressed in abnormal psychic visitations, including trances and aural and visual hallucinations, which are, in turn, "symptoms of nervous instability."[124] For James, however, phenomena produced in mystical states challenge the assumption that mental life is governed by a single consciousness in which all facts are delivered by sense-perception and suggest instead that there are hidden regions of the mind that deliver information independently of the senses. The lowly, pathological origins of such events compromise neither their spiritual nor their scientific significance. Empirical evidence of divine or ideal forces impacting the real events of the world as well as of psychological well-being in the "twice-born" demonstrates that the "facts" of the subliminal mind and the supernatural should not be ignored by psychologists. His argument echoes James Sully's suggestion in "The Dream as a Revelation" that the transition from waking to dreaming state should not be considered a temporary mental degeneration but rather as a "mental dissolution"[125] in which we are able to recover "the functional activities" of the "lower" organs of the brain that drive what is "instinctive, primitive, [and] elemental" and that have been suppressed by the controlling activity of regulative reflection.[126] Sleep thus unveils a collection of "primal" sensations and impulses that connect us "with the great sentient world."[127] With an overtly spiritualist emphasis, the prominent psychical researcher F. W. H. Myers similarly investigated the existence of a primitive subliminal mind housing forms of awareness that significantly outsized those of the supraliminal or conscious mind. For Myers, this mind contained the key to the survival of personality after death. Our study of human nature, he claimed, could be enriched by a "nascent science" investigating evidence of the afterlife.[128] Rather than diminished by its automatic activity, the primitive mind might reengage its ancient subliminal talent for perception enlarged beyond the ordinary dimensions of conscious experience.

III. THE REALIST NOVEL AND THE DREAMY MIND

Dreamy or "voluminous" mental states, Crichton-Browne proposed in 1895, are "of interest from a medical and psychological and a philosophical point of view" (*SL* 1). He might well have added "literary," since among the subjects and students of dreamy confusion he cites, he includes Scott, Dickens, Wordsworth, Coleridge, Hardy, Tennyson, and Coventry Patmore. On the face of it, the dreamy mind seems unsuited to the dilatory forms of prose fiction and narrative poetry, since its effects are generally "indescribable" and "almost invariably concerned with those ultimate ideas—space, time, matter, motion, and relativity—that are beyond the domain of certain knowledge and, according to Spencer, unthinkable." They produce, says Crichton-Browne, "momentary realizations . . . of Nirvana or the cessation of personal being or purgatorial pains more searching than any that Dante conceived" (7). Not only do they outdo the spiritual representations possible even in literary language, but they also obliterate all the anchors of consciousness that enable us to construct a sense of reality: personal identity, sense of time, the organization of the self in space, and the boundary between self and world. Yet in other ways they represent many of the objects of literary imaginative endeavor: "glimpses of real insight into an otherwise impenetrable past" (4), an uncanny identification of present and past (3), a "sense of reminiscence" that blends into "a sense of prescience" (1). The possibility of extracting forgotten details from the past or the myriad events that invisibly envelope a single moment in the present, as well as of assembling from these a vision of the future, might be said to constitute the spiritual dimension of realism—what Lewes describes as a power of representation beyond "the simple gatherings of sense."[129]

Crichton-Browne points out how such insight may be the morbid symptom of nervous disorder or degeneration, commonly epilepsy. Under the influence of the dreamy state, "the certitudes of science" dissolve into "the certitudes of faith" (*SL* 11). Such experience is symptomatic of disequilibrium in the nervous centers. Dreamy states are often precipitated by meditation on religious subjects and often dispelled by deliberately drawing the attention to some concrete element in the environment, as when Wordsworth reported that he might "grasp[] at a wall or tree to recall myself from the abyss of idealism to the reality" (11). Citing Jackson's account of voluminous mental events, Chrichton-Browne stresses that such exercises restore object consciousness, which has at least temporarily been overcome by subject consciousness, the usual symptom of an abnormal nervous discharge (24).

As unhealthy distortions of perception, dreamy experiences seem anathema to the forms of realist and naturalist narrative. Although these represent somewhat discrete movements in nineteenth-century literary history, I link them here as fictional endeavors to provide, not just a window on the world, but an account of the objective conditions that determine how characters experience that world—the conditions of the internal, physiological environment as well as the external conditions of heredity, social change, and biological adaptation that shape the events those characters must confront. The word "realism," as Levine has put it, is at once "dangerously multivalent" and "inescapable," describing simultaneously an effort to capture a preverbal, external truth, a loyalty to the ordinary over the exceptional, and a respect for facts, no matter how disagreeable.[130] Not only do realism and naturalism distinguish themselves from idealist literary form by asserting a reality independent of mind, but they also assume we can come to know this reality through systematic inquiry.[131] They are thus consilient, in E. O. Wilson's sense of the term, with neurophysiology and evolutionary theory as they "probe . . . the physical basis of the thought process itself."[132] As they trace behaviors triggered by nervous pathways that become overcharged or by the cerebral regions that become malnourished as the brain reacts to specific events and circumstances, they objectify the deepest levels of subjective experience.

Yet this is not necessarily what (broadly construed) realist narrative fiction achieves at all, as anyone picking up *Villette* or *Bleak House* for the first time will testify. Peter Brooks has argued that realism's limits are tested in the Victorian novel, as its loyalty to the ugliness of the everyday is strained by its competing attention to the "play of fancy . . ."[133] or to the social truths, whose dimensions are such that they can be grasped only in forms that do not belong to realism's system of representations.[134] The chapters that follow show that as realist narrative tries to accommodate the discoveries of Victorian mental science, new facts about the physical world paradoxically invite narrative forms that distort ordinary perception. "Objective" narrators are frequently unreliable or nervous subjects themselves, whose own episodes of reverie, ecstatic illumination, or cataleptic withdrawal are likely to bleed into their representations of characters and events. If, as Spencer claimed in the third edition of his *Principles of Psychology*, consciousness works through the antithesis of subject and object, barring our "knowledge of that ultimate reality in which subject and object are united,"[135] then novels repeatedly break the rules of consciousness: They deliver recessed memories, intuited connections, or clairvoyant glimpses into remote events and minds through the medium of either a first-person narrator who, "looking back," sees and knows more than she or he describes, or of free indirect discourse, in which awareness hovers in omniscience over thoughts assigned to particular characters. Such nervous narrative instability is characteristic not only of the distracted and dreamy voices of *Villette*'s Lucy Snowe or *Bleak House*'s Esther Summerson, but also of Dickens's haunting omniscient narrators who inhabit regions of space or time that do not represent ordinary waking experience, like the voice that moves with the fog across all of London at the beginning of *Bleak House,* or the observer of Coketown in *Hard Times* who records how the identical and repeated actions of its inhabitants today and yesterday and tomorrow matches the undifferentiated topography of the town. It is true of even of Eliot's intellectual narrators whose ironic depiction of their characters' narrow thoughts can become suddenly bloated with the imagery of past or distant events of which those characters must have little or no cognizance, like the "slow urgency of growing generations" and the "corpses of blooming sons" that succeed Gwendolen Harleth's discovery of Daniel Deronda's Jewish identity.[136] The narrators that describe Hardy's Wessex landscapes too can drift from naturalist matter-of-factness into a kind of intoxicated state in which those landscapes and the figures that inhabit them appear profoundly spiritual: the revelers who return to the d'Urberville farm before Tess's seduction, for example, show more of the narrator's state of mind than of themselves when they appear in an "opalized circle of glory"[137]; and Egdon Heath at the opening of *The Return of the Native* has the sublimity of Shelley's Mont Blanc.

Nicholas Dames has shown how the disciplinary overlap between psychology and literary criticism in the nineteenth century produced a "physiology" of novel reading that assessed activity in the brain as it responds to a lengthy text. Patterns of nervous receptivity or "rhythms of attention and inattention . . . buildup and charges of affect," make reading a nervous performance rather than a scene of moral instruction.[138] The dreamy, frequently inattentive, and cognitively lazy practice of reading that Dames identifies as a focus of literary and social criticism in the period also, however, shares some of the qualities that, for the Victorian audience, underlie artistic greatness. In his study of the physiological origins of dreams, reverie, and spectral illusions, *The Philosophy of Sleep*, Robert Macnish stresses the power of the dreaming mind to reach imaginative heights that ordinary consciousness represses. Even the most "dull and passionless" mind can be "lighted up with the Promethean fire of genius and romance; the prose of their frigid spirit is converted into magnificent poetry."[139] This homage to the power of the mind to generate ideal forms anticipates the principles of criticism outlined by E. S. Dallas in *The Gay Science* (1866), which integrate literary aesthetics and psychology. Arguing that criticism should be understood as a "science of pleasure," Dallas located the aesthetic experience in the hidden regions of the mind that do not enter the range of consciousness.[140] Imagination, thus understood, "is but another name for the automatic nature of the mind or any of its faculties," a set of "involuntary movements of thoughts unconscious or half-conscious"(GS 1:194–96). While art "portrays what we have seen and describes what we have heard" it differs from science because it "appeals to the unconscious part of us. . . . [a]wakening distant associations and filling us with a sense of mental possession beyond that of which we are daily and hourly conscious" (1:316). Art appeals to the "absent mind" that "haunts us like a ghost or a dream" (1:199), while science demands the prosaic and immediate work of conscious attention. Dallas contrasts this "occult power" of the poet, "suggesting something beyond and behind knowledge" (1:318), with the cruder art of the novel, which appeals merely to the pleasure of the palate. The association of the novel, and specifically of naturalist prose, with everyday awareness implicitly aligns it with science and its drudging attention to the objects of sense-perception and to consciousness built through the accumulation of knowledge.

Yet, in volume 2 of *The Gay Science,* Dallas sees the novel expressing the modern psyche and emphasizes the former's historical turn from the public and heroic to the private, the sensational, and the pleasurable. The novel is not exclusively the art form of the higher intellectual faculties. Alongside Eliot's depiction of the "higher consciousness which is known to bring higher pains" (2:123) and the novel of character, in which "man mould[s] circumstances to his will" (2:293), we find forms of modern popular fiction, particularly the sensation novel, in which character is ruled by plot or circumstance: In the spirit of Zola's radical naturalism, the sensation novel makes character and action the effect of milieu. In these same novels, it is not the reasoning mind but rather the disturbed and primitive minds of "idiots" or "half-witted creatures" that provide the crucial perspective on events and enable the plot to resolve (2:292). As modern readers "fly thought and cultivate sensation"(2:323), the novel delivers lower forms for lower minds and substitutes the involuntary pleasures of sensation for action and deliberation.

The nineteenth-century realist novel's attention to the "lower mind" does not quite subvert "Darwin's plots," as Gillian Beer argues of the jubilant, writerly dimensions of *Tess of the d'Urbervilles* that destabilize that novel's bleaker evolutionary themes.[141] It scarcely disturbs or "punctuates" the gradualist teleology that Levine recognizes as an (albeit unstable) "groundwork of nineteenth-century realism."[142] However, the representation of automatic or trance phenomena in these texts does suggest a countermovement to evolutionary progress that, while it positions spiritual experience within the physical history of the species, also haunts scientific observation with dreamy intuition. As the novels trace spiritualized, dreamy states to a primitive mental condition that persists alongside human evolutionary achievement, they identify intuition, mystical foresight, and clairvoyant imagination as atavistic powers of mind that either enhance or complicate empirically derived forms of knowledge. The naturalization of spiritual experience by nineteenth-century physiological psychology illuminates the recesses of the primitive mind. Yet in the very science-savvy narrative fiction discussed in the chapters that follow, this mind becomes an awkward object of study for evolutionist models of progress like Lamarck's principle of use and inheritance, which assumes a law of increasing fitness, or like Auguste Comte's sociology, which proposes the historical growth of human intellect beyond theology and metaphysics to positivism.[143] The haunting influence of the dreamy mind on narrative realism resists imperialist and eugenicist stories of advancing civilization and physical and moral perfection. It does so even as the theory of natural selection, with its emphasis on chance and contingency, removes the same stories of progress from evolutionary biology.

Carving moral and spiritual meaning out of an evolutionary understanding of the mind is the tall task that imaginative literature undertakes as it responds to medical science. The novels I have chosen to explore here in one way or another depict the social realities their characters navigate through the spiritualized dreamy states experienced by those characters. Despite Brontë's attention to the morally elevating power of will and its potential to overcome nervous momentum in the body, her heroines navigate their adverse circumstances and achieve their profoundest spiritual insights when in a state of near nervous collapse. Dickens's ghosts are comical in objective form, but as subjective "Ghost[s] of an Idea,"[144] they represent recessed dimensions of mental experience that illuminate social and familial connections imperceptible to ordinary attention. In different ways, George Eliot's and Thomas Hardy's studies of the effect of circumstance and environment on will, sympathy, and self-determination draw on episodes of suspended awareness, spiritual elevation, or reverie as much as on the myriad, minute events that compose the social and evolutionary histories within which characters are forced to play their part. In so doing, their novels endeavor to recover moral meaning from the physiological processes of nervous development and retreat, as they turn to the dreamy state—the visions, and episodes of prescience or reverie whose origin is profoundly physical but whose intuitive reach is often greater than the sum of its physical parts and whose force is sometimes socially liberating. Wilkie Collins and Arthur Conan Doyle adapt this menu of dreamy effects to the form of the detective novel, exploring how trance states and subliminal awareness complement the investigative tools of anthropometric and forensic measurement. Although Doyle became a convert to spiritualism sometime after he had buried Holmes for good, the substitution of dreamy intuition for moral discernment in the novel's depiction of character and conduct seems preliminary to the strong spiritualist themes of his later fiction. The detective stories, however, share the focus of this otherwise eclectic group of writers for which the depression of higher and more spiritual states to their humble physical origins is a signature of their physiological-psychological realism.

In "The Dream as a Revelation," Sully observed of night dreaming that, while modern science seeks to account for the irrational side of dream life, the latter must also be understood as an "extension of human experience [and] a revelation of what would otherwise have never been known."[145] The realist novel amplifies this double task of the psychology of dreaminess—though in this case of the dreamy states in which ordinary waking consciousness is so estranged and compromised. It endeavors to account for the biological origins of spiritual experience and at the same time to illuminate the recessed mental powers that make such experience possible. Here, distortions of the temporal and spatial relationships among characters and events reveal larger realities than social circumstance or conscious perception allow for. The spectral dimensions of these dreamy episodes deliver a spiritual transformation of the physical world even as they reveal the origins of such spirituality in the nervous pathways of the primitive mind.

CHARLOTTE BRONTË'S
HYPOCHONDRIACAL HEROINES

I begin with Charlotte Brontë's *Jane Eyre* and *Villette* because they are reluctantly realist. They share certain elements of Romantic-Gothic sensationalism: faux hauntings, scenes of physical and emotional incarceration, and barely navigable passageways that lead to episodes of horror or imagined horror. Both also depict the supernatural as a mental state brought on at once by the manipulative contrivances of others and by the effect of strained nerves. Each has a devout narrator whose perilous psychological condition is often shaped by fear of apostasy and whose heightened sensitivity sometimes gifts her with supernormal perception. Yet both novels temper their spiritualism with the demystifying forms of realist fiction: One subordinates its Gothicisms to the bildungsroman structure of moral growth and development, describing the heroine's struggle against her hostile environment and her endeavor to unite inner emotional and spiritual impulses with outer social forms; the other constantly subjects the spiritual states that stimulate the Romantic imagination to medical scrutiny, observing how particular nervous conditions are likely to trigger religious experiences or to sustain the reign of fancy.

This highly material understanding of mental experience, however, does not obscure Brontë's recognition that spiritual feeling offers a release from the oppressive social restraints that seek to confine the female imagination. Linking her heroines' aberrant psychologies with the "lower" minds that she identifies in children and primitive or degenerate peoples, she invokes developmental principles from both mental and racial science precisely to articulate and spiritualize the longings and sufferings that in many ways outlast her heroines' willed efforts at self-improvement. Even as nervous illness becomes associated with incomplete development or a lower racial type, it offers an escape from the oppressive institutions and personalities that structure the lives of Brontë's young, unmarried, and impoverished English heroines. The formal tension between realist and Gothic-Romantic tropes thus points to the contested site of the European female body, which medical knowledge fails to discipline entirely. Mental science, this is to say, does not fully demystify episodes of spiritual transport, however closely affiliated with sexual passion or mental illness it shows them to be. These spiritual episodes validate the Gothic forms associated with a resurgent primitive mind. They do so even within the realist framework that offers an objective medical diagnosis of its first-person nervous, but self-scrutinizing, narrator.

Much has been said about the strained realism in Brontë's novels and its gender implications.[1] Gretchen Braun recently challenged Mary Jacobus's well-known argument that realist forms are linked to patriarchal oppression in the novel and that this realism is threatened by a not-fully-suppressed Romanticism. Braun proposes that, in recording the silences and evasions in quotidian female experience, Brontë articulates the trauma of self-loss in the experience of the socially marginalized woman.[2] Yet for other critics, realism remains the formal expression of the technologies of surveillance and control against which her heroines struggle. Sally Shuttleworth recognizes its "penetrative authority" as the alibi of medical and social "cures" for aberrant minds and behaviors, causing her character-narrators to shun the very narrative omniscience that they are charged with securing.[3] And Heather Glen, like Jacobus, sees Jane's combination of narrative omnipotence and egocentric determination unsettled by the precariousness of her identity, arguing that her Miltonic oscillations between self-assertion and self-annihilation keep alive "the aspirations of Romanticism in a changing nineteenth-century world."[4]

In what follows, I argue that Romantic and realist forms together represent the double consciousness of hypochondriasis. The symptomatic flights of fancy belonging to the disease mentally remove their sufferers from the painful material conditions of their lives, yet remain readable to them as aberrant states that render them worthy objects of medical attention. As Shuttleworth reminds us, the Victorian medical understanding of hypochondria included "melancholy foreboding" in addition to its now more narrow association with excessive anxiety about one's own state of health.[5] In addition, the mind retains many of its reasoning powers even while it surrenders to wayward impulses, including reverie and rapture, and while it threatens to succumb to complete nervous collapse.[6] In one sense, then, the hypochondriacal mind-narrative is self-disciplining. Yet at the same time, it enables episodes of imaginative escape from the restricting circumstances of single, impoverished, female lives and the forces that silence and immobilize them. In the early Victorian language of mental development that parallels medical accounts of nervous disorder, the lower mind, which, like that of animals, knows nothing of its own workings, is temporarily ascendant over the higher mind, which observes and restrains its passions. The stuff of this more primitive nervous organization is the source of rapturous spiritual release.[7]

With a very different emphasis, Terry Eagleton has also shown how the formal tensions between Romanticism and realism in Brontë's novels point to wider thematic contradictions. The competition between "'preindustrial' imaginative creativity" and depictions of "actual relations" in exchanges among people of different social classes in her work, he argues, points to the way in which she had to "negotiate the rift between imagination and 'society.'"[8] Moreover, Brontë's fiction reveals two divided sets of values, with rationalism, self-determining individualism, and social protest ranked on one side against conservatism, religious submission, and piety on the other.[9] Eagleton situates Patrick Brontë's low-church Evangelicalism, with its combined hostility to proletarian dissent and to High Church formalism, in the context of these class and cultural tensions. He also emphasizes how, as women, isolated and educated, and daughters of a clergyman, Charlotte and her sisters were especially oppressed by their ambivalent social status and by the tenets of Calvinism.[10]

As Eagleton stresses, Brontë is often critical of organized Christianity. From the hypocritical austerity of Brocklehurst in *Jane Eyre* to the sensual self-indulgence and relentless surveillance on the part of Catholic characters in *Villette,* the representatives of Christian faith often reinforce the heroines' social exile or at best offer them only temporary emotional comfort and guidance. Yet both novels are structured by determining (Christian and pagan) spiritual as well as material events in the protagonists' lives and minds. *Jane Eyre,* in particular, reads as a kind of spiritual biography. In one recent view, the story records Jane's gradual acceptance of Mosaic Law as she abandons her idolatrous adoration of Rochester and discovers a "renewed servitude to God."[11] A less traditional interpretation tracks Jane's growth as a Christian individual, by tracing how private spiritual experience leads the way to social transformation as Jane internalizes Christ's teachings about human equality.[12] Brontë's female narrators assume scriptural authority and make it a platform for social protest.[13]

Like Eagleton, these critics position the life of the spiritual mind within the landscape of changing social relations. However, Brontë's shifting depictions of religious experience and Christian institutions also engage Victorian debate about the spiritual or material origins of the mind, debate that itself spills into the formal terrain of Romantic and realist aesthetics. In her challenge to various confining and oppressive forms of religious and social authority, Brontë deploys the Romantic figure of the liberated imagination both to capture the experience of spiritual ecstasy (whether divine or demonic) and to rupture the confines of gender-determined social and religious duties and expectations. At the same time, her narrative is sensitive to the question of how imagination figures in a materialist understanding of the mind. Her "realism" embraces the physical processes that determine motive, meaning, and sense of self and detachedly observes the play between inner and outer worlds in the minds of her narrator-characters. Although at times this observing voice brings imaginative vision perilously close to madness, it does not ever entirely pathologize the imagination, which remains the instrument of emancipation from insidious, brutal, and seductive forms of oppression.

This tension between medical-scientific observation and imaginative liberation plays out across the mental terrain of dreaminess in both novels. In *Jane Eyre,* peculiar mental states associated with childhood assume concrete forms in the events that subsequently structure Jane's life, even while the narrator herself becomes increasingly able to manage the fears and fantasies that earlier dominate her child's mind. In *Villette,* much of the story is told by a narrator who inhabits a series of dream states, including "waking dreams" and "reverie." These haunt the realist media of minute observation and memory with a sense of unreality and confusion. Such interplay between dreaminess and the scientific study of it is especially pronounced in the realm of spiritual experience. The heroines' ecstatic spiritual states, whether manifest as mesmeric clairvoyance or Romantic pantheism, indicate their susceptibility to nervous disorder. Both Jane and Lucy experience the might of God when in a state of physical and emotional exhaustion. Yet at the same time, nervous, dreamy spiritual vision transcends the "dry materialist views" of medical men like Dr. John.[14] Such states also challenge the emphasis shared by phrenology and Evangelical reformism on individual industry and moral restraint as the sole basis of mental health. The American psychiatrist Amariah Brigham observed in 1835 that religious excitement could "increase the action of one of the most delicate and important organs of the body,—one on which all the manifestations of the mind are dependent."[15] Although excessive passion, like the revivalist enthusiasm that overtaxed the nervous system and turned healthy Christian minds into mad, magnetized subjects, is frequently the source of emotional torment and even self-loss for Brontë's heroines, it also represents a route to the imagination and from there to a spiritual awakening that evades medical as well as ecclesiastical authority. Dreaminess, as she describes in "When Thou Sleepest," (1837), ruptures the ordered patterns of thought that separate internal sensations from external things. The effect can be rapturous:

> Sometimes, when the midnight gale
> Breathed a moan and then was still,
> Seemed the spell of thought to fail,
> Checked by one ecstatic thrill. (11.37–40)[16]

To suggest that Brontë relocates spiritual experience in the dreamy mental state and thereby liberates religious feeling from oppressive institutional forms is not entirely to return to Sandra Gilbert and Susan Gubar's association of madness with the woman writer's act of defiance against the patriarchal confinement of her sex.[17] In *Jane Eyre*'s implied paralleling of the heroine's unjust imprisonment in the red room at Gateshead with Bertha's incarceration in the attic at Thornfield, the novel in fact confirms the real dangers of moral madness; the unchecked child's imagination is one source of that infirmity and Bertha's insobriety and sexual appetite is another. Gilbert and Gubar argue that the attic-bound "madwomen" of *Villette*—the monstrous, scheming Madame Walravens and the garret-haunting nun— appear to stand in for Lucy's psychological incarceration and repressed rage.[18] Yet when Lucy does give voice to her feelings, we are usually invited to see these as signs of her nervous instability.

Neither do I echo those feminist critics who recognize a paradoxical narrative empowerment in the episodes of passivity, immobility, and silence that afflict Brontë's narrators, for these self-denying moments also encourage the reader's diagnostic skepticism.[19] Instances when Lucy is unable to act or speak indicate immanent nervous breakdown, just as the narrative syncope they produce suggests she is an unreliable cartographer of the city, its institutions, and the various erotic relationships on which her story centers. Indeed, it is well known that Brontë's less-than-trustworthy narrators conceal feelings or withhold information about events in ways that seem indirectly or, passively, voice their repressed desires.[20] Lucy, in particular, portrays herself as the victim of others' self-interested scheming, yet she is, in her own way, as busy a watcher as Madame Beck. She deliberately withholds Dr. John's identity from the reader despite her own discovery of it rather in the way that Catholic characters control information and conceal identities. Even the more emotionally stable Jane, who asserts that her own mental health depends on her drawing a realist self-portrait "faithfully, without softening one defect,"[21] delivers a story shaped by repression of the passions that throw her into nervous shock as a child; a tale no more "plain" and "unvarnished" (186), then, than that Othello told to Desdemona.[22]

The reference to *Othello* is particularly revealing of Jane's nervous disposition, and it hints at the racial thinking behind Brontë's texts, which, as I suggest later in this chapter, sees heredity and climate together influencing the capacity for nervous self-development. Despite frequent exertions of "wholesome discipline" (188) on her fanciful imagination, Jane's narrative exposes her frustrated longing and its nervous consequences in the imperialist fantasies of combined loathing for and identification with the racial other. She depicts both her dark-haired rivals, Blanche Ingram and Bertha Mason, as New-World Africans with, respectively, "inflated and darkened" (200) or "fearful, blackened, inflate[d]" features (327), even as she invokes the language of slavery to describe the oppression of English women.[23] In this respect, Rochester's insistence that Jane's midnight visitor is a figment of her nervous imagination is (notwithstanding his motive for concealing Bertha's existence) not in itself so improbable. After all, Bertha's appearance comes on the heels of a nightmare, and an earlier "apparition," when the gypsy woman throws off "her" disguise revealing Rochester himself, leading Jane to ask "did I wake or sleep?" (233). Behind both Jane's distorted representation of Bertha and her barely suppressed feeling of their shared oppression, the narrative offers both an objective scientific diagnosis of the symptoms of psychological disorder and a developmental theory of race that conflates the inhabitants of remote geographical regions with those from different temporal zones.[24] Even in the light of day, Bertha has a "savage face" (327) with "shaggy locks," a "wild visage," and "red balls" that Rochester begs his audience to contrast with Jane's "clear eyes" (339). As Sharon Marcus has argued, Jane's episodes of prescient reverie merge here with another kind of "abstraction" in the generalized representation of human physical and cultural differences essential to the movement of capital across the empire.[25]

Thus, even as the overly fanciful imagination helps to map the contours of empire in these stories, the critical recognition of such connections itself mimics the process of self-diagnosis and narrative realist restraint that characterizes one pole of the hypochondriacal text. What Marcus describes as the "displacement of an embodied self onto writing"[26] occurs with the detached reflections of the older and worldlier narrators observing the nervous habits of their younger selves. This correcting impulse is nonetheless countered in the novel by a Providential voice, in which, as Jane puts it, events can be seen to have unfolded according to "presentiments," "signs," and "sympathies" that register powerfully in the body. Lucy describes her flight from reason to "truant imagination" as a very physical experience: "Reason turned me out by night, in midwinter, on cold snow, flinging for sustenance the gnawed bone dogs had forsaken"(214), to be succeeded by "a softer spirit" who delivers her into the sensual delights of "eternal summer"—the aura of a vision of a "head amidst circling stars" in a "dwelling too wide for walls, too high for dome" (215).

Both novels explicitly link the unreliability associated with the body's nervous and dreamy tendencies to hypochondriasis, which involves above all a heightened sensitivity toward the body, whose symptoms seem "pregnant with future danger."[27] Jason Tougaw has shown how in free indirect discourse the hypochondriac's story is framed by that of the "physician" narrator.[28] Yet in Brontë's novels, the first-person voice represents both the patient's narrative and the physician's diagnosis. Jane experiences "hypochondriac foreboding" (320) when, in a "restless, excited mood" (318) and tormented by the previous night's visit from Bertha like "a foul German spectre" (327), she awaits Rochester's return before the wedding; Lucy projects her own mental turmoil both onto her description of the Belgian King, whose hypochondria, she says, is expressed in haunting visions as well as in melancholy, and the royal dreamer of the Book of Daniel, Nebuchadnezzar. Like these figures, both narrators allow the influence of precognition and Gothic apparition to partly shape their stories: Jane's reunion with Rochester is delivered by spiritual intuition; Lucy interprets others' words and actions within the labyrinth of malevolent motives and apparently supernatural influences that make up the Gothic landscape of Villette. At the same time, both narrators exercise realist restraint on their stories in the form of medical self-diagnosis, directly or indirectly inviting their readers to interpret their mental experiences as the result of nervous strain or excitement. "The Reader shall judge" (483)

Jane declares, whether her telepathic communication with Rochester was the effect of an overly stimulated imagination, and her more restrained adult mind looks back on the poor self-control she demonstrated in childhood and declares it a symptom of her then clearly overexcited mental state. Lucy self-consciously observes how she abandons reason to give "a truant hour to the imagination" (214), frequently confesses to being "constitutionally nervous" (343), and emphasizes how she finally "disdained hysteria" at the moment of her triumphant exposure of the ghostly nun as a worldly trick in "reality" and "substance" (439). Thus even as the episodes of clairvoyance, precognitive dread, or spiritual elevation point to the activity of the dreamy mind, that mind, hypochondriacally, preserves some objective awareness of the physical conditions that make such abnormal mental states possible. During such episodes, then, wild or undisciplined spiritual rapture and the scientific observing mind can comfortably, if curiously, coexist.

I. HYPOCHONDRIASIS, SELF-CONTROL, AND THE EVOLUTION OF CONSCIOUSNESS

The split awareness associated with hypochondria falls short of true madness because it preserves rational awareness of the mind's irrational wanderings. Hypochondriasis, like the later-coined "neurasthenia," was a cover-all diagnosis describing any nervous overextension or depression and was thought to diminish or even completely arrest certain mental functions, potentially leading to complete breakdown.[29] In the table of contents of *A Treatise on Insanity* (1837), James Prichard lists as "hypochondriacal illusions" those impressions that derive from a false judgment in turn traceable to the accumulation of images in the memory. Under the influence of morbid reverie, these images may assemble to "produce an effect similar to that of actual perception," and while the patient is aware of their difference from external perceptions, he "is so intent upon his reverie" that internally generated scenes have a much more powerful effect on him than external ones.[30] Prichard stresses that this kind of hallucinatory experience does not amount to madness, since the patient retains much of the faculty of reason and can recognize the difference between internally driven and external impressions.[31] Lunatics, on the other hand, have no such awareness, although in the condition he describes as "moral insanity," the practice of restraint can rehabilitate the mind enough that it becomes capable of correcting such error.[32] Other studies of the disease confirm this distinction between nervous disorders like hypochondria and insanity: In *Inquiry Concerning the Indications of Insanity* (1830), John

Conolly argues that people of too-active and vagrant imagination, ranging from dreamy poets with a "vivid sense of things not present"[33] to medical men who confront the phantoms of their own fever and artists who fix their attention so long on internal images that they project those images over external objects of sensation, all experience defects of the understanding that do not amount to insanity.[34] John Barlow's *On Man's Power over Himself to Control Insanity* (1843), explores forms of mental illness where "the patient retains so much of the reasoning faculty that the delusions of the sense are recognized by him as such."[35] He is thus capable of resisting the impulses caused by his delusions; his inner state is one of struggle between illness and reason. Similarly, Esquirol argues in *Mental Maladies* that, while hypochondriacs "have illusions which spring from internal sensations," they "never attribute their misfortunes to causes that are repugnant to reason."[36]

These accounts of hypochondriasis and its relationship to insanity overlap with the physiological study of dreamy states, including sleepwalking, waking dreams, and visions as well as ordinary dreaming. In *The Philosophy of Sleep* (1830), Macnish investigates the imbalance among mental faculties that occurs in states of partial sleep, such as reverie, daydreams, ennui, and hypochondriacally induced visions, as well as in full sleep, arguing that these states reduce certain powers of the mind while they elevate others. Both in ordinary dreaming and in partial sleep, the senses are either fully or partly inactive while certain thoughts and feelings, unrestrained by the faculties of reason and judgment, are given free rein. Thus the visionary phenomena of dreams must be understood not as they have been in the past as the work of spirits that "assault the soul in sleep" (52) but rather as an "unequal distribution of sensorial energy which gives rise to the visionary phenomena. One faculty exerts itself vividly without being under the control of the others," thus giving rise to "the most extravagant thoughts" (53). During sleep or other states of reduced consciousness, there is limited or suspended activity in the regions of the brain and nervous system responsible for sensorial power, diminishing the body's awareness of external circumstances even as it disables the faculty of reason. In waking dreams and visions, he proposes, imagination escapes the moderating influence of reason. Similarly, in sleepwalking, memory and imagination break free from judgment, even while some powers of volition, enabling the sleeper to go where he or she chooses, remain in play. Dreaminess is thus defined by diminished mental discipline and the greater or lesser failure of reason and judgment to prevail over the lower passions (186–207). Yet unlike Prichard's moral madness, dreaminess here denotes a state that we all inhabit regularly in one form or another and over which active mental discipline exercises little command. While dreamy minds habitually conjure up these visionary scenes and "imbue the most trite circumstances with poetical colouring" (277–78), they do not mistake illusion for reality. In contrast with those who suffer from spectral illusions, Macnish emphasizes, they do not mistake the impression created by the brain for one generated by external phenomena but are to various degrees aware that these images "exist only in their own imagination" (212).

Although Macnish is engaged in a medical study of dreams and dreaminess, he also reveals a Romantic attraction to the mental power they sometimes reflect. While dreamy visions are unequivocally the creations of an embodied mind, they also allow it to "mount the dizzy chariot" (277) even as that mind remains *aware* that it abandons reason to imagination. Having opened his chapter on waking dreams with the epigraph from *Lyrical Ballads,* Macnish begins by distinguishing between down-to-earth realist prose and the flights of imagination that are captured by poetry:

> Those gifted with much imagination are most addicted to waking dreams. There are some men whose minds are so practical and so thoroughly prosaic, that they seldom get beyond the boundaries of absolute reality; others are so ideal and excursive, that they have a perpetual tendency to transcend the limits of absolute truth—to leave this "visible diurnal sphere" behind; and on the pinions of fancy, soar away into the regions of poetry and romance. Waking dreams are merely the effect of unbridled imagination. The faculty, when exercised under common circumstances, is kept in strict subordination to reason . . . which never for a moment permits it to suppose that the fictions it brings forth are realities. (136–37)

Even as he demystifies the illusory states of waking dream, situating these within the "wide empire [of dreamy effects] between awake and perfect sleep" (52), he identifies imagination's liberation from reason, not as madness, but as the food of a Romantic mind. In a passage that allegorizes the dreamy imagination, Macnish describes its solitary journey through a sublime landscape in a way that will be echoed in Brontë's narrative voices at their most Romantic pitch:

> Now following the lone traveler in some narrow and venturous pathway, over the edge of the Alpine precipices, where a single slip is instant destruction, she tracks him alone by fitful flashes of lightening; and at length, struck by the flash, she beholds him tumbling headlong from rock to rock, to the bottom of the dread abyss, the victim of a double death. Or possibly she takes her stand on the jutting forehead of some bold terrific coast,

and eyes the foundering vessel straight below; she mixes with the spent and despairing crew; she dives into the cabin, and singles out, perhaps from the rest, some lovely maid, who, in all the bloom of recovered beauty, is voyaging back to her native land from the healing airs of a foreign climate, in thought just bounding over the scenes of her youth, or panting in the warm embraces of a father's arms. Such are waking dreams. (211)

Like Jane's extravagant musings on Bewick's birds or the paintings she draws from her "spiritual eye" (147) or Lucy's flights of imagination, these mental excursions liberate thought from the "stern and forbidding hues" of reality (*PS*, 210).[37] They reveal inaccessible landscapes and trigger Wordsworthian spots of time as they collapse the distance between domestic and foreign lands or rejuvenate the weary present with scenes from the past. In so doing, they soften the realities of—especially female—separation and loneliness. Macnish's Romantic admiration for the dreamy mind sometimes seems to overwhelm his scientist's interest in the brain's shifting patterns of activity, just as Lucy's infusions of spiritual meaning into a sublime landscape can rhetorically overpower the self-correcting diagnosis of nervous daydreaming that generally follow such episodes.

Nonetheless, both Macnish and Brontë stress the physiological basis of dreamy visions, which include prophecy and clairvoyant perception as well as poetic imagination. *The Philosophy of Sleep* was available to the Brontës through the Keighley Mechanics Institute Library, which additionally housed books by Thomas Reid and Dugald Stewart and Esquirol's *Mental Maladies*. The collection also included phrenology manuals and essays on consciousness and the nervous system found in volumes of *Blackwood's Edinburgh Magazine*, *Chamber's Edinburgh Journal*, *The Edinburgh Review*, and *Quarterly Review*; volumes on natural history, zoology, and plant physiology; George Cuvier's *Essay on the Theory of the Earth* (1813); and Charles Lyell's *Principles of Geology* (1833). The family's access to contemporary writing on natural and mental science through the library was complemented by Patrick Brontë's interest in science of the unconscious. He made notes on notes on sleep and nightmare that drew on Macnish's work together with William Buchan's *Domestic Medicine* (1784), frequently consulted in the Brontë household,[38] and was intrigued by the use of mesmerism and anesthesia as forms of medical intervention.[39]

Much of this eclectic reading in medical and mental science addresses how the competing influences of heredity, environment, and self-discipline could determine human success, including mental health. *Domestic Medicine* emphasizes that nervous affections, including hypochondria, can be controlled through changes in the patient's environment.[40] "Nervous afflictions," Buchan argues, "arise more frequently from causes which it is, in a great measure, in our own power to avoid than from diseases or an original fault in the disposition."[41] For this reason, children, whose "nerves are more susceptible of irritation"[42] than adults, should be protected against confinement and bad air, as well as against overindulgence, thereby "erect[ing] an early fence around the disposition of [the] child.[43] Buchan's emphasis on climate and self-management suggests a source for the differences in character development between Jane and Bertha. Yet Bertha is also mad because she comes from generations of mad women. Esquirol identified a range of moral causes for mental illness, including excessive study as well as disappointed affection and other passions,[44] but argued that these were usually accompanied by hereditary, physical, and environmental influences. Similarly, in his *Essays on Hypochondriacal and Other Nervous Affections* (1817), John Reid (whose work may be playfully referenced in the naming of Jane's childhood nemesis "John Reed") emphasizes that nervous symptoms are not ever entirely under the control of the will or able to be sufficiently controlled by education and environment. While we may shun circumstances that are likely to aggravate a bias in the personality toward mental disturbance, and "guard against the approaches of mental malady,"[45] by cultivating self-control at a young age, diseases of the mind cannot be cured by either external or internal influence where there is "an hereditary propensity to inflammation and consequent distortion of the mental faculties."[46] Mental disorders that fall short of full madness also demonstrate limited susceptibility to environment. To demand that a person burdened by nervous depression become cheerful is like commanding an overheated person to be cold, even while, like Buchan, he recommends that hypochondriacs avoid isolation and excessive study, both of which may exacerbate the disease.[47]

In *Jane Eyre* especially, Brontë seems to invoke Reid's shifting emphasis on heredity and self-control in the etiology and history of nervous diseases. Here the bildungsroman narrative traces the heroine's journey out of childhood impetuosity and nervous susceptibility (which manifest in the red room as full hysterical collapse) into a mature state of mind in which she is frequently able to control her strongest emotional urges. This deliberately contrasts her with Bertha, who has supposedly succumbed to her violent and lascivious propensities. Reid opens his book by observing that the "savage, rustic, mechanical drudge, and infant, whose faculties have not had time to unfold themselves . . . may be regarded as machinery regulated principally by physical agents," whereas "man, matured, civilized, and by due culture raised to a his proper level in the scale of being partakes more of a moral than an animal character."[48] Such confidence in the power of culture (both as nurture and as civilization) to correct the urges of nature, however, confronts two complicating developmental factors. The first is climate, which if too warm like that of the Caribbean enervates the moral senses or if too damp, like Lowood, compromises the health of the body. The second is heredity: For the Creole Bertha and her brother James, as well for Adele, the child of a loose woman, the promise of self-improvement seems feeble against the overwhelming influence of blood.

Medical investment in the idea of the civilized or mature will as foil to the deterministic influences of heredity and climate drew on debates in the 1830s and 1840s over the material history of the mind. James Ferrier's lengthy "Introduction to the Philosophy of Consciousness" appeared in an 1838 issue of *Blackwood's Edinburgh Magazine,* complaining that to make the mind an object of scientific investigation is to ignore a fundamental distinction between men and lower animals. Since animals are not capable of self-awareness and cannot "stand aloof in any degree from the influence to which [they are] subject,"[49] they have no self or moral agency. In particular, Ferrier attacks the "admirers of somnambulism and other depraved and anomalous conditions of humanity"[50] for focusing on unconscious processes that tell us nothing of the mind's powers or of man's free, moral nature.[51] In a similar spirit, the *Edinburgh Review* criticized Robert Chambers's anonymously published *Vestiges of the Natural History of Creation* (1844) for, in the style of phrenology, making a flesh-and-blood organ of the soul.[52] In Chambers's controversial account of evolution, mental phenomena "flow directly from the brain" and the "distinction between physical and moral is annulled, as only an error in terms."[53]

This idea that the very material structure of the mind is at the source of the human capacity to morally restrain or even reconfigure it is indeed at the heart of phrenology, which combines the concept of fixed, inherited traits with the principle of self-improvement. Phrenology proposed that the cultivation of particular mental faculties could actually restructure the brain. Sally Shuttleworth emphasizes how Brontë's novels tie phrenological knowledge to the literature on moral madness and nervous dysfunction through the doctrine of self-improvement. Phrenology claims that by following the principles of the physical and malleable mind and nurturing particular faculties, human beings can overcome the degenerative influence of an inherited tendency to insanity. Shuttleworth points out however, that the phrenological stress on self-management in Brontë's novels is tied to the narrator's tenuously unified self, which is always determined by a configuration of faculties and hence to Brontë's habits of narrative concealment.[54] The "realist narrative of self-improvement" indebted to phrenological positivism can easily turn into a parable of moral madness as the mind becomes a scene of unbalance in which powerful energies remain undisciplined. Brontë's recognition of the physical dimensions of mind, Shuttleworth proposes, is what lies behind the simultaneous impressions of helplessness and self-control in her narrators, whose behaviors are at once the sum of uncontrollable nervous activity and calculated mental restraint. In this way, "the secrets of the self are displaced from the spiritual to the physical domain,"[55] and physician displaces priest in the treatment of moral disorders.[56]

It is possible, however, to see Brontë's novels allowing some narrative force to the spiritual experiences they describe, thus resisting the regulatory regimes of phrenology and psychiatric diagnosis that Shuttleworth argues constitute technologies of selfhood for her heroines. As we shall see, *Villette's* refusal to entirely pathologize its narrator's attraction to the Romantic sublime, like *Jane Eyre's* unwillingness to surrender all experiences of rapturous self-loss to the diagnoses of medical science, suggests that we should also look to Bronte's interest in the physiology of imagination and the dreamy mind as sources of a narrative energy that sometimes outsize the realist scrutiny and self-correction of nervous tendencies. Even as Brontë maps spirituality onto the terrain of the body, revealing the sensational and embodied origins of mystical expression, her narratives climax at least as much in moments of ecstatic union with a "good angel" (215) or a "Mighty Spirit"(*JE*, 484) as they do in the scenes of realist triumph, when Gothic mysteries are unmasked. The dreamy descriptions of arctic or stellar landscapes that inspire her heroines to see beyond the confines of their drab schoolteachers' lives aesthetically outrun the "rude," "groveling" and "repellent" real about which Lucy complains (*V*, 100).

In this respect, her novels reflect the Romantic-era brain science of Erasmus Darwin, Franz Gall, and Charles Bell, which emphasized the evolved or physical basis of mind precisely in order to investigate its powers, including those of the elevated imagination.[57] Lucy's astral voyages combine Gall's biological model of the brain as a shifting arrangement of fully and less-active faculties with Darwin's account in *Zoonomia* of the effects of suspended volition and the exaggerated influence of internal over external sensations in dreaming.[58] Her moments of ecstatic transport echo Wordsworth's transformation of "outward things" by excited Spirit, occurring in the dreamlike state in which a combination of external scenes and internal sensations suddenly take "possession of the faculties."[59] Jane's childhood and early adult reveries, like the visionary events of *The Prelude,* occur in an interaction between "the growing faculties of sense"[60] and the natural environment, reminding us that the growth of the creative mind is organic as well as spiritual.[61] Such Romantic representations of mind recognize the confluence of physical forces that underlie that mind while simultaneously identifying the dreamy liberation of nervous energy that fuels creative greatness. They embed imaginative genius in mundane matter and observe its dangerous proximity to moral madness. Yet they allow the spiritual energies unleashed by the excited nervous system to imagine new psychic and social possibilities.

II. RAPTURE AND REALISM IN *JANE EYRE*

Brontë's first published novel responds to medical investigations of consciousness and spiritual experience by exploring how primitive, undisciplined expressions of anguish rupture the higher mental configurations of the European adult. In so doing, the narrative discovers continuity between a material understanding of the mind and the direct apprehension of God, through which Brontë attempts to release morality from convention, religion from self-righteousness, and "the world-redeeming creed of Christ" from "narrow human doctrine" (*JE*, 5–6). In her Preface to the second edition, Brontë aligns herself with the prophet Micaiah as well as with Christ's denunciation of the Pharisees to emphasize the peril of revealing truth outside human conventions and laws. Along with her publishers and readers, she also thanks those reviewers who have encouraged her, including G. H. Lewes, who praised the novel for its depiction of "deep, significant reality" (although he went on to complain of her tendency to melodrama).[62] By invoking her reviewers' praise even as she defends the spiritual truths of the novel, Brontë implicitly links phrenological accounts of mind that enable her to depict its most obscure and subtle movements with the "spiritual eye" (147) that foresees events, endeavors to follow the true Christian path independently of convention and authority, and asserts its own ardent interpretation of scripture. In the novel itself, much of this spiritual work occurs in a dream or in a dreamlike state, suggesting that, despite Jane's developing capacity for self-control, the mind's path to God involves those regions of mental experience that remain ungoverned by the faculties of will and judgment.

Jane's first dreamy episode occurs in the red room in which she is unjustly confined as punishment for fighting back against her bullying cousin. This incident obviously prefigures Bertha's incarceration in the Thornfield attic, since it follows upon Jane's "mutinous" defiance of John Reed, and since her struggle like "a mad cat" (15) against her captors will be repeated in

Bertha's "convulsive plunges" (339) when Rochester restrains her. Both the mistreated English girl and the displaced Jamaican Creole woman are prey to "ungovernable excitement" (44). When Jane is alone in the dark room she is overcome by the fear that she might awaken the "preternatural voice" (20) of the dead Mr. Reed, and her "wild, involuntary cry" (21) is succeeded by a fit that sends her into complete unconsciousness. This "vision from another world" (21) belongs to what Macnish calls the "unbridled imagination" of waking dreams, indulged at the expense of judgment and therefore threatening "the maddest and most extravagant thoughts" (53). The older, narrating Jane, recognizes that her child's mind was "prepared . . . for horror" (*JE*, 21) and that the vision of ghostly light is a product of the uncontrolled imagination. Reason, she adds, was only a "precocious though transitory power" (19). Her reflections echo Macnish's observation that children are particularly susceptible to dread and the mental phantoms it generates, as well as Buchan's claims about the nervous predispositions of children (54).

At the same time, Jane's dreaminess calls up a specter other than that of Mr. Reed, namely, the "half fairy, half imp" phantom in the mirror, a "strange little figure" (18) that she divorces from the observing "I." Appearing out of one of Bessie's nighttime stories out of "lone, ferny dells in moors . . . before the eyes of belated travelers," it presages the fairy Jane that Rochester will later blame for scaring his horse and that he will invoke in his infatuated teasing of her during their courtship. Jane has, he says, "the look of another world" (143). This does capture her susceptibility to dreaminess as, at key moments, the sensorial powers that link her inner with her outer worlds appear to weaken. Sometimes this takes the form of a feeling of disconnection from her own memories, as when she first arrives at Lowood and "Gateshead and my past life seemed to float away to an immeasurable distance" while the present remains "vague and strange." (58). Sometimes a sudden change in awareness will precipitate a feeling of unreality, as when Rochester throws off his gypsy disguise and she asks, like the speaker of Keats's "Ode to a Nightingale": "Did I dream still" (233). At other moments, she experiences a form of ego loss as when, having learned of Bertha's existence, she speaks of "Jane Eyre" as a remote third person, once again pale like the ghost-child in the looking glass (341). Rochester's accusations about pagan enchantment also seem to resonate in the "trance-like" sleep that she experiences on her last night at Thornfield. Dreaming that she is back in the red room at Gateshead, she once again sees the spectral light that, as a child she had expected to illuminate the ghost of Mr. Reed. This time, however, it reveals the spirit of the moon, who has replaced the child-Jane as the "white human figure" that meets her gaze.

Although Jane's dreamy states and experiences of spectral self-loss seem to draw her toward pagan spirituality, they are rapidly reconfigured as Romantic Christian mysticism. Alone on the heath, she seeks relief from "the universal mother, Nature" (172), but she is truly calmed by feeling God's presence in the sublime natural forms of the night sky. Looking up at the Milky Way, she feels "the might and strength of God." This revelation of divinity in the night sky invokes supernatural creation as it is laid out in the Book of Genesis. Such ecstatic intuition of God is also echoed in the final words of the novel from the Book of Revelations, "Surely I come quickly," and the response "Amen; even so come, Lord Jesus!" Although these words are given to St. John Rivers, they fill Jane's own heart "with divine joy" (521). St John also overwrites Jane's earlier cry to Rochester, "I will come" (483) with his repetition of St. John the Prophet's answer to Christ. Thus, even as the novel converts sexual back into spiritual energy in its concluding words, it also reminds us that Rochester and Jane are apparently united by divine fiat, both supplicating God before they hear the summoning or answering voice of the other. Jane's prayer then brings her close to a "Mighty Spirit" and her "soul rush[es] out in gratitude at His feet" (484). This is the summons and the answer, the direct communion of the soul with God, that Jane cannot properly hear or enact when it is communicated through Rivers's tyrannical will.

Rather than mediated by churchmen—whether in the form of Rivers's terrible devoutness or Brocklehurst's hypocrisy—this direct communion with God suggests the truth independent of convention, doctrine, and church or class hierarchy that Brontë invokes in her Preface. "Telling the truth" she announces at the beginning of chapter 12, means avoiding flattery, cant, and humbug. Yet "truth," in her narrative, is also opposed to "superstition" and Bronte's narrative realism depends on discoveries from mental science even as it describes from memory the heroine's moral and spiritual growth. Jane chastises her younger self for its proclivity to superstition. She notices her own experience of thrill at the Gothic mysteries of Thornfield, implying that such excitement is provoked by the stagnant and isolated life she has begun there and by the impoverished exercise offered to her faculties (130). When she hears Rochester's voice across the moorland, she apostrophizes superstition only to assert that this "is the work of nature" and not of witchcraft (483). The soul is not exalted at the expense of the body, as both Brocklehurst and Helen Burns, in very different ways, insist. Rather, soul can be located in the organization of the physical brain itself. The phrenological combination of faculties that constitute Jane's "peculiar" and "unique mind" (168) Rochester observes, enables natural sympathy between the lovers and hence, ultimately, their telepathic communication. Jane announces her skepticism of palm reading and magical arts when she meets Rochester in gypsy disguise, declaring that he is "coming to reality" when he begins to ground his reading of her character in phrenology and physiology (229). When she searches for the inner voice that will speak directly to her at moments of painful indecision, she orders her "brain to find a response" and then observes how in sleep or near-sleep it discovers that voice. This suggests the work of mental energies operating outside will and reason and not "the agency of spiritual beings or specters that assault the soul in sleep" (*PS,* 52).

Even as she proclaims the novel as prophecy, then, openly identifying with Micaiah and closing with the voice of St. John the Prophet, Brontë naturalizes intuitive vision and clairvoyant perception as the work of the undisciplined and undeveloped dreamy mind. In a chapter of *The Philosophy of Sleep* titled "The Prophetic Power of Dreams," Macnish declares the Book of Revelations "one magnificent dream" or "one gush of the Divine Spirit overflowing the mind of its author in sleep, and bringing the most distant ages in emblem before his eyes" (*PS,* 102). Mystical experience, he argues, must be seen to obey the fundamental laws of nature. In the novel, Rochester, of course, uses the science of sleep to disguise the truth about his imprisoned wife. When his guests inquire about the scream they hear from the attic, he blames a nervous servant who has "construed her dream into an apparition," and he does the same to Jane when she reports Bertha's ripping of the veil, protesting that in "half-dream, half-reality" Jane has "ascribed a goblin appearance" to Grace Pool.

Yet Rochester's efforts to obfuscate the facts by insisting on the nervous habits of women do not automatically cast all the narrator's descriptions of mental reverie in a skeptical light. Jane herself ascribes her feelings of foreboding to hypochondria (320), thus apparently concurring with Rochester's diagnosis that she has a nervous disposition. Nevertheless, she prefaces her account of the dangers of premonition-laden dreams about sickly children with a passage that unites the Puritan interpretation of signs with the science of the mind:

> Presentiments are strange things! And so are sympathies; and so are signs;
> and the three combined make one mystery to which humanity has not yet
> found the key. I never laughed at presentiments in my life, because I have
> had strange ones of my own. Sympathies, I believe, exist (for instance,
> between far-distant, long-absent, wholly estranged relatives asserting, not-
> withstanding their alienation, the unity of the source to which each traces

his origin) whose workings baffle mortal comprehension. And signs, for aught we know, may be but the sympathies of Nature with man. (254)

Here Jane elevates Bessie's folk superstition that dreams of children signify danger to oneself or one's kin from the realm of folk tradition into those of both Christian providence and mental science. The divinely arranged signs that illuminate Providence are potentially decipherable as natural mysteries, mysteries that as yet can be decoded only loosely through the principle of "sympathy" or the bonds among organic things, but which might eventually be fully unlocked.

In April 1850, Brontë acknowledged to her publisher George Smith "that there are certain organisations liable to anticipating impressions in the form of dream or presentiment I half believe."[63] What Rochester calls Jane's other-worldly character can be attributed to this kind of mental organization. She dreams nightly of a weeping infant before the news of John Reed's death is brought to her and again of a child whom she fails to protect on the night that Bertha appears beside her bed. The character's susceptibility to portentous dreams carries over into the narrator's half-conscious foretelling of events. She describes Mrs. Reed's dreaming of her son's "swollen, blackened face" (268) only to report, three chapters later, her younger self's horror at the "fearful, blackened inflation" (327) of Bertha's features. She depicts her wild defense against John Reed's violence in a way that foretells the physical struggle between Rochester and Bertha, as she "received him in a frantic sort" and, like Bertha, is pinned down at the arms before she is imprisoned in the red room. The sequence of events that incredibly restores her to biological kin appears to the character suddenly as a "chain that had been lying hitherto a formless lump of links . . . drawn out straight. . . . the connection complete" (443). As narrator, her task is to lay out the connections in sequence for the reader who, she observes, cannot be expected to have her "intuitive perception" or to "understand by instinct how the matter stood" (443). Here the often moralizing distance that the narrator Jane maintains from her younger self disappears and a mental gap emerges instead between Jane and her less-prescient reader. The real revelation does not occur in orderly narrative sequence but in an intuitive flash, suggesting that the narrator's retrospective interpretation of the events of her life can occur in the less-than-conscious process of what Rochester jokingly calls "second sight" (283) as much as through reflective judgment and the tracing of her own inner moral growth.

The naturalization of prophecy and second sight as productions of mental disposition and nervous organization positions spirituality and mystical insight in early-century theories about heredity and environment. These theories recognized heritable physiological characteristics as features of race difference—the effect of monogenetic organic variation from an original type rather than, as the proponents of polygenesis argued, evidence of multiple human origins.[64] In his *Researches into the Physical History of Man* (1813), Prichard stressed that characteristics unique to particular races are determined by cultural or climatic circumstance—determined by isolation or migration—and that these characteristics are generally hereditary.[65] Europeans (particularly women) transplanted into hot countries or descended from those who underwent such migration, he proposed, become debilitated and susceptible to disease.[66] Like Prichard, arguing that all human beings are descended from a single pair, William Lawrence and Thomas Hodgkin both proposed that differences in human type are the effect of inherited changes brought about through exposure to new climates.[67] In what he identified as a theory of "natural selection" that preceded Darwin's, Patrick Matthew proposed in 1831 that "a change of seed, that is, a change of place . . . [is] indispensable to . . . more sturdy growth and health"[68] and that there is "a power of change under a change of circumstances [in] living organized matter, or rather [in] the congeries of inferior life, which appears to form superior [life]."[69] He suggests that natural mechanisms of organic dispersal (change of place under favorable circumstances) can account for the superiority of the British "Caucasian breed" of human being, which maintains its sturdy growth through its "wide move across the Atlantic" where the "old breeds" of conquered countries sink "before the vigor of new immigration."[70]

Jane Eyre's bildungsroman form together with the phrenological readings Jane and Rochester make of each other emphasize the principle of individual development. Yet, at the same time, narrative allusions to the influences of environment and heredity pull against the themes of self-control and self-determination, juxtaposing the frail nervous states of the Jamaican Creole characters with Jane's ability to flourish even in adverse circumstances. Jane thrives at Lowood despite the terrible conditions and seems to grow with the "sweetest luster" (91) of spring, while so many of her classmates die of typhus and Bertha and Richard Mason succumb to the malignant influence of Jamaica. The latter has a "tame, vacant expression," (220) attributable to his life in the tropics, while his sister's moral indigence and mania is inherited from her mother and implicitly native to Creole ethnicity. Rochester pleads that his past, degenerate behavior should be attributed to "circumstances," rather than to his "natural bent" (159), and asserts that Jane can claim no credit for her mental strengths, which are only the work of "Nature" (158). Bertha comes "of a mad family; idiots and maniacs through three generations" (337); her youthful surrender to lust and intemperance only weakened her already innately frail faculty of reason. Jane, whose capacity for moral growth contrasts her with Bertha, pleads for the latter that she "cannot help being mad." Rochester admits that she is "singularly incapable of being led to anything higher, expanded to anything larger" (353). At the same time, "her character ripened and developed with frightful rapidity" (353). This confluence of inherited characteristics and innate developmental tendencies makes her Jane's opposite, since the latter, as Rochester has deduced from studying her face and brow, has powerful faculties of judgment and reason, which exert control over the passions, thus partly determining her own destiny by disposing her to follow her conscience or that inherent "inward treasure, born with [her]" (233).

Nevertheless, even as an adult, Jane is susceptible to "hypochondriac foreboding" (320), and, like moral madness, hypochondriacal nervousness is associated with a tendency to fall into mental states that escape the discipline of the higher faculties. Her innate "inward treasure" or self-disciplining moral compass surrenders to dreamy episodes that are especially likely to occur in an environment of confinement or isolation, or when she is threatened with these. One such circumstance is the terrible prospect of sexual enslavement as Rochester's mistress, when her fear manifests as an auditory hallucination; another accompanies the prospect of a life of exile as a missionary's wife—a life that St. John tries to impose on her and that she shakes off when she hears Rochester's voice on the heath. The dreamy apparitions she conjures at such moments are not managed by the rational observing faculty of the self. If they are the effect of "excitement," then that is, uncharacteristically, for the reader, not the narrator herself, to "judge" (383). What that reader is likely to conclude is that they are expressions of "the spiritual eye" (147) as she says of her surreal paintings, and as such they belong to a lower mental state in which the terrified imagination is ascendant and the governing faculties of reason and judgment suspended.[71] In her lower mind, Jane finds the means to liberate herself from the circumstances that threaten her as a single woman without the protection of her family and, paradoxically, the opportunity for greater self-definition.

In the final chapter of *A Treatise on Insanity*, Prichard investigates the ecstatic affections, describing the "obscure phenomena" of the mind ranging from simple daydream, in which there is a "voluntary abandonment of the mind to the leading fancy,"[72] to the luminous vision of the clairvoyant. While the perspective of the latter, which, like God, can penetrate the secrets of nature and see into the future or across any physical distance, defies all existing knowledge by observation and experiment and therefore cannot be subjected to proof,[73] we must assume that the answers lie in the natural powers of the mind and that such phenomena cannot be attributed to either miracle or some mysterious additional sense. The effects of animal magnetism, for instance, can probably be traced to the energies of the emotions and the imagination.[74] The visions associated with ecstatic somnambulism or trances, "are like those of a maniac or demented person," since the visionary scenes generated in the paroxysm blend with realities after the event. It is probable, he suggests, that impressions stored deeply in the memory merge with the creations of fancy when they are excited by the paroxysm.[75] Thus ecstatic states must be considered pathological and are closely related to disorders such as epilepsy and hypochondriasis as well as to madness.[76]

Jane Eyre at once recognizes the physical origins of ecstatic religiosity with their disturbing proximity to madness and affirms direct knowledge of God. Jane's clairvoyant powers, I have argued, have a natural origin in the dreamy state, where imagination and sympathy are liberated from the restraining influences of the higher powers. Yet Jane's story is mediated by scripture. She quotes Luke 2:19 in recording how she "pondered" the mystery of her clairvoyant communication with Rochester "in [her] heart" (516), and invokes the Song of Songs as she invites him to walk in the clear morning air. Most pointedly, she ends her narrative, not with the description of domestic bliss that her future holds but with the death of St. John Rivers and the quotation from Revelations. Although these words are given to Rivers, whose domestic tyranny is earlier linked to his reading from the Apocalypse, they also belong indirectly to Jane, who, in reading them, feels her heart fill "with divine joy" (521). The "fantastic dream" of St. John of the Apocalypse invokes, not the fire and brimstone of her cousin's reading or of Brocklehurst's threats but the ascendancy of Jane's own spiritual powers at the very moment that she rejects St. John Rivers's authority and as in prayer seems "to penetrate very near a Mighty Spirit" while her "soul rushed out in gratitude at His feet" (484).

In 1851, Brontë urged Harriet Martineau to mesmerize her. She told James Taylor that while she was not a convert to mesmerism, she had heard stories of its success and could not discredit everything she had been told. She also reported that "it was inferred in time I should prove an excellent subject."[77] Yet she was distressed by the "avowed atheism and materialism" of Martineau and Henry George Atkinson's *Letters on the Laws of Man's Nature and Development* (1851), whose "declaration of disbelief in the existence of God or of a future life" filled her with "instinctive horror." "If this be Truth," she told James Taylor, "man or woman who beholds her can but curse the day he or she was born."[78] In this book, Atkinson responds to Martineau's questions about the nature of mind but emphasizes that man is not essentially different from the lower animals, but only a fuller development of the "same fundamental nature or cause" (*Letters* 16). Mind is therefore not, some "brilliant existence" independent of the earthly environment of the brain (16). What we call "me" is "a thinking feeling substance" (132); sympathy, clairvoyance, and *prévoyance* are being traced by science to their place in the brain (123); and God, Martineau proposes, "is a projection of [our] own ideal faculty (217) or, as Atkinson argues of ecstatic visions, the creature of dreams and fantasies whose impressions are confused with realities (53). Where the *Letters* close by condemning organized religion as "demoralizing hypocrisy and cant" (290), Brontë's novels discover God through the peculiar mental talents of a devout mind, even as they recognize that God is encountered through a lower mind, vulnerable to hypochondriacal disturbance. Brontë respiritualizes material, evolutionist accounts of the mind and, in so doing releases her heroines from the patriarchal social structures with which mental science is often complicit.

III. *VILLETTE:* DEMONIC IMAGINATION AND THE REPELLENT REAL

In *Villette*, the heroine's ecstatic inspiration again feeds on scripture, only this time through the figure of the Apostle Paul. Like Paul, Lucy is exiled and often without friends; every journey leads her into the "vastness and strangeness" of a "wilderness" (38). In London, she sleeps homeless and friendless, not coincidentally, "in the shadow of St. Paul's" (40). Her sufferings, from the abuse and deception she experiences in her early journeys to the final possibility of the death of her fiancé M. Paul, might be said to echo those of St. Paul and the verses from Corinthians 2:

> In journeyings often, in perils of waters, in perils of robbers, in perils by mine own countrymen, in perils by the heathen, in perils in the city, in perils in the wilderness, in perils in the sea, in perils among false brethren;
> In weariness and painfulness, in watchings often, in hunger and in thirst, in fastings often, in cold and nakedness (2 Cor.: 24–29)

Such suffering (which Lucy also identifies with that of Job [48]) inspires the Pauline language that opens chapter 38: "who gives the shield of salvation, whose gentleness makes great" (410). For Paul, salvation is to be found by dressing in the "armour of God" (Eph. 6: 11–13). Yet this identification with Paul is profoundly unstable. It is not Lucy who bears his name, but her younger rival, Paulina, the child who prays "like some Catholic or Methodist enthusiast," yet who, when grown, becomes an "agent of God" without any excessive suffering (408). Despite the Protestant emphasis on Pauline justification by faith, the other namesake of the Apostle in the novel is the Catholic Paul Emmanuel, who accuses Lucy of worldliness and the "pride and self-will of Paganism" (283). Lucy's identity as a Christian sufferer is displaced by Paul Emmanuel's own story of sacrifice and diminished by the unsuffering goodness of Paulina, who not only finds earthly happiness but also earns "the blessing of heaven above" (409). She lives, in fact, the life that Lucy offered the reader as an "amiable conjecture" about her own future: "a bark slumbering through halcyon weather, in a harbour still as glass . . . face up to heaven . . . in a long prayer" (29). Meanwhile, Lucy's mental anguish, far from confirming her union with Christ, is more often expressed as a vulnerability to the miseries of the "rude real" (100). Moreover she reveals her repressed and projected jealousy of Paulina when she describes the latter's sewing thimble as "the golden head of some darting yellow serpent" (272). Jane realizes her own spiritual yearnings in part by becoming Rochester's guide and in part by displacing these yearnings onto St. John Rivers. Lucy, whose own name points to her troubled relationship with God, slips gradually away from her identification with St. Paul and becomes increasingly unsuitable as a Protestant spiritual mentor either to the pupils whom she half despises or to her Catholic lover.

Like Jane, however, she is subject to episodes of dreaminess, as when she finds herself in a state of "lonely calm" which can "steal meaning from the page, vision from [her] eyes, and lure [her] along the track of reverie, down into some deep dell of dream-land" (121). Such reverie is sometimes moderated by the more rational awareness of the narrator who contrasts her visions with the external realities that her character would like to escape and can observe how she is "snatched . . . back to consciousness" (121). Yet even as narrator, Lucy is often directed by an inner voice, one that tells her, in the absence of friends or home, to "go out hence" (37); she hears the sound of the wind as something "almost articulate to the ear" heralding apocalyptic flood, fire, and disease (32). As she tells her story, she dwells on the dreamy episodes that mix daydream with clairvoyant powers of sight, such as the vision of Europe spread out "like a wide dream-land far away" (49) or that release her from the pain of her circumstances by conjuring up ideal figures or "angels" (100) to dull her longings and fears. Like Jane waking from her rapturous experience on the heath to the cold reality of hunger, Lucy is startled out of her dreams by the external senses that make her aware of the activity around her. This is an awareness of the real, "all evil, grovelling and repellent" (100). She observes that she seems to "hold two lives—the life of thought and the "life of reality" (68).

For Jane, these two lives eventually become simultaneously livable. She achieves both earthly and spiritual fulfillment: In her union with Rochester she vicariously experiences the delights of the senses, as his sight is restored and he can appreciate the ordinary as well as the beloved objects around him; in her closing identification with St. John, she can give free rein to her ecstatic affections. Lucy, on the other hand, claims she can limit herself to satisfying the most primitive wants of the body so as to indulge the "necromantic joys of fancy" (68). What she represses here is of course the very need for sympathy, whose fulfillment, for Jane, joins the ecstatic life of the mind with the mundane wants of the body, including those of sexual desire. Later, when she is made companion to the cretin, whom she describes as a "strange tameless animal," Lucy states quite openly her need for communication with a "human being" and she hides from the natural elements that she cannot make "comrades" "nor yield them affection"(144–45). In a feverish state, she imagines that sympathy between lovers could sustain "a fine chain of understanding . . . through a separation of a hundred leagues—carrying across mound and hollow, communication by prayer and wish" (145). Lucy's lack of shared sympathy with any other human being transforms what should be ecstatic devotion into necromantic fancy. Without sympathy, her hypochondriacal despair reaches a pitch, and her formerly dreamy visions now become demonic: a "nameless experience that had the hue, the mien, the terror, the very tone of a visitation from eternity" (146). The nightmares that oppress her while she is left alone in Villette during the summer vacation are then rekindled at the theater when she witnesses the demoniac possession of the actress Vashti, something that is at once marvelous and mighty, low and immoral.

Lucy lurches between the miseries of the material world and the spiritual torments of a mind strained by physical illness. These competing levels of awareness in turn are attached to the competing generic forms of realism and Gothic. Vashti's incarnation of the fallen Lucifer is a projection of the demonic obsessions that haunt Lucy herself. Moreover, the Gothic twists and turns in the novel, from the appearances of the "ghostly" nun to the confusing narrow streets of Villette map in the external world the mysteries and terrors of Lucy's internal landscape. Hence, when she is lost in the old part of the city, Lucy loses consciousness and falls into a state of suspended animation (172). Meanwhile Dr. John, the man of science, can pilot these streets with ease and "penetrate . . . every door which shut[s out] an object worth seeing" (185). Although the visitations of the ghostly nun turn out eventually to be a hoax, she carries enormous psychic weight for Lucy, signifying, in medical terms, her own nervous condition, which Dr. John also penetrates as he speculates that she simply saw something that impressed her imagination. Lucy is less sure that she has had a hallucination of the presence of the nun, but she does link the latter's appearance with her own tendency to "romance and unreality" (235). Indeed, until she is exposed at the end of the novel, the nun herself embodies the unnavigable double life of a narrative that straddles Gothic romance and realism, raising the competing possibilities that she is either a thing "beyond the grave" or else "a child of malady"(235).

There are moments in the story when it seems that the sheer aesthetic power of Romance will win out over realism. By transcending the limits of the body in her performance, "convulsing a perishing mortal frame" (243), Vashti too is an immortal spirit, one who fills Lucy with fascinated terror. More than just another incarnation of the nun, however, Vashti is an artist. In one of the first moments that she allows herself to be critical of Dr. John, Lucy notices that his reaction to the actress is callous, because he judges her as a woman rather than as an artist. It was, Lucy declares, "a branding judgment" (242), reducing to the objectifying mark of the professional eye what for Lucy has the power to tear the soul out of its earthly chamber. Vashti's Romantic genius has a magnetic effect on Lucy, drawing her into a Shelleyean sublime where the mind abandons the mundane directives of hope and desire and discovers spiritual union with a "power like a deep swollen, winter river, thundering in cataract, [which bears] the soul, like a leaf, on the steep and steely sweep of its descent"(242). Yet medical sense ultimately prevails. When Vashti's artistic rage apparently reaches such a pitch that it sets the theater on fire (reviving the figure of Bertha Mason) it is superseded by Dr. John's authoritative calm, which in turn renders Lucy still and sensible, "neither hindrance nor incumbrance" (244).

Oscillating between wild Romantic imagination and calm realist awareness, Lucy is at once vicarious artist and nervous subject. Her indifference to the Rubenesque "Cleopatra," in all her bulky glory, and her disgust at the paintings representing the four stages of a woman's life from coquette to widow contrast with her enthusiasm for the truth of Flemish paintings that capture Nature's power in a landscape, or that reveal genius in a portrait artist. M. Paul, who shares her taste, nonetheless accuses her of an interest in the "Cleopatra," thereby provokingly associating her with de Hamal, the womanish man of sense who is drawn to voluptuous forms. As poor a reader of Lucy's character as M. Paul, driven by his own obscure passions, appears to be at this moment, he is nonetheless right that Lucy cannot completely abandon herself to her visions or transcend the mundane truths of the flesh, as can the Satanic-heroic Vashti. When, in sleep, or dreaminess, she allows "a truant hour to Imagination" (214), she is brought soundly back to the realm of the senses: She hears the sound of rain on the windows, feels the cold of the morning air, tastes the "ice-cold" of water (215). The daylight of the senses banishes Imagination, whose province is dreams, whose 'flowers cannot fade" and whose "day needs no sun" (215).

The tensions between Romantic Imagination with all its Gothicisms, on the one hand, and the realist awareness operating variously through reason, "groveling" materialism, or medical science, on the other hand, are themselves pathologized as evidence of Lucy's hypochondriasis. In *Villette,* the spirit that declares, as Rivers did through Jane, "I come" (199) is the specter of Hypochondria. Lucy recognizes her own silent suffering and nervous melancholy in the face of the King. She accepts Dr. John's diagnosis of hypochondria as the source of her nervous fever and syncope, although she dislikes discussing the subject of her nervous health with him. Like his real-world medical colleagues, John Graham prescribes cheerful society and exercise. Yet however willing Lucy may be at times to follow Dr. John's lead and practice self-diagnosis with the hope of improving her mental health, she resists his firmly realist stance on the nature of mental phenomena. Not only does she give Hypochondria an allegorical power that "on that stage" (199) anticipates the spectacle of Vashti, but she also associates it with vision and prophecy, donning Nebuchadnezzar with the title of "imperial hypochondriac" (255) even as she reaches for a simile to convey the nervous agony of solitary confinement. As a hypochondriac, she is at once vulnerable to the ungoverned force of the imagination and, at the same time, a calm observer of her own delirium. This is true, not just of the character, whose partial insanity is balanced by the shame that comes with self-awareness, but also of the narrator. Lucy-narrator at one moment reaches for the sublime heights of unfettered imagination and at the next becomes the cool diagnostician who can at once speculate on the nervous origin of what she thinks she sees and assemble her account of events so that the everyday causes of apparent mysteries will be resolved.

Like the revelation about Rochester's mad wife in the attic, the real events behind mysterious happenings shift from the realm of the supernatural to the activity of the mind. Ghostly apparitions and sinister intrusions upon Lucy's privacy turn out to be nothing more than the work of romantic and Jesuitical conspiracy, yet they have an afterlife in Lucy's bewitched perceptions that, stimulated by a drug supposed to sedate her but rouses her imagination, infuse everyday scenes with a sense of "mystery" and the "ghost[ly]" (434).

Under the sway of an opiate whose effects seem only to mimic her sponta-neous nervous episodes, Lucy wanders like an invisible onlooker through "a strange scene, stranger than dreams," a "land of enchantment" (423). She secretly watches her friends, not with the eye of the realist observer but as a dreamy bystander watching figures in a pageant like Prospero's, who will suddenly "vanish like a group of apparitions" (424). Although, in her detachment, she feels she "penetrates to the real truth" (435) and that "there is a kind of presentiment that never is mistaken" (436), she arrives at false conclusions about the arrangement of characters in the scene she observes. Finding that the ghost of M. Paul's former love, that other nun—Justine Marie—is merely reincarnated in her namesake, the ward of M. Paul, she is swayed by figments of her imagination as she misconstrues the relationship between M. Paul and the young Justine Marie, thus playing her own part in the romantic-comic "sylvan scene" (436) before her. This in turn hearkens back to her performance in the play at the École, when she became absorbed in the part "as though lifted in a trance to the seventh heaven" abandoning her customary role as "mere looker-on at life" (129).

That her apprehended "truth" is bound up with imagination's figments is a reminder of how little trust can be placed in a narrator who habitually withholds key pieces of information from her readers. Just as she fails to tell us when she recognizes Dr. John as the John Graham from her childhood, she gives no hint that her coming disclosure is a product of the dreamy mind and that it will lead her into error. In fact she seems to treat the reader as an unwelcome intruder on her dreamy episodes—one who, like M. Paul, coerces her into a particular form of writing and threatens to discredit her strange turns of fancy. Of that reader, she asks wearily, "must I tell . . .?" (447), as she introduces her account of the strange events of the fête. Yet as a hypochondriac, like her character, Lucy-as-narrator is also a reasoning observer of her own ecstatic episodes. As she describes the series of memories and impressions feeding her presentiment that Justine Marie will somehow rise from the dead, she asks:

> Ah! when imagination once runs riot where do we stop? What winter tree so bare and branchless—what wayside, hedge-munching animal so hum-ble, that Fancy, a passing cloud, and a struggling moonbeam, will not clothe it in spirituality, and make of it a phantom? (433)

Such self-consciousness, with its down-to-earth account of presentiment as a phantom of the brain also releases the reader from any obligation to heed the "signs in the sky" (462), which portend M. Paul's likely death at the end of the novel. This final refusal to divulge essential facts paradoxically pays homage to the creative imagination even as it highlights the hypochondriacal origins of Lucy's narrative and announces that "man cannot prophesy" (460). Indeed, hypochondriacal imaginings are the stuff of autobiographical art, as memories from key moments in our lives, "when reviewed, must strike us as things wildered and whirling, dim as a wheel spun fast" (454). Unlike Paulina, who claims to remember every moment of her childhood in exquisite detail, Lucy freely admits that she cannot recall experiences from the early days of her life and translates this imperfection of memory into the narrative syncope that may eliminate the ten minutes following M. Paul's gift of a schoolroom, or the several days of unconsciousness that she spends in the Bretton household. The realist check on hypochondria's flights of fancy does not quell the ecstatic imagination any more than Lucy's alternately Pauline and Miltonic episodes of spiritual transport are silenced by the mundane sensualism or accumulation of worldly knowledge through surveillance that she associates with Catholicism.

Yet there is a profound loneliness to Lucy's dreamy states, and we are left with a strong sense that she will remain unmarried and childless. This reader intuition has its roots in the pronounced mental difference between her and the happy and reproductively successful Paulina, whose intellectual talents put her firmly on the side of science even before she marries John Graham. The child Polly loves the book the older John shows her for its wonderful illustrations of the wide world and the deep history of species—painting everything from "wild men" (24) in faraway countries to mammoth bones; the natural wonders of the past being once again associated with the geographically remote primitive of the present. In this scene of hers and Lucy's childhood, the union of Dr. John and Polly is plotted. Her wonder at all he can tell her about natural history and geography resurfaces when the grown Paulina/Polly pulls an old book of his from the shelf and her looks of delighted recognition confirm at once her remarkable power of recall and her faithfulness to Graham himself. Paulina, Lucy tells us, "loved the Past" (270), meaning, presumably, not just the past of her own life but also, given the reading matter that inspires it, the deep past whose traces can be found in both dead and living evidence from the present.

Through the success of this marriage, the novel quietly articulates connections among the rational mental faculties, successful attachment, and the future progress of the European bloodlines. Paulina's "scientific turn" (3) is inherited from her father, Mr. Home, who in turn derived it from a maternal uncle. While Home himself made an unsuccessful match, falling for a beautiful but irresponsible woman from whom he formally separated, their daughter chooses a man who, Home remarks, is descended from a High-lander chief, and whose "tongue of wile and the brain of wile, are all come down [to him] by inheritance" (406). (Matthew praises the Scots among the "native[s] of the north of Europe [who have] a superior development of person, and a much longer reproductory life than the native of the south."[79]) This man of science and this scientifically minded woman, well-matched in their mental precision, will produce "healthy and blooming" offspring who will, Lucy assures, grow up "according to inheritance and nurture" (409). Despite his earlier infatuation with the coquettish Ginevra Fanshawe, he has a native clear-sightedness that protects him against pursuing a union that will lead, as it did for Home, into emotional decline. Dr. John will prove a good father because he "does not with time degenerate; his faults decay[], his virtues ripen[]" (408). The positivist cast of mind, which Comte argued in 1844 represents the last social-evolutionary stage of human intellectual progress, is specifically linked here with heritable qualities of mental and physical strength and is explicitly contrasted with the degenerate mind and body. Oblique references to the uncivilized world—the "wild men" of Gra-ham's book and M. Paul's fatal mission to the West Indies—do not threaten to link the hypochondriacal heroine with the savage degenerate as power-fully as they do in *Jane Eyre*. Yet Lucy's episodes of spiritual ecstasy are so impenetrable to the scientific mind, as she explains to Paul, that she is implicitly, by her own reckoning, developmentally inferior to Graham and Pauline. Moreover, their story, which Lucy carries chronologically beyond the endpoint of her narrative, is entirely legible, where her own is left unfin-ished and obscure. As unfruitful as she herself is reproductively unsuccessful, Lucy's narrative portrays nothing, as Brontë confessed, of public interest or a philanthropic or moral scheme, and its characters are as unrounded as its plot seems often unreal.[80]

For all its self-conscious allusions to narrative failure, however, *Vil-lette*, like *Jane Eyre*, refuses to succumb to the tyranny of the real. After the publication of *Jane Eyre*, Brontë wrote a hurt letter to G. H. Lewes, responding to his criticisms of melodrama and improbability. She protests that in her earlier writing, she had taken "nature and truth as [her] sole guides . . . restrained imagination, eschewed romance, repressed excitement." The result, she observed, was that publishers complained of a deficiency of "startling incident" and 'thrilling excitement." "Then too," she goes on,

> Imagination is a strong, restless faculty, which claims to be heard and exer-cised: are we to be quite deaf to her cry, and insensate to her struggles? When she shows us bright pictures, are we never to look at them, and

try to reproduce them? And when she is eloquent, and speaks rapidly and urgently in our ear, are we not to write to her dictation?[81]

Jane observes that such eloquence of the mind's eye is not equaled in the execution by her artist's hand. Brontë lamented that the "colours dashed onto the canvas" lacked "the proper amount of daring."[82] Yet despite the difficulties in realizing through art what is inspired by imagination, "the *real* should be sparingly introduced in pages dedicated to the *ideal*."[83] Lucy's and Jane's dreamy, spiritual attraction to the ideal may be disciplined by the restraining influence of the will, yet both characters manage nonetheless to protest their social confinement by linking stories of psychic struggle with the triumphant imagination. They do so though the diagnosis of hypochondria—that strange complaint in which reason maintains some foothold within the body-driven, interior landscapes of premonition and ecstatic vision. This lower, automatic nervous organization, invoked by Brontë in the image of writing to nature's "dictation," will become the source not only of clairvoyant vision but even social transformation in two novels by Charles Dickens.

SPIRITS AND SEIZURES IN
BLEAK HOUSE AND *OUR MUTUAL FRIEND*

*D*ickens had no patience with spiritualism. His periodical commentaries berate the "credulous persons who are abasing their intellects under the feet of that grossest of all impostures."[1] The converted spiritualist narrator of "Well Authenticated Rappings" in *Household Words* describes a ludicrous "visitation" in which he discovers that the spirit rapper knows the contents of his recently eaten lunch.[2] Whether the product of weak-mindedness or indigestion, belief in spirit communication, he derided, belongs to the primitive superstitions of the "idle" and "silly" and to the poor judgment of respectable men who fall prey to the impostures of scam artists and criminals.

Yet while, in his journalism especially, spectral events are frequently the projections of an infatuated spiritualist persona, they also invoke the materialism and monism of physiological psychology: "Wonders will never cease," an article from the September 1859 issue of *All the Year Round* cautions its readers, but perhaps eventually they will belong to the "manuals of science" rather than the "curiosities of superstition."[3] Hence Dickens expressed his intolerance of celebrated mediums such as D.D. Home or their Christian advocates like William Howitt and insisted on segregating the "preposterous state of mind" from the "medical, legal, or other watchful experience."[4] Contemporary interest in the apparently supernatural, he argued, must move beyond "bald credulity" into an energetic spirit of inquiry that respects the "vast unexplored ocean" of mental science.[5]

This interest in the physical origin of spiritual experience begins to explain the narrators and characters in his narrative fiction who sometimes display dreamy awareness, including "spiritual" episodes of clairvoyance, prophecy, and ghostly visitation. Dickens's treatment of these phenomena, I propose, draws on a theory of dissolution (the counterpart to evolution) that anticipates later neurological studies of epilepsy. Although triggered by nervous dissolution, dreamy events are neither held up to narrative scorn nor dismissed as the meanderings of a disturbed mind. In fact, they enable anticipatory revelations in the novels' plots and allow for intuitive connections among characters inhabiting vastly different social worlds. Even where these spirit manifestations are transparent plot devices or where they are absorbed into metaphor (John Harmon was never literally dead; the "Ghost's Walk" at Chesney Wold is a legend animated by the scandal of Lady Dedlock's past), they retain their otherworldly reference in narratives that are elsewhere driven by ghostly sightings, visions, and voluminous mental events. During such episodes, consciousness expands to an awareness of relations and connections that defy ordinary perceptual limits.

In this sense, Dickens's segregation of the watchful from the preposterous is not fully enforced in the dreamy environment of his fiction, whose divining narrative structure allows for the curious connections among seemingly unrelated stories and the unfolding of intimate connections between present, past, and future events. Such spiritualizing of expansive social truths encapsulates what Dickens famously described in the preface to *Bleak House* as "the romantic side of familiar things."[6] Omniscient as well as the first-person narrators, who sometimes pretend to impartiality and watchful observation, are all vulnerable to a sense of unreality or to visions that disturb the order of the observable physical world. In dreamy disturbances of spatial and temporal narrative organization, objective knowledge dissolves into apparitional landscapes as often as spirits are disciplined to obey the laws of physical nature. These spectral events intrude into stories that are otherwise firmly committed to the realist portrayal of the motives, eccentricities, and other psychological habits that not only make up individual human lives but that also determine the shape and scope of social institutions. Yet the many connections and conjunctions around which these broader social portraits coalesce are fully illuminated only by a clairvoyance that penetrates beyond the natural limits to perception imposed by time and space.

Lewes said of Dickens that he had, despite his perfect saneness of mind, a "vividness of imagination approaching . . . closely to hallucination,"[7] enabling him to represent ordinary objects like a street, or a house, or a room "not in the vague schematic way of ordinary imagination, but in the sharp definition of actual perception, all the salient details obtruding themselves on his attention."[8] "Psychologists," Lewes added, will understand both the extent and the limitation of the remark."[9] In identifying the point at which realism becomes hallucinatory in Dickens's style, Lewes combines his aesthetic evaluation with a diagnosis of mental abnormality. Such remarks are in keeping with the author-centered focus of Lewes's criticism. Yet they also suggest the engagement of literary form with mental science that characterized not only Lewes's career but, more broadly, a periodical-driven, intellectual culture in which fiction and scientific journalism were consumed by the same readership. In this interpretive context, not only the vividness but also the dreamy unreality of Dickens's "hallucinatory" writing is central to his realism. The dreamy forms in his narratives point naturalistically to his engagement with the psychic symptoms of a nervous disturbance; his writing explores the nervous pathways that shape perception and character. At the same time, the suspension of ordinary sensory encounter with the environment and the perception of phenomena that exist beyond the reach of the senses reveal intimate connections among characters who appear unrelated or seem remote from the central action of the novels.

Much has been written about this paradoxical aspect of Dickens's realism: his use of the ghost figure to answer the narratives' urge for connections or to chart disintegration in the social landscapes of *Bleak House* and *Our Mutual Friend.* An occult vision, critics have shown, oversees the fantastic realities of social and biological intercrossing that unite the disparate characters and settings of, especially, *Bleak House.*[10] *Our Mutual Friend* romances its realist themes of material collapse and degeneration with the observations of narrators and characters reanimated from the dead.[11] The omniscience in both novels, Audrey Jaffe argues, is akin to a supernatural perception in which voices attached to individual minds dissolve into ones that emanate from nowhere.[12] Many readings that tie the spectral forms in Dickens to particular psychological mechanisms focus on Freud's theory of the uncanny, where the mind encounters once-familiar objects that have been long repressed.[13] Some, however, have concentrated on the psychology of the time, citing studies of hysteria, the effects of stimulants or narcotics, and circulatory or digestive malfunctions that accounted for the origin of ghosts in the body.[14]

Yet despite the range of nervous disorders invoked by Dickens's representations of spiritual episodes (in which I include déjà vu, double-consciousness, and the previsions of trance states as well as actual spectral phenomena), there are several reasons why I read them here as symptoms of epilepsy. The first and probably least compelling of these is biographical: Dickens himself suffered what may have been epileptic seizures as a child.[15] He also witnessed the phrenologist John Elliotson's magnetic treatment of the epileptic Elizabeth O'Key in 1838, and in 1845 he conducted his own experiments in mesmerism, treating the Genoese Madame de la Rue for symptoms that included convulsions and catalepsy.[16] The second reason is that several of his characters suffer from grand mal seizures. For Mrs. Snagsby's servant Guster, in *Bleak House* these are set off by some reference to her parentage or by a sudden awareness of her implication in a network of events or characters. For the more prominent characters of Bradley Headstone in *Our Mutual Friend* and Monks of *Oliver Twist,* the "fits" are a physical expression of enormous mental anguish caused by suppressed familial, financial, or other close relationships. Dickens's depictions of "fits" as nervous episodes brought on by an obsessive preoccupation with something or somebody, by a horrified discovery of the subject's implication in a larger story, or by response to a psychic trigger (like Monks's loathing reaction to the sound of thunder) suggest that fanaticism, fixation, and sudden shifts in identity, along with falling and writhing, may be interpreted within the medical landscape of epilepsy.

The third reason is that nineteenth-century neurologists became increasingly interested in the dreamy states of mind precursory to or even constitutive of an epileptic seizure. By identifying the dreamy episode in which abnormal or fantastic memory penetrates awareness as something almost universally experienced, Dickens invites us to read his depictions of advanced epilepsy into the fabric of the larger stories in which they appear. These episodes are shadowed by those of characters who experience only dreamy awareness or recognition: Oliver's sleeping discovery of Monks and Fagin, Esther's intuitive discovery of her parentage in *Bleak House,* or the precognitive fear that affects many of the characters in *Our Mutual Friend.* Such episodes are instances of psychic voluminosity whose penetration of the ordinary workings of consciousness suggests levels of awareness operating below the inhibitory threshold of consciousness, even as they point to forms of nervous malfunction among those whose symptoms are slight enough that they do not provide evidence of disease.

Although the voluminous minds that produce premonition or discover unexpected links between characters and events in these stories do not inhabit falling bodies, they express symptoms of what Victorian neurology would describe as epileptic nervous dissolution—a pathology in which subjective states of mind are liberated from the objective truths of their environment. It is now commonplace to observe that we read Dickens's social worlds, not through the conscious mind of an individual character or narrator but in the impersonal network of overlapping events.[17] My focus on a nervous disorder as the narrative origin of this expansive social vision restores perception to individual minds, but to minds whose physical substratum has suffered trauma.[18] Epileptic dreaminess is paradoxically the means by which realities larger than those available to a single healthy consciousness become discernible: realities of hidden heredity, systemic corruption, and social disintegration.

I. GHOSTS IN THE BRAIN

Dreamy consciousness represents the conditions of heightened subjectivity and loss of cognitive awareness that is often associated with petit mal or what we now know as "complex partial" seizures. A passage from *David Copperfield* describes this experience of dreamy detachment as a clairvoyant connection between past, present, and future events and the remote histories that have brought these events into being:

> We all have some experience of a feeling which comes over us occasionally of what we are saying and doing having been said or done before, in a remote time—of our having been surrounded, dim ages ago, by the same faces, objects, and circumstances—of our knowing perfectly what will be said next, as if we suddenly remembered it.[19]

In this description, which has been quoted several times in medical literature on epilepsy and dreamy states, such mental episodes appear so slight that they barely disrupt the continuum of healthy mental experience.[20] Moreover, as Dickens emphasizes, they are almost universally experienced. The déjà vu is an everyday manifestation of the dreamy state that seems, for a few passing moments, to summon up memories of a former life. Here, although a healthy mind may barely pause to notice it, surrounding objects and people assume a heightened significance, manifesting as figures and events from a past so remote that it could not possibly inhabit a single memory.[21] Objects in the external environment appear simultaneously to belong in that dim past and to stimulate predictions of the immediate future, like forewarning ghosts. As John Hughlings Jackson was to argue in his essays on epileptic dreamy states in the 1870s and 1880s, subject consciousness is so heightened and object consciousness so compromised during these states that present surroundings vanish, giving way to a sense of expanded awareness.[22] This may include "a feeling of being somewhere else" or "in some strange country"[23] or "a blending of past and present. . . . as if reminiscent of a former life" or of having "two minds."[24] One of Jackson's patients talks about experiencing "curious sensations . . . a sort of transportation to another world, lasting a second or two."[25] The fit may take the form of various visions when not quite unconscious.[26] Jackson would propose that the disease may manifest in something as slight as an "overconsciousness" or dreamy recognition of "some other and quasi-former surroundings."[27] In large part the dreamy state is ignored, he suggested, because it represents only "slightly raised activities . . . of healthy nervous arrangements."[28]

Through his contact with asylum physicians,[29] Dickens was aware of studies of mental illness that identified overlap and potential diagnostic confusions among epilepsy, hysteria, and monomania.[30] It is reasonable, however, to interpret the dreamy episodes depicted in novels that include epileptic characters as "petit mal" epileptic seizures, given that nineteenth-century medicine increasingly recognized epilepsy in the manifestation of psychic symptoms. Among the British physicians studying epilepsy, including James Prichard, Richard Bright, and Robert Bentley Todd, convulsions ceased to be considered its essential symptoms.[31] "Spasms," Herbert Mayo likewise observed, are always liable to be combined with a trance state in which the mind takes on an abnormal relationship with the nervous system.[32] One of the key continental studies, Esquirol's *Mental Maladies,* declared that epileptic attacks might involve only the milder premonitory or early symptoms such as "a simple convulsive movement of a limb, the head or lips, with a momentary privation of thought,"[33] while in *Des accès incomplets d'épilepsie* (1867), Théodore Herpin explored manifestations of Esquirol's "vertiges" in the form of an altered consciousness immediately preceding an episode of syncope.[34] Indeed, minor attacks, including those so slight that they might be barely detectable, increasingly came to be identified as seizures in their own right. By the 1880s, even loss of consciousness, which was nearly always identified as a key symptom, had been expanded in definition to include "alterations of mental activity" and "disordered . . . intelligence."[35]

Jackson's theory of epileptogenesis, based on the evidence he found that function is localized in the cerebral cortex, argued that epilepsy should not be identified with any particular group of symptoms but rather by the "*sudden, excessive* and *rapid* discharge of gray matter of some *part* of the brain."[36] Even loss of consciousness, he argued, may not be essential to a diagnosis of epilepsy, since the disease may cause a "*defect* of consciousness" only.[37] Thus there was no reason to classify dreamy states or "intellectual aura" as they were more commonly known as premonitory or abortive symptoms of epilepsy. In large part the dreamy state was formerly treated as a precursory symptom or ignored, Jackson suggested, because in itself it represents only "slightly raised activities (slightly increased discharges) of healthy nervous arrangements."[38]

In his account of the physical substratum of mind, nervous centers—lower, middle, and higher—provide increasingly layered representations of different regions of the body.[39] In the highest centers, each unit represents all parts of the body at the same time that it represents one specially, thus allowing for a complex objective awareness of the self.[40] When, for example, a man is pricked on the back, he experiences both the nervous stimulation in the region affected, and the stimulation as affecting the self—an object (the body) and a subject of conscious awareness: The prick is to *his* back. Jackson speculates that if the whole body is represented in the units making up the division of the highest centers, with each part of the organ containing nervous arrangements for movements of the whole body, then it can be said that each unit is "the whole division in miniature" but "each of it is the whole of it in *different* miniature."[41] Thus each unifying or synthesizing center is "a series of miniature higher centers, each of which is in some degree 'potentially' the whole organism . . . in a different degree and order of representation of all parts."[42] These units, essentially the material basis of mind, therefore exist as potential, as much as they do actual, triggers of particular nervous and mental states. Reduced activity, or dissolution, in these centers is likely to increase automatic behavior. Elsewhere, this theory of nervous representation suggests an origin for the voluminous mental phenomena that he calls "dreamy." Objective awareness, choreographed by a higher center, selects particular objects in the environment for attention partly by choosing among the sensory images stored in the memory. When a higher center disintegrates and this objective awareness recedes, the mind is flooded with a multitude of subjective or sensory states that are normally "stored" in potential nervous configurations. Dreamy states, his case studies show, are nearly always experienced as a kind of expanded consciousness or "a diminished object consciousness with increased subject consciousness."[43]

The novels I discuss here predate Jackson's publications on epilepsy by some years. However, his studies are indebted to the physiological psychology of Dickens's contemporaries. In particular, Herbert Spencer's evolutionist account of the mental faculties was crucial to Jacksonian neurology, since Spencer emphasized principles of divergence and increasing heterogeneity in response to associative triggers, arguing that the brain developed more complex forms through its interactions with the environment. Spencer's proposal that cortical activity was governed by the same sensory-motor mechanisms and the same adaptive principles as the rest of the body provided the basis for Jackson's clinical investigations of malfunctions in higher order nervous activity. Like Jackson, Spencer also emphasized the origin of mental events in discrete areas of the brain. Combined with a theory of nervous development, the phrenological principle of cerebral localization enabled both to link all psychological phenomena to specific nervous activity.

In *The Principles of Psychology* (1855), Spencer animated his phrenology with a detailed account of the evolutionary process causing organic change across time. He describes "the evolution of intelligence by the multiplication of experiences"[44] as a "progression of the lower to the higher instincts . . . towards greater specialty and complexity of correspondence."[45] The cumulative effect of these nervous changes influences the character of the species as well as of the individual:

> Let it be granted that this tendency is, in however slight a degree, inherited, so that if the experiences remain the same, each successive generation bequeaths a somewhat increased tendency, and it follows that, in cases like the one described, there must inevitably be established an automatic connection of nervous actions, corresponding to the external relations perpetually experienced if from some change in the environment of any species, its members are frequently brought into contact with a new relation.[46]

By introducing the principle of "mental evolution,"[47] Spencer updates both associative psychology (where all knowledge is the product entirely of experience) and phrenology, which makes too-discrete correlations between different regions of the brain and mental faculties, ignoring the processes of coordination among different regions that occurs in complex intellectual events.[48] The development of mind in the higher animals from reflex activity to intellect, complex emotions, and will (as psychical changes become less definitely coordinated and less automatic) is consistent with the general principle that "life in its multitudinous and infinitely varied embodiments, has arisen out of the lowest and simplest beginnings."[49]

Although not formulated as a mechanism for describing nervous disorder until some years later, Spencer's concept of "dissolution" appeared in the context of political organization in *Social Statics* (1851)[50] and then as a general principle of evolutionary processes in *First Principles: A New System of Philosophy* (1862). In the latter, he argued that by means of adaptive responses to the environment, all phenomena evolve from "an indefinite, incoherent homogeneity to a definite, coherent heterogeneity."[51] This means they tend toward increasing complexity, becoming increasingly more differentiated, specialized, and heterogeneous. In dissolution, however, the reverse occurs as heterogeneous objects move back to indefinite, incoherent homogeneity: Complex molecules break up and their constituents take on looser structures; living organisms are subject to death and decay (and solid constituents assume gaseous forms); states are dissolved through social unrest; political collapse returns societies to a crude division of labor.[52] Such reversals, he argues, are integral to the evolutionary process. Indeed, the very condition of knowledge implies grasping not only the present nature of a thing but also its earliest, imperceptible state and its future, decayed state. "Intellectual progress consists largely . . . of widening our acquaintance with this past and this future."[53] Hence, in the 1873 edition of *The Principles of Psychology*, he added to the earlier account of mental evolution a description of the dismantling of the complex nervous arrangements that make higher and more deliberate processing possible, where there is an imprecise charging of the nervous system caused, for example, by feeble blood circulation (to which those with nervous complaints are particularly vulnerable) and producing failure or paralysis in the highest plexuses. The effects of this failure include monomania and strong disturbances where consciousness, loosened from its surroundings, "becomes a torrent of intense thoughts and feeling."[54]

Dickens was undoubtedly wary of Spencer given the latter's association with the philosophical radicalism of the *Westminster Review* (while *All the Year Round* contained three reviews of Darwin's *On the Origin of Species*, it did not review any of Spencer's work on evolution). However, Spencer's early phrenological studies, in particular his contributions to *The Zoist*, position him in the same circle within which Dickens maintained friendships with the leading British phreno-magnetists in the 1830s and 1840s, Chauncey Townshend and John Elliotson.[55] In keeping with the themes of *The Zoist*, which Elliotson edited, Spencer's articles examined not only several phrenological matters but also the trance phenomena of insensitivity to pain and spectral visions. Among other essays on these subjects, he wrote "A Theory Concerning the Organ of Wonder" (1845), which argued that spectral encounters could be traced to a region of the frontal lobe where wonder or "reviviscence" enabled reanimation of past impressions. This faculty, a powerful agent to the imagination, and thus physically visible in the skull shapes of great writers, could cause the revived impressions to be confused with real perceptions. Visionaries and prophets, whose mental organization also privileges this faculty, thus believe they communicate directly with spirits. Household ghosts appear when "during the gloom of night and under the influence of appropriate feeling, every dimly distinguished object calls up in the mind some pre-existing impression [and the] . . . mental image is mistaken for the thing seen."[56]

Spencer's phrenological investigation of spectral and other dreamy events complement Elliotson's inquiries in *The Zoist* and elsewhere into the organic origins of trance phenomena. In *Human Physiology* (1840), Elliotson reports how, whether as a result of nervous disorders such as epilepsy or by means of artificial somnambulism, subjects can become either insensible to external stimuli, partially sensible as in the case of sleep walking, or else manifest exalted power in one or more faculties. These altered states can also house an alternative state of consciousness or "double consciousness," in which a second personality emerges with a set of memories independent of those that belong to the original state. In 1837 and 1838, Elliotson and Charles Dupotet conducted experiments at University College, London, in therapeutic mesmerism, especially as treatment for the symptoms of epilepsy.[57]

In *Human Physiology*, Elliotson cautions that scientists investigating reports of marvelous phenomena—such as where subjects speak a language they have never learned or experience lucid vision wherein they observe events belonging to a distant time—must be alert to the possibility of fraud.[58] Nonetheless, he organized secret séances in which the phenomena of table turning and mesmeric clairvoyance were observed under experimental conditions. His lengthy report in issue 2 of *The Zoist*, the "Various Trials of the Clairvoyance of Alexis Didier," presented accounts of lucid vision witnessed by numerous dependable gentlemen including medical men "all of whom were perfectly satisfied of the fairness of the experiments."[59] In the 1846–47 issue he reported on a study of double states of consciousness in which he identified how both artificially induced and spontaneous trance states reveal the abnormal excitation of a particular region of the brain associated with a particular faculty.[60]

Dickens's own library reflected a combined interest in material and supernatural accounts of the exotic productions of the mind. It housed books that investigated the nervous and evolutionary origins of dreamy states like Macnish's *Philosophy of Sleep* (1840), Elliotson's *Human Physiology* (1840), and William Engledue's *Cerebral Physiology and Materialism* (1842). Yet it also contained copies of Beaumont's *Treatises on Spirits, Apparitions, Witchcraft, and Other Magical Practices* (1705), Augustine Calmet's *Phantom World; or*

The Philosophy of Spirits, Apparitions &c (1850), Robert Owen's *Footfalls on the Boundary of Another World* (1860), and Frank Seafield's *The Literature and Curiosity of Dreams* (1865).[61] The studies in the second list all propose the existence of genuine spiritual phenomena even as they explored the physiological conditions for experiencing them. Seafield alternates accounts of the material causes of dreams with those of their divinatory significance. Calmet declares that apparitions may be delivered by angels and "spirits of the blessed" or they may be the products of a powerful imagination, overly subtle senses, or the derangement caused by madness or fever.[62] And Owen proposes that abnormal conditions of sleep, which include coma, somnambulism, trance, and ecstasy, revealed an exaltation of mental powers whose modified form we experience in normal sleep in which "every night . . . we pass the threshold of material existence" and where "the grave restores its dead."[63] Such dreams cannot be the "purposeless wanderings of a vagrant imagination"[64] or the product of old associations "drawn from the forgotten depths of the memory," because they never existed there.[65]

Like these studies, Dickens's novels investigate the question of ghosts in the brain. In so doing, they replicate the kind of spiritual phenomena that medical scientists witnessed in nervously or artificially induced trance states and interpret "supernatural" events as nervous episodes in what seems like a literary articulation of the evolutionist neuropsychology that Spencer and later Jackson developed. Nervous disorder permeates the narrative voices in *Bleak House*, which are sensitive not only to the self-improving potential of the mind but also to its opposing tendencies—episodes in which the self splits into more than one personality or where object consciousness gives way to moments of heightened subjectivity. In *Our Mutual Friend*, the prevailing metaphors of dust and disintegration penetrate narrative consciousness, as dreadful anticipations and heavenly visions alike align disparate plots and unrelated characters. The disorganization of matter becomes the means by which little events achieve larger significance. In Dickens's nervous portraits, a principle of dissolution animates dreamy connections and projections made between and among characters, even as it links their mental suffering to the crumbling and corrupt edifices of the modern metropolis.

II. EPILEPSY AND THE VANISHING SELF: *BLEAK HOUSE*

In Tennyson's *The Princess*, "weird seizures" deliver the speaker into "a world of ghosts."[66] In Dickens's novels, revelations of identity provide the conditions for a similar kind of epileptic disturbance as they precipitate a feeling of nonself, or of a ghost of the self, whose knowledge of past events and buried associations is larger than the sum of individual experiences in the mind that contains them.[67] The altered perceptions, ghostly visions, and prescient awareness that sometimes attend the alterations of subjectivity in the dreamy state are especially pronounced in the narrative organization of *Bleak House,* since the division of narrative labor between third- and first-person voices alerts us to how the subjective mind negotiates the objective world. At the same time, connections among the many improbably related characters and their stories unfold through hazy presentiments as much as they do through the accidents and coincidences of the plot: dreamy minds make connections across time and space, linking the poorest of London's poor with a great country family, orphaned nobodies with titled somebodies, and the multigenerational suit in Chancery with the ancient line of the Dedlocks.

Such revelations are linked to instances of suspended selfhood in the novels. George Levine describes the way in which "scientific" characters, like Inspector Bucket, manifest the Baconian self-abnegation, or "clearing of idols," essential to objective understanding.[68] Such renunciations of self can be achieved through "the moral strength of self restraint" (and are therefore sometimes successfully performed in *Bleak House* by Esther, as they are by Inspector Bucket) and through self-annihilation, as in *Our Mutual Friend,* where John Harmon is able to observe the behavior of other characters from the position of a "dead" man.[69] Levine's argument can be linked with that of Catherine Gallagher, who shows how, in the latter novel, bioeconomic value (derived from living and laboring human bodies) is stored up in nonvital and nonorganic forms. This process of commodification, which Gallagher recognizes as "life in abeyance" is manifest in "apparent lapses in identity, breaks in the continuity of the self and moments of self-alienation associated with the marketplace."[70]

As a character whose self is suspended at once through her powers of self-restraint and her social nonexistence as orphan and illegitimate daughter of a man known as "Nemo" or "nobody," *Bleak House*'s Esther embodies the crossed-out identity achieved both through the self-abnegation and suspended animation that Levine and Gallagher describe. Yet the discovery of her parentage, however socially disgraceful it remains, triggers an intensified subject consciousness, whose psychic ferocity in turn precipitates experiences of dreamy unreality. This other kind of self-loss, or dissolving of identity, enables neither detached observation nor the accumulation of value. On the one hand, as narrator, Esther becomes suddenly interested and connected where formerly she had been morally impartial and removed; on the other hand, her dreamy mind offers nothing like regenerative promise either in the form of reproductive biopower (both Jarndyce and Woodcourt admire her instead for the self-restraint and moral strength that "all around . . . see in Esther Summerson" [866]) or in the form of useful information, since, as she says of the perceptual confusion she suffers when she is almost dying of smallpox, the less she says of her "strange afflictions," "the more intelligible" (514) she can be. The barely intelligible, dreamy voice that represents the mind under the pressure of dreadful self-recognition threatens the very order and revitalizing potential of narrative meaning, promising to overwhelm objective knowledge and to substitute portent for profit. Like the abyss of Chancery, this voice plots hazy possibilities and dim connections more than it does outcomes and advantages.

Esther, on the face of it, does not seem a likely candidate for nervous disturbance. She exercises a powerful self-control that suggests the active engagement of her will with the activity of her mind. A decade ago, Timothy Peltason rescued Esther from the charge of relentless selflessness by highlighting episodes in the novel that reveal her "force of self . . . under the names of will and desire."[71] Yet whether understood as self-control or self-expression, her will is sometimes overcome by dreamy episodes during which her mind, suddenly flooded by subjective awareness, becomes attuned to a range of possible identities or phantom selves, past, present, and future. As Esther's objective awareness of her surroundings recedes, her will falters, and she is temporarily unable to look at herself sternly as an objective observer or to fashion her social position as the "useful, amiable [and] serviceable" (569) "little woman" (640) of obscure origins to whom friends turn for comfort and advice.

Many such moments occur in her story. The most obvious instance is during her illness when divisions of time between childhood, adolescence, and youth "became confused with one another" (513) and when her sense of independent self dissolves into an image of the terrifying connectedness of everything: "a great flaming necklace" that is "strung together somewhere in great black space" (514). Yet these experiences of unreality and the altered sense of self that signals the onset of the illness are not entirely new for Esther. When she and Charley first leave to visit Jenny's cottage and help the orphan Jo, they pause at the gate leaving Bleak House, where Esther observes a strange light in the sky overhanging the darkened skyline of London. The spectacle is both "beautiful and awful," "immovable and heaving," revealing the terrible worldliness of London's "waste" with the light of a seemingly divine fire (450). Struck by this strange conflation of opposites, Esther experiences a doubleness in her own psyche, as she has "for a moment an undefinable impression of myself as being something different from what I then was," even though she is quite sure that she had no thought of "what was soon to happen"—referring perhaps to the symptoms of the illness but more probably to the discovery of her parents' identities (450). Here, in a subjective response to an atmospheric effect (as Monks responds to thunder in *Oliver Twist*), Esther's objective consciousness is flooded by that subjective awareness. She then undergoes one of those not-quite-describable moments of detachment from identity that Jackson would record, in this case linked to form of a peculiar clairvoyance, in which she experiences viscerally the effects of the knowledge of her parentage that is yet to come.[72]

Her dreamy states and the revelations they entail are always characterized by a feeling of indistinctness, whether something "undefinable," as it is at the garden gate; or the haziness of the light under the atmospheric conditions of dawn, twilight, fog, or shadow; or by a dreamlike or confused state of mind. The first time she meets Lady Dedlock, the latter's face is "in a confused way, like a broken glass to me, in which I saw scraps of old remembrances" (268); the second time, just before the mother reveals herself to the daughter, Esther "cannot say what was in my whirling thoughts" as she is struck by "something in her face I had pined for and dreamed of as a little child" (532). While she and Inspector Bucket are searching for Lady Dedlock at the end of the novel, premonitions of her death take on physical symptoms as "thoughts [that] shudder through me" (804), but they also have an unreality to them, as "I was far from sure that I was not in a dream" (803). Recalling the walk to the burial ground where they will find the body, Esther admits to "confused impressions"; "it was neither night nor day" (844). Almost-everyday fluctuations of consciousness, Esther's memories of events are here like her memories of childhood: indistinct and fragmentary yet overflowing with premonition. Or they are like her still more ordinary state of sleep in which objects become "indistinct and mingled" (57), and the separate identities of others as well of herself dissolves.

In all of these moments, her awareness of the external world is overwhelmed as her subject consciousness is intensified, while her strange sense of not-self, or of a ghostly self, is sometimes prelude to a strong premonition. Even when she has not the faintest idea of her connection to Lady Dedlock, she feels that "*I-I,* little Esther Summerson, the child who lived a life apart, and on whose birthday there was no rejoicing—seemed to arise before my own eyes, evoked out of the past by some power in this fashionable lady" (268). Earlier, the first morning she wakes up in Bleak House, she watches objects within and outside her room emerge "from the indistinctness of last night, disclos[ing] the scene over which the wind had wandered in the dark, like my memory over my life"(105). She is referring to a moment the previous night, when she had allowed her mind to wander back over her childhood and then "raise[] up shadowy speculations" (95) about her parentage. The simile draws the dim forms of the external world—the objects in the dawn light—into the territory of her wandering mind, where thoughts of the past summon up the ghostly figures of her parents.

Such apparitional moments, or simply the confusion and indistinctness that often accompanies them are, nonetheless, sometimes defeated by Esther's will, suggesting Dickens's confidence in the moral treatment of madness promoted by progressive asylum doctors like John Conolly.[73] She evades the disarming "shadowy speculations" about her parentage by recalling "Esther, Esther! Duty, my dear!" (95). She avoids the "fitful, dazzling"(244) habits of mind that destroy her cousin Richard, by exercising the "application and concentration" that he lacks, and she recovers from the auralike "dread and faintness"(532) that precedes her mother's revelation by reflecting on her "sacred obligation" (538) not to alert others to her discovery. Perhaps most powerfully, when she first looks at herself in the mirror after the illness has altered her features, she overcomes the estrangement from her own image by reminding herself firmly that she must begin life afresh as something other than a beauty. At such moments her story announces the victory of will over mental confusion and self-loss.

There is, however, a character that experiences a far more extreme loss of volition than Esther, experiencing not a dreamy state, but rather grand mal epileptic attacks. Guster has "fits," attributable, the narrator suggests, "to a tender heart, and a susceptible something that might have been imagination" (164) if it had not been for her stifling upbringing at the hands of the parish. In Jackson's cartography of nervous disorder, such emotional and intellectual undernourishment results in less activity in the higher nervous centers, suggesting that Guster might be more susceptible to a disorder in the lower and more automatic centers. Like Esther, and like Jo, whose unhappy plight "sends her into a fit of unusual duration" (164), Guster is an orphan. Unlike Esther, however, she communicates the distressed state of her nerves and mind only through her convulsions, and her ghostliness is that of the improbable séance specter so derided by Dickens: When she announces the visit of the Chadbands, she "comes rustling and scratching down the little staircase like a popular ghost" (281).

In "The Uncommercial Traveller," Dickens seems to speculate about the interiority of the female epileptic that he denies Guster in *Bleak House*. Here, the narrator visits a ward for the "idiotic and imbecile" in the Wapping workhouse, full of women who "drop," "roll," and "tear."[74] Among these, the one who reputedly has the worst attacks of them all, is a young woman who sits "with her face turned up, pondering." The traveler wonders:

> Whether this young woman, brooding like this in the summer season, ever thinks that somewhere there are trees and flowers, even mountains and the great sea? Whether, not to go so far, this young woman ever has any dim revelation of that young woman who is not here and will never come here, who is courted and caressed, and loved, and has a husband, and bears children, and lives in a home, and who never knows what it is to have this lashing and tearing come upon her? And whether this young woman, God help her, gives herself up then, and drops like a coach-horse from the moon?[75]

The traveler's compassion for the girl—his dismay at the bleakness of her life—is expressed here, not in a satire on the poverty of institutional care, but rather in an imaginative description of an alternative life of domestic contentment that she will probably never live. As the creation of the sick woman's mind, this other self arises as a "dim revelation." This spectral self then in turn signals the onset of a grand mal seizure. The odd thing is that it is the narrator himself who earlier claimed to have encountered the ghost of a drowned man on the swing bridge over the locks near the workhouse. Although he describes this "apparition" with not a little irony—it too appears like a séance grotesque with "a ghastly grin and a sound like gurgling water in its throat"—the ghost functions as a premonition, warning him about the desperate condition of the female residents of the workhouse.[76] To read this encounter as a clairvoyant episode is also to recognize the narrator's own implication in the scene with the epileptic girl: the speculations about what might have been come from him, and the "other young woman" is the apparitional creature of his mind as much as it is of the girl's.

Just as manifestations of the dreamy state become the property of not just cerebral disease but the ordinary observing mind in this scene, in *Bleak House* epilepsy inflicts not only Guster's and Esther's stories but also the quality of large portions of the anonymous narrator's tale. The fog that covers all of London in the opening paragraphs of the novel famously provides a metaphor for the murky conduct of Chancery. This fog makes forms indistinct and undistinguishable. It is the first of many of the narrator's descriptions of atmospheric effects that estrange the observer from a familiar environment, like the "dilating" (654) effect of dusk over Tom-all-Alone's or the twilight over Chesney Wold that changes known forms into "distant phantom[s]" (593). In this last description, the evening landscape is in sympathy with the ghostly presence haunting the house and its contents, in particular casting a menacing shadow over the portrait of Lady Dedlock. Curiously, in describing the way that Chesney Wold is still inhabited, in portrait form, by the generations of Dedlocks who have lived there, the narrator's omniscience expands speculatively from the present, visible world into the worlds of the lived past, the future, and the dead:

> The present summer evening, as the sun goes down, the preparations are complete. Dreary and solemn the old house looks, with so many appliances of habitation, and with no inhabitants except the pictured forms upon the walls. So did these come and go, a Dedlock in possession might have ruminated passing along; so did they see this gallery hushed and quiet, as I see it now; so think, as I think, of the gap that they would make in this domain when they were gone; so find it, as I find it, difficult to believe that it could be, without them; so pass from my world, as I pass from theirs, now closing the reverberating door; so leave no blank to miss them, and so die. (592–93)

Here the narrator breaks the rules of third-person anonymity, not in the limited mode of free indirect discourse, where anonymity enables the penetration of characters' consciousness but by projecting his voice into the body of a Dedlock and there inhabiting his own subjective, first-person "I." This spectral intrusion into the objective world then itself becomes the occasion for an imaginative, if not clairvoyant, representation of the dead ancestors that moves simultaneously into the past and into the future. It is the moment in this narrator's tale that parallels Esther's vertiginous reflection following her illness that "I felt for myself as the dead may feel if they ever revisit these scenes" (653). The narrator's Dedlock imagines himself as a dead ancestor, who in turn tries to imagine a future in which he is no longer the living master of the house. This layering of spectral voices and the collapse of linear time it temporarily effects is dizzying. Reader and narrator recover their balance only when the living and the dead are separated again by the closing of the "the reverberating door" (593). Then the portraits assume a comfortably caricaturelike quality as they come to satirical life in the light of the sunset: a Justice winks; and an ancestress in high-heels assumes a halo.

The narrator's prescience is sometimes manifest in the subjunctive mood of the voice that asks, as it does in the preceding passage, about what a character, real or imagined, "might have" thought or whether, for instance, Tulkinghorn *would* see a woman pass if he looked out the window at a certain moment. It is the voice that suggests "it *may* be the gathering gloom of the evening or it *may* be the darker gloom within herself" that casts a shadow on Lady Dedlock's face "*as if*" she wished for Tulkinghorn's death (598, my emphasis), and it is the voice that examines the scene of Tulkinghorn's murder with cinematic precision while imagining the ghost stories that the details it notes will spawn. This voice sacrifices both omniscient knowledge of the minds of characters (the knowledge that Tulkinghorn himself, "always at hand, haunting every place" [681], possesses and uses to his own dark ends), as well as knowledge about the visible world based on forensic evidence of the kind Guppy assembles, for intuitive anticipation of possible revelations or events to come. Hence, even as the narrator describes how Bucket "mounts a high tower in his mind" (798) to deduce the whereabouts of Lady Dedlock in the dramatic closing scenes of the novel, that narrative voice almost imperceptibly slips away from the detective's rational, speculating mind to uncover the mystery for the reader well in advance of Bucket and Esther's too-late discovery. At this moment, Bucket's reasoned deduction surrenders to a subjunctive mood that carries the reader beyond ordinary perception and discovery, not by penetrating the objective and subjective worlds of all places and all characters, but by inhabiting a field of the possible:

> Where is she? Living or dead, where is she? If, as he folds the handkerchief and carefully puts it up, it were able, with an enchanted power, to bring before him the place where she found it . . . would he descry her there? On the waste, where the brick-kilns are burning with a pale blue flare; where the straw-roofs of the wretched huts in which the bricks are made, are being scattered by the wind . . . there is a lonely figure with the sad world to itself. It is the figure of a woman too, but it is miserably dressed, and no such clothes ever came through the hall, and out at the great door, of the Dedlock mansion. (798)

Such dissolution, manifest in the drifting away from definite forms and signs, complements the images of physical change across time. The first chapter opens with the twin images of a megalosaurus wandering up Holborn Hill and of "new deposits to the crust upon crust of mud" (11) created by London's foot walkers, collapsing the comings and goings of the present into the vastness of geological time and intimating the interconnectedness of events as they are shaped by inevitable and unchanging natural forces. "What connexion," the narrator asks, "can there have been between many people in the innumerable histories of this world, who, from opposite sides of great gulfs have, nevertheless, very curiously been brought together!" (235). Given the mid-century popularity of Robert Chambers's *Vestiges of the Natural His-*

tory of Creation and the fact that Charles Lyell's *Principles of Geology* had gone through seven editions by 1851, it is hard not to interpret the "gulfs" he invokes here as those among natural forms and species as well as among social classes. Yet nothing in the novel suggests either natural or social progress. Instead neglect and indifference return creatures to their most primitive forms. Even the "lower animals" at Chesney Wold, the narrator speculates, might have more "motions of fancy" (95) than the stunted imaginations of the servants and stable hands that take care of them, and an "educated, improved, developed dog, who has been taught his duties and knows how to discharge them" (238) can, unlike the poor, uneducated orphan Jo, respond to his environment with more than brute sense. Hence too the dog, we are reminded, if turned wild, like Jo, will produce descendants that lack any of these domestic talents. Because he is continually being "moved on," Jo's mental and physical condition ironizes the very idea of evolutionary progress in a city where everything is "moving to some purpose" (291).

This social dissolution, imaged as a descending hierarchy of social beings, traverses the episodes and descriptions of mental dissolution. When Guster offers Jo food, asks him whether he has any parents, and lays the "first decent hand" on him, she has to repress "symptoms favorable to the fit"(384). Meanwhile Jo himself is rendered, as he so often is, mute and "petrified" (383). Both have suffered, like Esther, because they are orphaned, and both are most vulnerable to a psychomotor dysfunction at the moment they experience feelings of domestic tenderness, just as just as Esther is affected by her own inklings of familial connection. Yet neither, like her, has the capacity for self-direction that can summon her to duty with a commanding, "Esther!" Esther's superior mind (the result of the education and affection she has received as much as of native determination) often enables her to restrain her own mind's tendency to dissolution—a tendency that, as we have seen, gives her an expanded awareness of the relationships among people and places. Jo is also paired with Esther, however, as a character that belongs to the improbable connection between Chesney Wold and Tom-all-Alone's. He is "unconscious of the link" and he "sums up his mental condition, when asked a question, by replying that he 'don't know nothink'" (235). Esther, on the other hand, has a "knowledge of details perfectly surprising" (624) and the capacity, however dreadful she finds it, to understand her own place in the unfolding mystery.

Looking back on her illness, Esther reflects that her object in reporting its horrifying symptoms is to contribute to medical knowledge: "It may be that if we knew more of such strange afflictions, we might be the better able to alleviate their intensity" (514). This reflects her effort to shape her narrative as an expression of duty rather than hubris. But when the activity of her mind escapes the disciplining exercise of her will, her story becomes something other than the record of "progress" it claims to be by the title of her first chapter. Ostensibly, the ending secures the providential narrative, as the "goodness and tenderness of God" (911) reveals itself in the blessing and restoring of good characters who have suffered: Ada, Charley, and Caddy. This blessing is expanded in the formation of something like a Rousseauean *petite société* around the marriage of Esther and Woodcourt, whose goodness ensures the happiness of all those whom they touch: patients, friends, and children alike. Chesney Wold is left to "darkness and vacancy" (910), while Bleak House becomes the scene of new life and a generation liberated from the moral quicksand of Jarndyce and Jarndyce. Yet Esther's closing reflection seems to shift the narrative emphasis on moral restraint and its domestic and social rewards back to the more peculiar activity of her mind. In response to her husband's suggestion that the mirror should show her that, despite the scars of her illness, she is prettier than ever, she responds privately in the form of an incomplete phrase whose mood is subjunctive: "they can very well do without much beauty in me—even supposing—" (914). This abandoned reflection ends the novel with moral as well as semantic uncertainty: What if she *were* as or more beautiful than before her illness? The mirror suddenly ceases to be an instrument of self-discipline. It is possible to read this closing speculation as another moment of dissolution, a form of knowing that is neither that of third-person narrative omniscience nor of first-person moral self-fashioning. Instead it represents a heightening of subjectivity as awareness of the objective world becomes confused. Esther's closing half-thought, in other words, invokes the ghostly form that represents the dissolving of a conscious moment into a host of potential states.

III. THE DISEMBODIED VOICES OF *OUR MUTUAL FRIEND*

Ghosts are everywhere in *Our Mutual Friend*. Shortly after she meets John Rokesmith, Mrs Boffin sees the faces of old Harmon and his children all over the house; Lizzie appears to hear her father's voice calling her at the moment of his death; Jenny Wren sees her Jewish father substitute Riah as a dead man stepping out from the grave; Riderhood at one time saw towing posts turn into ominous figures in the gloom; and of course the reportedly dead John Harmon rises from the ashes to inhabit several new identities and hover around the lives of those to whom he was formerly connected "like a ghost."[77] This figurative ghost is the keystone to the plot, absorbing and transforming the myriad events in the novel into a single narrative. Yet ghosts have psychological origins too in the story. The visual and auditory hallucinations that Mrs. Boffin and Lizzie experience are, as Mr. Boffin suggests, the effect of "thinking and dwelling on that dark spot" (240). In Spencer's terms, they loom out of a mind in which wonder or reviviscence has taken an excessive hold, overwhelming impressions conveyed by the immediate senses with those delivered by the memory. Such specters arise like the images that come to Lizzie out of the hollow of the fire. Her foreknowledge of "dreadful things" (72) "comes like pictures" (71). Charley reproaches her with being a "dreamer" and tells her instead to "look into the real world" (278) and control her clairvoyant "fancies" (279). But she cannot control them. When she looks into the fire she sees visions of her life or of lives that might be hers that make her "exalted and forgetful" (405). The mesmerized state that comes upon her when she stares at the flames liberates old impressions from the exercise of her will and she becomes enraptured by them.

Lizzie's trance states summon up images of herself or an alternate self (the rich woman that might love Eugene) whose vividness makes them seem apart from herself. This out-of-body experience approximates that of the "dying" John Harmon, who later recalls how, under the influence of the stupefying drug that Riderhood gave him, "I saw a figure like myself lying dressed in my clothes on a bed" (426), and that "[t]he figure like myself was assailed, and my valise was in its hand" (426), and "[t]his is John Harmon, drowning" (426). In a description of dreamy dissociation that echoes Tennyson's, he recollects that "I could not have said that my name was John Harmon—I could not have thought it," but then demands of himself, "This is still correct?" (426). The narrative is accurate, he reflects "with the exception that I cannot possibly express it to myself without using the word I. But it was not I. There was no such thing as I, within my knowledge" (426). These "deranged impressions," he reflects, "are not pervaded by any idea of time" (425). As he moves through this series of hazy recollections, John Rokesmith does indeed raise the ghost of John Harmon, to whom he addresses this narrative and whom he apostrophizes with a desperate "Don't evade it, John Harmon, don't evade it" (423). This is not an indulgence in the metaphor of his death and "rebirth" as Rokesmith, the "fanciful side of the situation" in which he can describe his loneliness in the figure of a ghost who has no place among the living. It is the "real side" (422) of that circumstance, in which his dreamy consciousness, unable to integrate his former state of mind with his present one summons that older self up as a specter, one that is as remote from his subjective experience as the first-person narrative is from the dreamy unreality that it endeavors to capture through the artificially imposed pronoun "I."

Although artificially induced, this division of self approximates the many instances of "double consciousness," or divided personality, that Elliotson records in *Human Physiology*, whose cause may be nervous disease.[78] Harmon's split self is also bound to the broader pattern of doublings and substitutions that structure the narrative: Bradley Headstone not only disguises himself as Riderhood, looking "in the clothes of [another] man, as if they were his own" (697) but is united to him in death by the iron ring that causes it; Mr. Venus's trade in human parts parallels Gaffer Hexam's business in drowned bodies; Silas Wegg and Charlie Hexam are consumed by the same desire for "getting on" (127); Eugene Wrayburn's obsession with "the lonely girl . . . by the fire" (211) is not contrasted but rather coupled with the uncontrollable passion of her other lover, and like Lizzie herself, both men are entranced by gazing into the "charmed flame" (872), whose mesmeric power seems to be a stand-in for the enchanting beauty that awakens a new personality in each of them. The plot depends on these usually unlikely doubles as much as it depends on coincidence to bring together its very disparate players and unrelated places.

This nervous symptom of double consciousness—or the oscillation between two entirely different states of mind—is another expression of the dreamy disturbance that at once prevents the integration of self and divorces it from the social world. Perhaps the most unexpected link is between Harmon and Bradley, since despite their shared experience of social and self-alienation, only the latter suffers from a diagnosable disorder. In Harmon's efforts to make sense of what has passed, of who he is, and to make himself more substantial than the ghosts of the churchyard he is walking through, Harmon ventriloquizes an "I" that "was not I" (426). This is precisely the state of epileptic nervous collapse that Bradley falls into by the end of the novel. His condition first manifests in the *idée fixe* that strips him of all "power of self-command"(396), and becomes full-blown under the influence of rage and fear after his failed attack on Eugene in "fits" wherein he becomes seized with giddiness, and begins "biting and knocking" (821). Despite the loss of moral and then motor restraint, Bradley retains a state of consciousness in which he is profoundly aware of his own mind and, in this respect, never approaches madness. "The state of the man was murderous, and he knew it" (609). Like Harmon, he preserves some intellectual awareness, recognizing his two selves belong to one body even as he experiences them as two. By day, in the schoolroom, he maintains his "disciplined show," even as he contemplates his other, nocturnal state, "perfectly comprehend[ing] that he hated his rival with his strongest and worst forces, and that if he tracked him to Lizzie Hexam, his so doing would never serve himself with her. . . . And he knew as well what act of his would follow if he did, as he knew that his mother had borne him" (609). His core sense of identity—reason and self-perception anchored in the knowledge of his birth—survives the assault on his power of self-government by his passions, yet only by substituting detached awareness of these dueling selves for the integrated self that can align feeling with moral judgment. By the end of the story, when he "twists" and "falls" in front of his pupils, such awareness disappears with consciousness, yet its trace remains in an even further-removed point of self-recognition, as he sees his own facial distortions in the reactions of the horrified boys. This dreamy fit, in which Bradley knows himself only while being outside himself, follows on the two acts of violence that precipitate all other events in the novel.

Given this prominence in the plot, it is scarcely surprising that the narrative voice too sometimes slides into dreamy uncertainty in which thought becomes unmoored from identity. A full chapter before the discovery of Gaffer's body, Lizzie hears her father call her: "She opened the door, and said in an alarmed tone, 'Father, was that you calling me?'" This premonition is then revived in the narrative memory directly after Eugene, Mortimer, Riderhood, and the Inspector pull Gaffer from the water. Here, in an exaggerated, otherworldly form of free indirect discourse, not only direct quotation, but even the pronouns that might at least temporarily anchor the voice in a character are abandoned to a stream of images ranging across the consciousness of several witnesses to the scene and then left to drift away from all human awareness entirely:

> Father, was that you calling me? Father! I thought I heard you call me twice before! Words never to be answered, those, upon the earth side of the grave. The wind sweeps jeeringly over Father, whips him with the frayed ends of his dress and his jagged hair, tries to turn him where he lies stark on his back, and force his face towards the rising sun, that he may be shamed the more. A lull, and the wind is secret and prying with him; lifts and lets fall a rag; hides palpitating under another rag; runs nimbly through his hair and beard. Then in a rush it cruelly taunts him. Father was that you calling me? Was it you, the voiceless and the dead? Was it you, thus buffeted as you lie here in a heap? Was it you, thus baptized unto Death, with these flying impurities now flung upon your face? Why not speak, Father? Soaking into this filthy ground as you lie here, is your own shape. Did you never

see such a shape soaked into your boat? Speak to us, the winds the only listeners left you! (222)

This passage, preceded by a description of the dead body on the windswept shore and followed by the direct speech of the inspector, presents a dreamy interlude on the otherwise direct depiction of this dramatic event. Given the echo of Lizzie's earlier cry, it appears to represent her lucid vision of the scene, for she is not present. Yet the high diction of "sweeps jeeringly" and "hides palpitatingly" is not Lizzie's; nor is it the inspector's, although he too might be expected to observe the shape and the position of the body with exceptional scrutiny. Considering his demonstrated ability, when roused, to create "reviving impressions"(54) with language and given that it was he who witnessed Lizzie's earlier cry, it seems for a moment that it could be Eugene's. Yet Eugene, as Lizzie observes, has little-to-no capacity to enter imaginatively into the suffering of others. Eventually we are told it is the winds that speak, but their "prying" and "taunting" of the body is incommensurate with the cries of distress they carry. Voice is configured in the spectral conflation of words recalled from an earlier episode and present impressions recorded by a mind liberated from the sensory limits of a single being. Oddly evoking the hybrid figure in Mortimer's dream, "M.R.F. Eugene Gaffer Harmon" (224), this is the voice that belongs to no living body in particular and that, mediumlike, addresses "the voiceless and the dead."

Another such spectral intrusion occurs in Book 3, when Bella and Rokesmith are returning from their visit to Lizzie. Here the narrative voice recognizes their impending union, a voice that is once again routed through the "awareness" of a nonhuman agent:

The railway, at this point, knowingly shutting a green eye and opening a red one, they had to run for it. As Bella could not run easily so wrapped up, the Secretary had to help her. When she took her opposite place in the carriage corner, the brightness in her face was so charming to behold, that on her exclaiming, "What beautiful stars and what a glorious night!" the Secretary said "Yes," but seemed to prefer to see the night and the stars in the light of her lovely little countenance, to looking out of the window.

'O boofer lady, fascinating boofer lady! If I were but legally executor of Johnny's will! If I had but the right to pay your legacy and to take your receipt!—Something to this purpose surely mingled with the blast of the train as it cleared the stations, all knowingly shutting up their green eyes and opening their red ones when they prepared to let the boofer lady pass. (594)

The railway's "knowingness" seems at first a projection of Rokesmith's pleasure, which imagines the inanimate world to be working in his interest, engineering circumstance to bring him physically closer to the object of his desire. Yet in the first paragraph, the voice pulls away from the Secretary's conscious experience as it ponders that he "seemed to prefer" looking at the girl to looking at the stars. Moreover, the invocation of the "boofer lady" in the second paragraph could represent Rokesmith's thoughts only if he were morbidly invoking the figure of the dead Johnny, the boy that Mrs. Boffin hoped to adopt as a substitute for the younger, "dead" John Harmon. The identity of "I" is ambiguous here, as is the person referred to as "Johnny," since the diminutive form of the name suggests not the elder Harmon, who is of course the author of the will, but rather the dead child or else the younger Harmon in his infancy. Even the identity of the "boofer lady" is obscure, since the dying Betty mistook Lizzie for Bella, calling out to the "boofer" as in her confused state she appears to inhabit the mind of her dead great-grandchild, Johnny. Once again, impressions recorded in earlier scenes are revived in a floating consciousness that seems as incapable of fixing an identity to the figures it describes as it is unable to distinguish the living from the dead. Strangely combining the thoughts of a dead child, a dying woman, and a hopeful lover, this voice then blends with and animates the sounds of the train—the nonhuman object that, like the wind of the earlier passage, belongs to the visual content of the scene itself.

These descriptions, part hallucinatory revival of earlier impressions, part self-conscious omniscience that brings the usually invisible narrative voice into ghostly half-presence, suggest that the dreamy state and the physiological conditions that underlie it infect the very medium of narrative. Mary Poovey has shown that Dickens resists the interpolative role of narrative fiction, whose function is to diffuse disruptive impulses, particularly fear.[79] She argues that, like other formal modes of analysis that navigate the relationship between human impulses and sociality, imaginative literature obfuscates real sources of danger—those that are too painful or too terrifying to contemplate—by displacing these into abstractions such as "human nature" or "the market." Structurally equivalent to the Freudian ego, these abstract forms protect the subject by blocking it from its true source of danger. However, Dickens uses free indirect discourse, Poovey suggests, to reveal rather than obscure, unstated emotions and anxieties. When voices begin to merge, unpredicted relationships and unmanageable affects may suddenly appear. Narrative becomes both socially destabilizing and cognitively disorienting. Yet if we restore Dickens's narrative to the scientific contexts in which he wrote and read, we can see alongside this scorn for imaginary forms that "obliterate free will," another kind of emphasis. What is risked in free indirect discourse is not the inhibitory structure that manages individual passions but rather the diagnostic quality of narrative—its observation and labeling of nervous disorders. As the narrative voice assumes a ghostly, non-human form that rolls across other minds, collapsing differences in space and time, its investigative and explanatory powers are overwhelmed by a state of dreamy confusion which suspends the higher faculty of judgment—a phenomenon that is comically encrypted, perhaps, in the early scene at the Veneerings where narrative attention is apparently gratuitously turned to the "Analytical Chemist's" contempt for the Harmon story.

An essay by Edmund Dixon that appeared in the April 10, 1858, issue of *Household Words* offers a prototype for Dickens's peculiar kind of dreamy storytelling. In "A Microscopic Dream," a natural scientist finds himself transformed into a microscopically small life form. The dream, he implies, is the combined effect of associative connection and the nervous state into which his work has thrown him. Circumstance, however, offers the possibility that the "vision" was delivered to him by the direct influence of a clairvoyant magician, who exercises power and insight "over men and things" and to whom he has promised, at peril of such transformation, to explain the mystery and purpose of lower and smaller forms of existence.[80] In the dream, he undergoes physical dissolution "much like a lump of sugar might feel when it is dissolved in a glass of cold water" to become finally "an animated droplet" with "no definite shape or form." In this primitive state, he is able to assume any shape he pleases and attach himself to any life form he comes into contact with. Like Scrooge in *A Christmas Carol*, he is released from the vision the same way he was drawn into it, by the sound of the clock striking the hour. This dreamer is the scientist-counterpart to the spectral narrator of *Our Mutual Friend*. Through the dissolution and recombination of miniature life forms, he experiences multiple identities and states of awareness, all of which are tenuously attached to a single subjective "I." The physical transformation into a more primitive condition also parallels the novel's depictions of nervous retreat as it is expressed in the dreamy state.

Moreover, by invoking the figure of decay, Dixon's essay draws attention to the link between nervous decline and dust in *Our Mutual Friend*. Dust is the primitive residue of larger, more complex forms that are either dead or discarded, yet in this story it also conceals the revivifying treasures that promise to enrich and transform present lives. Bloated corpses, like the household detritus and vegetable refuse of the dust heaps become "meat and drink" (45) to the living. Hence Rokesmith's musing thought that "if the dead could know, *or do know*, how the living use them" (429, my emphasis), the best and worst of motives would become transparent. The prevailing figure of dust suggests that, in keeping with the perpetual cycle of evolution and dissolution, the dead do not quite stay dead. Hence Jenny Wren's cry to Riah: "Come back and be dead . . . come up and be dead" (335). Jenny, whose ecstatic moments of "lightness" when she is "taken up" by her "blessed children" (290) are so many deaths from which she returns to the pain of life, belying Riderhood's conviction that he who has once been drowned cannot die from drowning a second time. Jenny returns, however, as something half-angelic herself, "looking down out of a Glory of her long bright hair" (335) to call the living back to death, while Bradley orders Riderhood to "Come down" and be drowned again (874). As though to emblematize these efforts to keep down the dead, Lizzie's miserable interview with Charley and Headstone takes place in a raised church graveyard where the dead sit "above the level of the living" (451).

Although there is no megalosaurus in *Our Mutual Friend* to hint at the manifold hidden, material connections between the monstrous secrets of the past and the mental demons of the present, the novel shares with *Bleak House* an interpretation of visions and voices from beyond the grave as the effects of nervous disorganization. As lives and fortunes are reconstituted out of dust and rot, so are the dead reanimated in the dreamy visions precipitated by suffering and delivered by the dissolution of complex structures in the brain. Where dreamy self-loss in the first novel produces divinatory glimpses into ghostly lives that might have been, disembodied voices merge the worlds of the living and the dead, in the second. In this way, both stories mimic the marvels of the séance room even as they illuminate the cerebral origins of the spiritual events that it unleashes.

SUSPENDED ANIMATION AND SECOND SIGHT

Daniel Deronda and *Silas Marner*

n identifying the hallucinatory quality of Dickens's realism, Lewes indirectly links his style with George Eliot's. In her mature novels, Eliot largely abandons her empiricist confidence in "the humble and faithful study of nature" to a narrative form that respects the microscopic or invisible coordinates of external reality;[1] such form equates narrative perspicacity with an intuitive and imaginative power of vision rather than with the keenness of the common eye. Where dreamy minds in Dickens's novels discover the broad web of connections or the forces of disintegration that escape ordinary sense perception, Eliot's fiction animates the scientific eye to uncover the minute influences beneath observable forms.[2] For Dickens, the narrators and focal characters that communicate this extraordinary reality are nervous subjects, where for Eliot, ostensibly at least, they are higher-order thinkers who open the sensible world to its imperceptible elements. In so doing, they advance positive knowledge even as they aim to activate the sympathetic fibers of a vast social organism. Sympathy is a form of second sight because in addition to registering the unseen, it requires the intuitive selection of the highest and most affecting forms from a vast assembly of stories and events. This is a form of imaginative vision, or prophecy, rooted in the social whole.

Yet in the strain to discern and order those microscopic truths, her fictions also explore the limits of narrative acuity. In *Daniel Deronda*—a novel that depicts the loosening of thought from the narrow portal of the ego into imaginative vision, or prophecy—there are also episodes of nervous arrest. Here the mind becomes overwhelmed by the minutiae that have no place in a fantasy of self. Such episodes tie the novel to Eliot's study of nervous states in earlier works, particularly *Silas Marner,* which focuses on the little understood disorder of catalepsy. For Eliot, catalepsy is the inverse of sympathy: In its radical arrest of all but the most automatic nervous functions, it also suspends social potential as it interrupts virtually all interaction between an organism and its environment. Although it is the nemesis of Eliot's visionary realism, catalepsy can be seen as a reaction to a shocked, sudden awareness of the larger stories in which the single life participates.

This interpretation engages some of what critics have already said about the dismantled identities at the heart of Eliot's narratives. Sally Shuttleworth has compared the loss of order and meaning in the life of the cataleptic Silas Marner to the dissolution of the shaping will in *Daniel Deronda,*[3] while more recently, Leona Toker has described *Deronda*'s "dialectics of self-loss and self-transcendence" as the ethical space for spiritual vocation.[4] Focused on the consolations of textuality, deconstructionist accounts of Eliot's novels have shown how the self's encounters with the sublime objects of world history or social whole engenders a destabilization or near-destruction of the self, whose "recovery" occurs as a scene or allegory of writing.[5] This chapter investigates the traumatized identities in Eliot's novels in terms of what David Carroll has described as a "prevision[ary] . . . primitive, superstitious self"—a self that pulls the novel in the direction of the unknown "unmapped country" of the mind's relationship to the world as much as it disperses the once confident, egoistic self into the immensity of its milieu.[6] As it reduces the human nervous system to an evolutionarily primitive organization, catalepsy marks the precarious quality of the visionary mind, which threatens not just the integrity of a willful, shaping ego, but the most fundamental motions of the inner life. In Eliot's sophisticated realism, as Levine has put it, "reality is inaccessible to mere common sense" and "the ideal becomes an essential component of [that] reality."[7] A true understanding of the intricate relations among things is made possible through "positivist idealism."[8] Yet even *Daniel*

Deronda, whose incisive narrative vision draws together a myriad of events from multiple lives and disparate social worlds, carries an undertow of nervous retreat. Like *Silas Marner,* it also depicts mental episodes in which there is little-to-no capacity for imaginative reach and the penetrating forces of science and second sight shrink into unfathomable facts and superstition.

I. GREATER AND LESSER MINDS

In a chapter of *Phantoms in the Brain,* V. S. Ramachandran and Susan Blakeslee put one of the yet unsolved mysteries of neuroscience back into the context of a two-century-old debate about religiosity, creativity, and evolution.[9] Having described how electrical storms in the limbic system provoke emotional charges that might be experienced as religious rapture, they then look at a case history in which mystical experience coincided with an extraordinary expansion of memory, speculating on the possibility of a neural correlation between spiritual transcendence and certain savant phenomena. Such miracles of the mind, they propose, should be interpreted within an evolutionary framework that can explain the development of compensatory mechanisms and specialized talents. They conclude, however, with an observation about creative genius, pointing out that this represents expanded areas of general intelligence, rather than extraordinary, isolated acts of mental brilliance. The source of this intense creative activity remains as obscure to scientists in the twenty-first century as it did to Darwin's colleague, Alfred Russell Wallace, who attributed it finally to God. In an odd way, the noncommittal nature of Ramachandran and Blakeslee's closing remarks are in keeping with the broad intellectual contours of Victorian debate about evolution. Their surrendering of scientific ground to the unknown, heightened by a tip of the hat to William Shakespeare and the mystery of his unrivaled gift for metaphor, implicitly invites other disciplinary modes of investigation, including art and literary criticism, to help make sense of some of the most obscure and extraordinary products of the mind.

Ramachandran and Blakeslee's cluster of speculations about mysticism, creativity, and mental strength revisits not just Victorian discussion of the relationship between art and science but also inquiry into the mental processes that produce these different forms of knowledge. Like Ramachandran and Blakeslee's investigation of the savant, George Eliot's novels explore connections between the exceptional and the primitive mind, tracing where recessed mental talents are realized through the expanding web of human social lives and where they point, in reverse, to the diminishing of social experience. The contrast between greater and lesser minds is partly what structures the plots of *Daniel Deronda* and *Silas Marner,* yet in both texts the opposition is repeatedly tested. Both scientific and artistic imagination, the capacity to see larger connections, predict likely outcomes and distinguish key events, express the intellectual progress of the species as it is driven by sympathy. Yet these gifts, which belong to Eliot's narrators as well as to many of her principal characters, can also draw the mind away from the social world that nourishes it. At such moments, even narrative realism, which in Eliot's terms represents the most developed form of artistic expression, becomes vulnerable to a kind of sympathetic arrest or paralysis. The physiological counterpart of this suspended narrative animation is catalepsy, a condition that inflicts some of the most "evolved" as well as the most primitive characters in her novels.

In his literary criticism, G. H. Lewes identifies "vision" as the source of both scientific aptitude and artistic greatness. Vision originates in the general capacity of mind to transform sense perceptions, via the agency of inference, reasoning, and imagination, into knowledge about that which lies beyond the senses. In science, this projection moves across much greater distances than ordinary inference can travel. The rigorous interrogation of nature "requires intense and sustained effort of imagination" ("Vision," 573). Similarly, the artist "renders the invisible visible by imagination" (576), and unites what sense observes as two isolated objects into two related objects. The artist has the power to gather the "numerous relations of things present to the mind" (575) and form images beyond the promptings of the sense while nonetheless remaining true to the originating force of their impressions. Like science, great literature supplies "the energy of sense where sense cannot reach" (576) but is restrained by its duty to the accurate representation of experience. Literature's configuration of relations among objects and invention of new objects from the raw material of memory must be both distinct enough and true enough to human experience so as to arouse memories and kindle powerful emotions in a reader, "paint[ing] pictures which shall withstand the silent criticism of general experience" and "fram[ing] hypotheses which shall withstand the confrontation with facts" (579). Idealism is thus not opposed to realism but rather a "vision of realities in their highest and most affecting forms" (588); conversely, the capacity of great artists and exact scientists to see beyond immediate relations and reason beyond local experience, to work through "selection, abstraction, and recombination" (586) rather than memory, is a vital part of coming to know and communicate things as they really are.

This perspicacious, if not to some degree mystical,[10] realism therefore demands that the art object is embedded in social experience:

> [T]he fine selective instinct of the artist, which makes him fasten upon the details which will most powerfully affect us, without any disturbance of the harmony of the general impression, does not depend solely upon the vividness of his memory and the clearness with which the objects are seen, but depends also upon very complex and peculiar conditions of sympathy which we call genius. Hence we find one man remembering a multitude of details with a memory so vivid that it almost amounts at times to hallucination, yet without any artistic power; and we may find men—Blake was one—with an imagination of unusual activity, who are nevertheless incapable, from deficient sympathy, of seizing upon those symbols which will most affect us. (586)

Artistic genius is rooted in sympathy: the capacity to distinguish the most affecting elements from a "multitude of details." Unlike the realism that "confounds truth with familiarity and predominance of unessential details" (589), true artistic vision is in accord, not with the simple "gatherings of sense" (576) but with the imaginative experience of ordinary men of whom all but the most mentally sluggish exercise the power of forming images or bringing objects and ideas into existence that are not present to the senses. The poet's remarkable powers of selection, in other words, may demonstrate a special distinctness in the objects, relations, and emotions they bring to life, yet they remain true to the imaginative conceptions as well as the sense-based experiences of the whole body of sensitive, creative, and visionary social beings to whom they must appeal.

Lewes joins this confidence in the creative power of mind to give shape to the unknowable with Lamarckian principles of adaptive improvement.[11] His account of realism, which echoes Comte's claim for the progress of human thought from theology and metaphysics toward positivism, rests implicitly on a developmentalist argument that ranks human beings from the most sense-bound and mentally primitive to those most capable of profound sympathy and exquisite imaginative vision. "A man of genius is one whose sympathies are unusually wide." He embraces the thoughts and feelings of all those around him and out of these "greets the dawning of a new idea upon his soul."[12] In *Problems of Life and Mind,* Lewes makes this relationship between sympathy and human development explicit. Arguing that psychology must investigate not simply the organic or physiological conditions of subjective experience but also the "modifications which arise from experience and history," he emphasizes that mental states and talents can be properly understood only with reference to the "social medium" that informs them (*Study of Psychology*, 25). What he calls the "spiritual" conditions (25) or the results of experience that frame all mental events are in turn shaped by social influences. It is through these influences, he argues, "that the highest powers are evolved" (26). Hence the difference between "a Goethe and a Carib" (27) is not one of organic structure but of faculties developed in a social medium that allows for "wide-sweeping intelligence with a sympathetic conscience" (27). Mental maladies, he then claims, are not, as the alienists have mistakenly and narrowly assumed, simply a matter of brain disease. If the patient is considered as a spiritual as much as an organic being and "the product of former generations," then the psychologist will recognize both the biological influence of ancestral abnormalities and the "sociological" influence of "the General Mind"(37). Psychology "must study man as a social animal," taking into account his "stages of development from the simple emotions and conceptions of rude, barbaric social states to the ever-increasing complexities of civilized states" (38).

For Eliot too, the imaginative creation of true relations among objects has an evolutionary history.[13] In a notebook essay on the principles of artistic form, she argues that the selection of images and rhythms that depict mental states in, especially, poetic form represents a higher or conscious version of the spontaneous grouping and selection that constitutes the natural growth of the mind itself.[14] Moreover, even as the invention of such form demonstrates a higher order replication of a fundamental organic process, this superior consciousness is nourished by the living emotions and sympathies, past and present, of the social organism it represents, just as "the beautiful expanding curves of a bivalve shell are not first made for the reception of the unstable inhabitant, but grow and are limited by the simple rhythmic conditions of its growing life."[15] Artistic form, in other words, is not created by near-divine fiat as a fixed frame for holding emotional content but is rather a dynamic response to the emotional rhythms of human organisms as they in turn adjust to the conditions of their environment. In place of the preposterous dualism that Eliot ridicules in her essay on "Silly Novels by Lady Novelists," which declares that the gifted lady artist can see more in the "soul of man" than merely the urgings of an advanced polypus, she identifies an organic interdependence between the creations of the gifted mind and the evolved social feelings out of which these forms emerge.[16]

However, as for Lewes, such artistic creation for Eliot involves selection and combination. The artist discriminates tones, rhythms, and sequences that best express the myriad human passions she seeks to represent.[17] This act of discrimination is like those of empirical science, "knowledge [that] continues to grow by its alternating processes of distinction and combination, seeing smaller and smaller unlikenesses and then grouping or associating these under a common likeness."[18] The highest form is therefore an organism that binds the most varied constituents into a whole that in turn assumes multiplex relations with all the phenomena in its environment. Thus, even while the exquisite form of the ballad points back to the primitive huntsman's "rhythmic shouts" and "clash of metal," it also points forward to the formal expression of increasingly complex relations that in turn unlocks higher ranges of moral feeling.

In this respect, Eliot's organicist aesthetics reflect Spencer's Lamarckian evolutionism more than they do the principles of natural selection in Darwin's *On the Origin of Species*. Gillian Beer and Michael Davis have both shown that Eliot's fiction echoes key Darwinian themes, especially complexity and variety in the evolutionary process and the disruptive influence of chance on the idea of inevitable progress.[19] At the same time, Davis points out, her emphasis on the influence of habit on inherited forms, on the adjustment of the inner relations in an organism to the pressure of its environment, and the increasing tendency to "heterogeneity" and thus adaptive flexibility as that organism develops out of its primitive, more "homogenous" existence point to the influence of Spencer even as she critiques his rather rigid progressivism.[20] In her review of R. W. Mackay's *The Progress of the Intellect*, Eliot argues that civilization advances by infusing "living ideas" into the "lifeless barbarisms" that we inherit from the past.[21] Such development, which promises to produce Comte's "positive truth," reflects an increasing complexity in human knowledge, drawing sustenance from each and every event in the history of human experience as "an experiment of which we may reap the benefit."[22] Eliot approvingly cites Mackay's account of religious development, which argues that science and true faith are inseparable; while credulity rests on unquestioning submission to religious authorities, genuine mystical faith depends on "evidence of things unseen," evidence that in turn depends on the "data of experience."[23] The exceptional mind, which can combine minute knowledge with expansive vision, is the instrument of both intellectual and spiritual progress.

Lewes too demonstrates a closer affiliation with Spencer than Darwin. His four complimentary articles in *The Fortnightly Review* on "Mr. Darwin's Hypotheses" downplay the arbitrary elements in selection that Darwin recognized. Rather than focusing on the latter's contention that evolutionary change is the product of random mutations on which the pressures of selection act to determine survival and reproductive success or failure, Lewes emphasizes that the theory of natural selection provides a powerful articulation of what Spencer christened the "Development Hypothesis": namely, that when a species discovers new environmental conditions, it will immediately undergo changes that fit it for those new conditions and that these changes are then communicated in permanent form to the next generation.[24] Lewes does criticize Spencer's sloppy reasoning that organic structure *follows* from function, arguing instead that an organ changes shape in tandem with increased activity, just as when a person's ability to walk great distances improves not because the muscle has been enlarged by extra activity but because it has enlarged *with* such activity.[25] Yet despite this correction, he broadly echoes Spencer in stressing the relationship of function to structure and remarks that Darwin focuses "somewhat too exclusively on the adaptations which arise during the struggle for existence," thus neglecting the laws of organic growth, just as Lamarck fixed his attention exclusively on the influence of external conditions and wants.[26]

Developmentalism provides Eliot with the framework for character. Despite her recognition of the chance occurrences that may determine the trajectory of an individual life, her narratives are frequently organized around the difference between primitive forms of existence, whose internal motions are instinctive and narrow and whose relations with external phenomena are few, and intellectually animated beings whose internal impulses are directed by the higher, conscious regions of the mind and a complex and expansive sympathy. The sluggish, automatic character of simpler minds, which her narrators often figure as insectlike, contrasts with the active sympathy of social beings who "make all knowledge alive" (*DD*, 533). As Nicholas Royle has pointed out, however, Eliot allows the insect to represent a "telepathology of everyday life"—its mysterious powers of communication suggest spiritual forms of connection that remain as dark to us as they do to it.[27] Even where this superior mental state transforms inert ideas into living social forms, it is shadowed by the primitive mind, whose narrow understanding expresses nervous disorganization strangely similar to that which may attend the highest grasp of reality. At its most acute, this disorganization manifests as a peculiar state of arrest.

II. VISION AND DEANIMATION IN *DANIEL DERONDA*

In her earlier novels, Eliot positions "spiritual" phenomena in the evolved capacity for sympathy. Thus, rather than the "divine beauty" of "prophets, sibyls and heroic warriors," the narrator of *Adam Bede* declares, the novel should show "that other beauty . . . which lies in no secret of proportion, but in the secret of deep human sympathy" with its "faithful representing of commonplace things."[28] Taking her inspiration from the subjects of Dutch realist art, the narrator who aspires to represent this commonplace world "should have a fibre of sympathy connecting [her] with that vulgar citizen who weighs out sugar in a vilely assorted cravat and waistcoat," with the "common labourer" and the "perhaps too corpulent" clergyman of her own parish.[29] The narrator's attention to the "monotonous homely existence" of ordinary lives is faithful because both she and they belong to the same social whole whose progress rests on minute interactions among manifold human actors.[30] Despite the novel's tenderness toward its Methodist heroine, Dinah, this narrator's sympathy, which recognizes her own place in the same evolving social orbit as her characters, contrasts with Dinah's revealed religion, whose passive voice separates world, mind, and soul from a remote agent of change: "I felt a great movement in my soul, and I trembled as if I was shaken by a strong spirit entering into my weak body. And . . . I spoke the words that were given to me abundantly. . . . And many wept over their sins and have since been joined to the Lord."[31]

In *Daniel Deronda,* prophecy or second sight replaces *Adam Bede's* respect for the common eye. Exploring the "disputed ground" of second sight, the narrator suggests that there may be persons

> whose yearnings, conceptions—nay, travelled conclusions—continually take the form of images which have a foreshadowing power: the deed they would do starts up before them in complete shape, making a coercive type; the event they hunger for or dread rises into vision with a seed-like growth, feeding itself fast on unnumbered impressions. They are not always the less capable of the argumentative process, nor less sane than the commonplace calculators of the market: sometimes it may be that their natures have manifold openings, like the hundred-gated Thebes, where there may naturally be a greater and more miscellaneous inrush than through a narrow beadle-watched portal. (471)

This power of prophetic vision, like the narrative recognition of and selection among myriad relations of characters and events, represents what Lewes identifies as the work of an exceptional mind. Describing Mordecai's visionary belief in Deronda; the narrator uses the same word again—"inrush"—to describe the belief that "possesse[s]" Mordecai following his early impressions of Daniel, suggesting that such belief is formed out of the manifold histories and imaginings of the General Mind of his people and that it transforms this host of mental experiences into a more transcendent image or a revelation. "Prophetic consciousness" (529) is thus mystical only in the sense that it can perceive historical sequences with extraordinary perspicacity.

At the same time, the vision itself becomes part of a living thing. Superstition, Mordecai declares, gives way to "the illumination of great facts which widen feeling, and make all knowledge alive as the youngest offspring of beloved memories" (533). In his passionate search for the ideal face, he searches the collective memory of the scattered people whose nation is an "inheritance that has never ceased to quiver in millions of human frames" (536), embodied in "the experience our greatest sons have gathered from the life of the ages" (537). Responding to the English-Jewish "philosopher" Gideon, who insists that enlightened reason will eventually extinguish religious prejudices, Mordecai answers:

> But what is it to be rational—what is it to feel the light of the divine reason growing stronger within and without? It is to see more and more of the hidden bonds that bind and consecrate change as a dependent growth— yea, consecrate it with kinship: the past becomes my parent, and the future stretches towards me the appealing arms of children. (528)

Second sight, like evolutionary science, traces the organic origins of the great events of history to the small events of biological descent and sympathetic fusions among minds. As the inlayer Goodwin puts it, ideas "work themselves into life and go on growing with it, but they can't go apart from the material that set them to work and makes a medium for them" (524). As the ideas of national identity and destiny are transmitted across generations and enlivened by sympathy, ideas take root and become feelings. In Deronda, Mordecai recognizes the "hidden bond" both in the sense of a biological inheritance that will be revealed in the former's birth and in that of the sympathetic kinship through which the idea of the nation is realized in feeling.

Yet at the same time as it refuses to separate the visionary from the ordinary minds from which he draws sustenance, the novel's account of second sight evokes a developmental history of the human race that does distinguish rudimentary from more fully evolved elements of consciousness. Mordecai turns from "superstition" to "growth, completion, [and] development" (534); visionaries, the narrator announces, are "the creators and feeders of the world, molding and feeding the more passive life which without them would dwindle and shrivel into the narrow tenacity of insects unshaken by thoughts beyond the reaches of their antennae" (685), suggesting, as Deronda does, that Mordecai's religious enthusiasm represents "the highest order of minds" (567). At the same time, greater and lesser forms of the visionary can be found, just as greater and lesser forms of mammalian life are bound together by evolutionary ties or "great mental or social types" are related to "specimens whose insignificance is both ugly and noxious" (471). As Pamela Thurschwell has argued, the links between second sight and scientific knowledge in the novel are double edged, rendering the former "on the one hand prophetic, elevated, nation- and vocation-forming, and on the other hand uncontrollable and unwanted, or banal and mundane."[32] From Eliot's evolutionary perspective, the gifts of a Mordecai find their lower analogue in the narrow mind of a Gwendolen, with her susceptibility to fits of spiritual horror. These occur at moments when her egotistic consciousness is penetrated by an unwelcome recognition of the larger stories in which she plays so insignificant a part. Dread, which Deronda urges should be her moral guide, is the diminutive form of prophecy, endowing her with horrified premonition about future events (Grandcourt's death) or the effects of her past sins (the "ghastly vision" of Mrs. Glasher's life [152]) even as these are diminished by a conscience that refers all external events to her own private suffering. In a feeble replication of Mordecai's mental powers, her feelings of social triumph are haunted by "some dim forecast, the insistent penetration of suppressed experience" (357).

In this respect, Gwendolen has a more pronounced affinity with Mordecai than with Deronda. In his early life, Deronda has a "subdued fervour of sympathy" that yearns after "wide knowledge" (178) and that habitually puts his imagination to work for others, while his social privilege in combination with his uncertain identity stand between him and the focus or purpose. Later, his bond with Mordecai and meeting with his mother enable him to bend this knowledge and sympathy to a purpose, turning his "inherited yearning—the effect of brooding, passionate thoughts in many ancestors" to the task through which he becomes "the heart and brain of a multitude" (750). Yet Deronda is often more like the *creation* of an exceptional mind than he is himself an artist-creator. In the animation golem tales of Jewish mysticism, the creature is the vessel for accumulated wisdom or the idea that the creator wants to transmit.[33] Deronda will carry the "sacred inheritance" beyond Mordecai's "narrow life" on which "the generations are crowding" (500). Mordecai selects his face out of the crowd of faces, identifying in Daniel the object of physical beauty that he believes will embody the greater future of his people; as art object, Deronda becomes the expression of Mordecai's marvelous vision—the creature who emerges from the collective mystical yearnings of that vision, literalizing, as it were, what Lewes describes as the "spiritual conditions" of social life.

> Tracing reasons in [him]self for the rebuffs he has met with and the hindrances that beset him, [Mordecai] imagined a man who would have all the elements necessary for sympathy with him, but in an embodiment unlike his own: he must be a Jew, intellectually cultured, morally fervid—in all this a nature ready to be plenished from Mordecai's; but his face and frame must be beautiful and strong, he must have been used to all the refinements of social life his voice must flow with a full and easy current, his circumstances must be free from sordid need: he must glorify the possibilities of the Jew, not sit and wander as Mordecai did. (472)

Such vision emerges less from a conflation of principles of biological descent with Romantic idealism than in the specific figure of metempsychosis, the longing to transmit the spirit of Judaic restoration and "complete ideal shape of that personal duty and citizenship" (512) that absorbs his entire being into some other body through which it will be truly realized. This passion is therefore "something more than a grandiose transfiguration of . . . parental love" (533). Ironically, then, it is Deronda's *lack* of second sight that makes him, rather than Mordecai, the messianic figure. He longs for "some ideal task" in which "[he] might feel himself part of some great movement," but this can be realized only through Mordecai's inspiration, without which "the ancestral life would lie . . . as a dim longing for unknown objects and sensations" (750). Such unfocused sympathy clearly contrasts with Mordecai's recognition of the precise human form in which those histories will be realized as national destiny.

Although the closest plot connection Gwendolen has to Mordecai is her sexual rivalry with Mirah, she is taxonomically linked to him as an inferior specimen of the same mental type.[34] In the first half of the novel, Gwendolen is "little penetrated by feelings of wider relations"(149), yet her mind is such that it draws all the minute events of her social experience toward the object of her passion, so that "everything is porous to it; bows, smiles, conversation, repartee, are mere honeycombs where such thought rushes freely" (602). Later, in the days leading up to Grandcourt's death, the images of her past wrongdoing surface to forecast "some fiercely impulsive deed, committed as in a dream" (674), her prescient dread and ensuing mortification providing the antithesis to Mordecai's visionary anticipation and subsequent exultation. What she describes to Deronda later is a realization of her vision at the moment of her husband's drowning, when "I saw my wish outside me" (696). Where Mordecai has the power to realize new spiritual truths through his capacity for mental imaging, Gwendolen, it seems, will bring crimes to pass through the agency of her own horrified imagination.

This pairing of Mordecai and Gwendolen is most pronounced in the effect each has on Deronda. Where Gwendolen's influence on the latter is to paralyze him with compassion because he cannot save her, Mordecai animates him, transforming his "yearning disembodied spirit, stirred with a vague social passion" (365) into "a definite. . . . action" (180). Again in keeping with the myth of the golem, an indefinite, amorphous, deanimated substance assumes definition and active power. Mordecai's vision delivers Deronda, like the awakening mortal in the epigraph from Browning's *Paracelsus* that opens Book VII, from his frozen state (617). Yet despite the dubious associations with this Frankensteinlike animation (oddly reminiscent of Charles Meunier's marvelous revivification of the villainous Mrs. Archer in *The Lifted Veil*), Mordecai's gift is analogous to the methods of true science: "His exultation was not widely different from that of the experimenter, bending over the first stirrings of change that correspond to what in the fervour of concentrated prevision his thought had foreshadowed" (493).[35] He animates Deronda with the spirit of the Jewish nation, assembled from the great storehouse of sufferings and hopes that make up the history of his people, and transforming manifold experience into idea as the scientist's imagination transforms innumerable facts into laws and projections.

This affiliation between seer and scientist parallels that between the deductions of science and the clairvoyance of narrative itself. This analogy is established in the first chapter of the novel: the epigraph reflects on the shared disingenuousness of science and storytelling, both of which really begin *in medias res,* despite their pretensions to beginnings; the narrator describes the characters' mutual scrutiny through the language of scientific observation and classification, as the novel's opening aesthetic question about the form and nature of Gwendolen's beauty rapidly shifts to one about her rank in the animal kingdom and Daniel looks at her as though she were "a specimen of a lower order" (10).[36] Explicitly linking herself with the figure of the seer, the narrator directly boasts of an expansive vision that "connect[s] the course of individual lives within the historic stream" (88).

Yet this is not always possible. At other moments, her confidence in the artist's capacity to navigate unknown regions of the physical world with the same precise observational tools as science, or to synthesize the minute events of history, is less certain. The epigraph to chapter 16 begins:

> The astronomer threads the darkness with strict deduction, accounting so for every visible arc in the wanderer's orbit; and the narrator of human actions, if he did his work with the same completeness, would have to thread the hidden pathways of feeling and thought which lead up to every moment of action, and to those moments of intense suffering which take the quality of action. (164)

To illuminate the innumerable sensible and mental events that lead to an action or its equivalent in feeling would be like "hearing the grass grow and the squirrel's heart beat" that describes the impossibly "keen vision" in *Middlemarch*, or Latimer's wearying clairvoyance in *The Lifted Veil*, which intrudes the "frivolous ideas and emotions" of others onto his consciousness like "the loud activity of an imprisoned insect."[37] These are the "unessential details" that Lewes claims crowd works of false realism. They are the minutiae that Deronda himself is able to subdue so that they assume their proper place as diminutive phenomena: "an insect-murmur amidst the sum of current noises" (187). Yet they threaten to encroach upon the narrative consciousness, just as, at times, the obtrusive external world presses upon and threatens to crowd Mordecai's inner vision. Thus, even as the creative mind draws from the multitude of details that make up history and that arrive at thought and sensation, it must also, to some extent, shut out the external world and narrow its portals. In both Mordecai and Gwendolen this process takes the form of near-complete physiological arrest, or catalepsy.

Locked into his passionate search for a spiritual successor, Mordecai is frequently unaware of the way ordinary events unfold around him: Deronda's appearance at the Cohen's has no meaning for him beyond the realization of his vision; he has trouble going to unfamiliar places where "the outer world . . . narrows the inward vision" (521). The club of philosophers is the only public place where he feels truly comfortable since its familiarity enables him to resist the pressures of his mundane environment and gives free rein to his enthusiastic spirit. Here, even as he argues with his skeptical fellow Jews about tradition, prophecy, and racial destiny, he becomes less and less aware of what is immediately around him, until finally he is thrown into a cataleptic fit by the force of his spiritual vision: He becomes insensible to the movements and farewells of his companions, his head sinks upon this breast as his mind wanders through past events that have brought about this moment, and he becomes "rapt and motionless" (539). This state prefigures the hours before his death, when, having announced that he has transmitted his soul into Deronda's he neither speaks nor moves for several hours before he ceases to breathe. As Toker argues, his spirit "consumes his fragile body," putting him in need of an "executive self," whom he finds in the healthier body of Deronda.[38]

Mordecai's cataleptic withdrawal from the living environment is strangely doubled in Gwendolen's episodes of paralyzing fear. Despite her toxic vanity and social snobbery, and notwithstanding her indifference toward institutionalized religion, she is nonetheless subject to "fits of spiritual dread" (63), during which the narrow world that she governs through her will dissolves into a wider horizon over which she has no influence and in which her petty ambitions are swallowed up in a sudden overwhelming awareness of an "immeasurable existence aloof from her" (64). The Shelleyean awe that she feels when alone in a landscape where the light makes a sudden dramatic shift, is one kind of prompt to this feeling of dread; the discovery of her insignificance to the larger destinies of humankind through her contact with Deronda, is another. At such moments, she has a visionary grasp like Mordecai's of the manifold histories that collectively announce the future, although in Gwendolen's case, the vision is horrifying and apocalyptic:

> There comes a terrible moment to many souls when the great movements of the world, the larger destinies of mankind, which have lain aloof in newspapers and other neglected reading, enter like an earthquake into their own lives—when the slow urgency of growing generations turn into the tread of an invading army or the dire clash of civil war. . . . Then it is as if the Invisible Power that has been the object of lip-worship and lip-resignation became visible, according to the imagery of the Hebrew poet, making the flames his chariot, and riding on the wings of the wind, till the mountains smoke and the plains shudder under the rolling fiery visitation. (803)

Here her nervous tendencies become charged with Protestant revelation. Convinced that she is responsible for Grandcourt's death, Gwendolen confesses to Deronda a terrible ecstatic awakening to her own sin, declaring "it was not my own knowledge, it was God's that had entered into me" (692) and that "[i]t was all like a writing of fire within me" (695). Yet it is not through submission to the spirit alone that Gwendolen is humbled. Having always been afraid of anything aloof to her own petty ambitions, she experiences the discovery of Deronda's mission to the East as a shrinking of her own life before the enormity of national destinies. At this moment, Gwendolen's still-egotistic assumption that confession of her sin will somehow bind Deronda to her is overwhelmed as the force of "growing generations" enters her consciousness. This is the "sort of crisis," the narrator tells us, in which apocalyptic vision, a "rolling, fiery visitation," takes form as "something else than a private consolation" (804). For Gwendolen, as for Mordecai, the private spiritual ecstasy that arrests all other activity in the mind is tied to the large-scale processes of organic change whose indifference to the individual ego is as dreadful to her as it is inspiring to Deronda.

Critics who focus on Gwendolen's nervous condition have suggested a subterranean, hysterical counternarrative in the larger story of her moral and spiritual reformation.[39] Yet although often identified as a hysteric symptom, the rigid and unresponsive state of catalepsy does not suggest a subversive body speak because it represents extreme nervous retreat.[40] When Gwendolen learns of Deronda's plans, her diminished sense of self expresses itself in mental and physical arrest, as she sits "like a statue with her wrists lying over each other and her eyes fixed—the intensity of her mental action arresting all other excitation" (804). This scene directly echoes an earlier episode in the novel when her performance as the awakening statue of Hermione is interrupted by the accidental opening of a moving panel to reveal a painting of a dead and a fleeing figure, and she resembles a statue "into which a soul of fear had entered: her pallid lips were parted; her eyes, usually narrowed under their long lashes, were dilated and fixed" (61). When Deronda hints at his pending marriage to Mirah, Gwendolen is able to fuse the narrative threads of a greater plot in which she (and for some early time we too as readers) previously imagined she was central. "A great wave of remembrance" (804) passes over her, and Mirah, who had formerly appeared to her as an inconsequential figure in Deronda's life, suddenly assumes her rightful place in the larger story. After this revelation, Gwendolen, "dull[ed to] all other consciousness" (806) becomes insensible of the movements that she had once been in the habit of executing with calculating self-awareness. Her stupor thus records her discovery of the weaving of multiple events into a series of interlocked outcomes rather than, as the early sections of the novel seem to promise, a story in which she remains firmly at the center. Unable to select meaning from these events without her own fortune as a point of reference, she is frozen by them.

Gwendolen's cataleptic episodes are initially a response to the dreadful premonition of her own spiritual despair, but increasingly they express her horrified recognition of the greater landscapes in which she appears so insignificant and the broader web of lives over which she exercises no mastery. At such moments it is as though she were being pulled out of the narrative frame to address the questions about stories, characters, and destinies that preoccupy the narrator and that drive Eliot's epigraph selections. The narrative voice itself, linking single histories to one another and to the larger evolutionary story of the human mind's overcoming of selfish passions, inhabits both the minor divinatory and the fully clairvoyant states that both inflict and enlarge the minds of its major characters. This is the voice that can describe the evolution of second sight; that links poetic fervor with "a mind . . . which thrills from the near to the distant, and back again from the distant to the near" (205) and that can both discern the way its characters experience dread in relation to the unknown and anticipate how they will grow in their efforts to embrace it. In addition to present-tense omniscience, in other words, it supplies the voice and vision of evolution and prophecy. It manifests the strength of the superior mind that Lewes identified in the capacity to intuit beyond the local, the immediate, and the sensible. Yet even this clairvoyant voice is sometimes silenced by the too-intricate threads of connection that it cannot ever make fully visible. It can no more describe the origins of Gwendolen's "fits of timidity," than the scientist can use a word like "heat" to override the web of differences that constitute the universe (64). Such moments of narrative self-awareness about the potential of higher minds to retreat from the too-thick and pressing phenomena of the outer world are rare in *Daniel Deronda*. They are more prominent in an earlier and, for this reason perhaps, much shorter novel.

III. CATALEPSY IN *SILAS MARNER*

Silas Marner might be read as a story about the problem of representing a consciousness with little-to-no capacity for the imaginative reach that Lewes calls "vision." Not only the cataleptic Silas but indeed all the characters that belong to his world are limited to the "perpetual, urgent, companionship of their own griefs and discontents," and "the ever trodden round of their own petty histor[ies]."[41] A mind that encounters the world through such a narrow window will, as Eliot describes it elsewhere, "exalt feeling above intellect" and will have, in religious life especially, a "sense of truthfulness [that] is misty and confused."[42] The difficulty, then, for this story is how to represent its primitive subject matter—the undeveloped regions of consciousness—and yet allow the telling of it to do the work of sympathy that *Daniel Deronda* does for Gwendolen and her kind, illuminating and expanding darkened and narrow mental or social landscapes. Here, narrative deanimation is not triggered by the overwhelming capacity for vision but instead represents a response to the evolutionary gulf between minds.

Silas Marner, Eliot wrote to her publisher, was "a story which came *across* my other plans by a sudden inspiration."[43] This acknowledgment of a debt to the mysterious workings of the creative mind might be said to find its negative imprint in the strange vacuity of mind that characterizes catalepsy. In what seems, at least provisionally, like a formal endorsement of this bond between the miraculous and the vacuous, the plot of the novel is driven by the sudden, inexplicable appearances and disappearances of people as well as precious objects. These are mysteries whose natural cause is only sometimes apparent to the narrator and a few skeptical characters on the periphery of the narrative. Thus, while this story describes social life in thoroughly organic terms, its very narrative structure respects the force of the mystical, reflecting what the narrator identifies as a primitive mental state, in which "vagueness and mystery" (9) or simply a "fearful blank" deliver incomplete or fantastic meaning (22). Again, for Eliot, art is high or low, depending, like the form of an organism, on the level of complexity of parts that are bound into an "indissoluble whole."[44] This narrative's focus on the retreat of an extremely complex organism—a human being—to its most primitive structure, undergoes a reverse process. The narrative voice itself falls back into what Shuttleworth has recognized in Silas's condition as Comte's first period of social evolution: the fetishistic, polytheistic stage in which order and meaning belong only to divine beings and individuals take "no far-sighted responsibility for their action."[45] Such organic and narrative dissolution occurs in the withdrawal of the mind from its social environment and in the shriveling of sympathy, scientific knowledge, and intuitive foresight that follows.

Silas's catalepsy seems to befuddle both narrative realism and medical science. We are offered no rational explanation for the attacks that render him as incapable of psychological as of physical movement. The possibility that they are the result of divine inspiration, however, is immediately removed by Silas's honest testimony that he had no vision from God; indeed, there was no mental content to the episodes whatsoever. The story apparently sides neither with scientific enlightenment nor with Protestant awakening. Instead, it provides a bare-bones depiction of a sudden, inexplicable suspension of the inner life, "a mysterious rigidity and suspension of consciousness" (9) that only the rudest-minded of its characters interpret as signifying either divine or demonic influence. We cannot credit these primitive interpreters—neither the fiercely judgmental members of the isolated Lantern Yard community nor the benignly superstitious Raveloe villagers—with any special knowledge of the condition. And yet with no Tertius Lydgate in the novel to speculate on the minute behavior of nervous pathways and so begin to explain this strange condition of emotional and physiological arrest, it is hard to see how catalepsy can have any currency in the narrative economies of psychological and social realism either. In Eliot's longer novels, the growth and flexibility of minds as well as the subtle interactions among them bring the subjective state into relationship with its larger environments, creating new social possibilities through what the narrator of *Middlemarch* calls "unhistoric acts."[46] *Silas Marner,* on the other hand, puts the blank mind of catalepsy at the heart of a world unchangingly shaped by tradition, superstition, and the tendency to describe that which is unknown as "dark to the last" (169).

The narrator's reticence about the physiological circumstances of Silas's condition is especially striking given how long trance phenomena have featured in the dialogue between faith and medical science. Both in Catholic mysticism and in Protestant revivalism, the deathlike trance testifies to a direct intuitional experience of God, where the soul is so absorbed in the divine that it fails to animate the body. For Protestant reformers, catalepsy, along with epileptic seizures, speaking in tongues, trance, visions, and clairvoyance, signified the "indwelling" or "witness" of the Spirit, in the language of eighteenth-century Protestant evangelism. Numerous eighteenth- and nineteenth-century published accounts of deep trance or apparent death, in which the subject was shown the horrors of hell and the glories of heaven, provided textual support for this experience of Spirit. In *Memoirs of the Reverend William Tennent,* for example, an apparently dead man revived after several days, and reported that, in what seemed like a much briefer period of "unspeakable rapture," he found himself "in another state of existence, under the direction of a superior being."[47] In the account given of her experience during a five-hour trance, Sarah Alley recalled that she was led by a heavenly guide to see the burning lake and then to heaven, where she saw Christ surrounded by angels. In another episode, she was commanded by Christ to return to the world and teach sinners to repent.[48] A poem called *The Prodigal Daughter,* depicts a young woman guilty of swearing, whoring, Sabbath breaking, and attempted murder who falls into a swoon from which she apparently cannot be revived, and only a cry from her coffin frees her from the fate of being buried alive. When she is restored to life, she reports on the flight her soul took through heaven and hell, and she is restored to grace and repentance.[49] In each of these episodes, the cataleptic attack marks the moment of spiritual transformation as that in which the mind withdraws from its physical environment and finds union with God.

Such testimonies to immediate religious experience were supposed to contrast with the spiritual lethargy of High Church formalism. They were also scrutinized by naturalizing discourses that identified ecstatic states as symptoms of physiological disorder. From Richard Burton's *Anatomy of*

Melancholy (1620), which interpreted such states as symptoms of religious melancholy, to scientific skepticism about animal magnetism and the trance medium in the 1850s, medical philosophy and later physiological psychology endeavored to naturalize religious experience and to strip trance phenomena of their supernatural content. Even within the revivalist movements themselves, such phenomena might be explained naturalistically, if only to point more indirectly to the presence of Spirit. Ann Taves has shown that moderate reformists like Jonathan Edwards, John Wesley, George Whitefield, and James Robe drew upon the naturalistic explanations made by anti-enthusiasts in order to distinguish true religious experience from its enthusiastic counterfeit.[50] Along with scientific skepticism and religious naturalism, some revivalist movements themselves advocated a measured interpretation of spiritual ecstasies. Rapture, in itself, was no guarantee of divine influence. It might be merely a symptom of physiological disorders or a naturally enhanced state of mind. John Wesley, for instance, cautioned that the Witness of the Spirit should be complemented by the fruits of experience.[51] Prophetic episodes might well signify divine inspiration, but they were also indicative of a condition of mind physiologically triggered by the saturation of consciousness with an *idea* of transcendence.

The relationship between natural and supernatural explanations for the visions and insights that often accompany trance states receives what is probably its first thorough exploration in Meric Casaubon's *A Treatise Concerning Enthusiasme* (1655). Casaubon suggests that natural causes can be identified for ecstatic experience without denying the truth and reality of supernatural influences or their possible manifestation in the prophetic content of that experience.[52] Yet he distinguishes the sudden alienation of mind and the strange raptures it provokes from the "true divination," and the "highest gift of God . . . [in] sound reason" (62). God's immediate presence is less probably felt in the strange phenomena generated by most varieties of enthusiasm than in that "sound reason and discerning spirit [that] is a perpetual kind of divination" (63). Hence the likely explanation for divinatory experience lies in those natural causes, ordinary or extraordinary, that remain obscure to us. We can conjecture, however, that "[m]any natural things, by some natural foregoing signes, may be known, felt or discerned by [such] men or creatures, that have a natural disposition or sympathy, whether constant or temporary, to those things or their signes, though unknown unto others that have not they be altogether unknown" (55–56). Casaubon proposes that ecstatic prophecy, in its natural form, is of the same class of phenomena as the sensitivity of animals who can anticipate storms well in advance of the human senses. Prophecy can be attributed to the power of an exaggerated natural sense, or sympathy. In this way, apparently supernatural phenomena are subjected to both known and unknown natural laws, both of which are of God's making.

Casaubon identified enthusiastic "divinatory fits" as "incidental" to the natural diseases of, among others, melancholy, mania, and hysteria (36). Such conditions, however, render the patients especially vulnerable to demonic possession, and natural causes are "not wholly sufficient to produce this effect" (42). Nearly two centuries later, Macnish's *Philosophy of Sleep* identifies almost exactly the same physiological origins for divinatory trance, adding that medical science has not been able to fully account for all manifestations of trance phenomena:

> The remote causes of trance are hidden in much obscurity; and generally we are unable to trace the affection to any external circumstance. It has been known to follow a fit of terror. Sometimes it ensues after hysteria, epilepsy, or other spasmodic diseases. . . . Nervous and hypochondriac patients are the most subject of its attacks; but sometimes it occurs when there is no disposition of the kind, and when the person is in a state of the most seeming good health. (202–3)

The possibility of malign supernatural influence that Casaubon concedes has disappeared, but medical knowledge remains unable to trace the etiology of the disease. Since, he argues, the apparently suspended activity of the heart and lungs during the trance must be "more apparent than real," continuing to support life at a level below that which our senses can detect, the causes of such trance cannot be uncovered by current technologies of observation (202). In keeping with the larger theme of his study, Macnish does suggest that the clairvoyant content of some trance experiences might be attributed to the same mental cause as that of apparently prophetic dreams. If the mind is not in a state of torpor, as it usually is during a trance, it might be in a condition analogous to the state of dreaming, and thus call up memories of impressions that the conscious mind has long since forgotten. Yet most of the accounts of catalepsy—stories of people who apparently return to life moments before burial or others who can fall into a trance at will—while they might be related to prior conditions, like hysteria, remain for the most part "astonishing and inexplicable" (205).

In his *Observations on Trance or Human Hibernation* (1850), James Braid is more ambitious than Macnish about discovering the natural origins of suspended animation. He recommends that scientific men suspend their skepticism about the extraordinary accounts of the fakirs who survive voluntary burial for days or weeks and, rather than dismissing such accounts as fraudulent, "endeavour to arrive at a satisfactory solution of the phenomena on physiological principles."[53] Like both Casaubon and Macnish, Braid suggests that catalepsy is linked to hysteria, and thus that it can be brought about by shock or terror as well as by religious enthusiasm. More specifically, however, and in part so as to distance his own study and practice of hypnotism from the occult strains of mesmerism, he suggests that by a combination of suppressed respiration and fixing the mind on a single object, the human body can reduce all its vital functions to the same condition as that of hibernating animals. "The unfortunate extravagance of the Mesmerists," who claim gifts of clairvoyance, thus making "a mockery of the human understanding and all the known laws of physical science," has compromised that genuine study of the remarkable phenomena of trance, including catalepsy.[54] The "wonderful exaltation of the natural faculties" that can occur in the trance state—the suspension of vital activity, the remarkable heightening of memory, the extreme vividness of imagination, and even the intensification of reasoning power—are "only exaggerations or exaltations of functions or faculties which are possessed by all of us in a less degree in the ordinary or waking condition."[55] Such states and the phenomena that sometimes accompany them are particularly likely to be triggered by powerful religious experiences, as in the case of the Hindu fakirs, because the subject is so isolated from the external world and so intensely concentrated on the internal world that the senses barely respond to external stimuli.

Braid insists that "unlimited skepticism" about the remarkable instances of human hibernation is as "equally the child of imbecility as implicit credulity."[56] Neither superstitious nor narrow-mindedly skeptical, science should make incomplete knowledge about the human mind and body valid to the investigation and treatment of disease. Yet the problem remains of what exactly to do with phenomena that remain so far outside the orbit of current medical knowledge that, if they do not point to the influence of the supernatural, they do seem to highlight science's feeble grasp of the operations of nature. Even as late as 1896, an account of some instances of premature burial declares that "of all the various forms of suspended animation, trance and catalepsy" are described as "the least understood. . . . the laws which control them . . . appear to be as insoluble as those which govern life itself."[57] The radical differences of opinion over modern instances of catalepsy even within medical academies, its authors go on to say, "are sufficient to show that all the culture and the scientific instincts of the present age have not quite inaugurated the 'reign of law' nor established finally that 'miracles do not happen.'"[58]

This argument might be seen less to authenticate religious experience at the expense of scientific inquiry than to gesture to the "visionary" elements of evolutionary science itself. Our interpretation of nature, our imposition of laws upon all its vagaries, William Carpenter insists, must in turn be understood in terms of the "mental processes, by which are formed those fundamental conceptions of matter and force, cause and effect, law and order."[59] These conceptions are representations framed by the mind, and as such they are formed out of a combination of the impressions made upon the senses by external objects and commonsense views that are "the generalized experiences of the human race."[60] Such cultural banking of knowledge is what enables inquiry to proceed beyond the gathering of empirical data. Common sense, "one of our most valuable instruments of scientific inquiry; affording in many instances the best, and sometimes the only, basis for a rational conclusion,"[61] is thus at the core of scientific knowledge and, like Lewes's conception of "vision," a fundamental, cultural-evolutionary mechanism: "The intellectual intuitions of any one generation are the embodied experiences of the previous race."[62] According to this reasoning, catalepsy will be understood by a future generation of educated men who are able to grasp the as yet impenetrable natural laws that encompass its strange manifestations. At present, it is accessible to science only through the more strictly empirical agency of an "*un*common sense."[63] Citing Braid's study of the fakirs, Carpenter observes that those who have some special medical knowledge of self-hypnosis, or of the experiments that have been conducted on mammals underwater, or of how an organism might survive in the soil temperature of certain regions of India, can observe Braid's Hindu devotees surrender voluntarily to a deathlike torpor and survival burial for days or weeks on end without either offending that acquired intuition that refuses to believe such a feat is possible or resorting to supernatural explanation.[64]

Yet even as scientific method, "that trained and organized common sense,"[65] is transforming the basis of belief in religious inquiry, substituting the principle of continuity for supernatural cataclysms and interruptions, Carpenter's psychology points out that the mind can tend to self-deception. Under the influence of a mental prepossession, a subject may actually produce sensations, as the higher mental states exercise a downward influence on the sensorium. The prepossessed mind thus "dwell[s] on [its] own imaginings,"[66] producing hallucinations and revelations, which as long as common sense is suspended, seem unquestionably real. Contemporary testimony to the supernatural phenomena of table turning and other miracles of the séance as well as the ancient faith in dreams, visions, and trances can be attributed to this tendency of the mind to "prepossession" or "ideational states."[67] Even the mind of the scientific observer, he suggests, is vulnerable to the seduction of its own ideations: "We are liable to be affected by our prepossessions at every stage of our mental activity from our primary reception of impressions from without to the highest exercise of our reasoning powers."[68]

Carpenter's warning echoes Francis Bacon's: We should be wary of the idols of the mind in both the objects and the subject of scientific inquiry. Even as the mind evolves under the influence of common sense, it might also come under the equally powerful influence of ancestral idols; it might, in other words, become more superstitious rather than more scientific. This possibility in turn suspends the conjectural history that puts "primitive" societies at one end of the human evolutionary chain and "civilized" nations at the other, suggesting that the primitive is a condition of mind whose features appear in the very evolutionary pathways that should overcome them. As a manifestation of such mental dissolution, catalepsy pulls the figure of the primitive out of the remote past and into the present tense of scientific modernity.

Silas Marner's turn to the primitive occurs at the level of narrative form, where mind is incapable of discerning the intricate forms it encounters. The novel is therefore not quite "a secular fable demythologizing . . . puritan allegory," for it finds no more answers in science than it does in religion.[69] Rather, it might be said to confound both allegorical and realist forms, as Silas's mind, entirely disconnected from the surrounding world and unmoored from all external references, remains impenetrable to the psychologically savvy narrator. In the pathology of catalepsy, the organism retreats to its most primitive condition as only the automatic elements of the nervous system are able to function, enabling just the minimal interaction with the environment necessary to immediate survival. This evacuation of mind, including the functions of memory, thought, and will, from the physical body results in a state of social as well as physiological arrest, since there are no longer any available channels of sympathy through which human subjects can interact. Unable to find movement or shape in Silas's consciousness, the narrator is consequently incapable of bringing subjective and social realities into sympathetic connection, and her characters are correspondingly incapable of the kind of emotional growth achieved by Dorothea or Gwendolen.

There is *some* such growth in the novel. The Raveloe community becomes kinder and more accepting, in step with the emotional development of its central characters: An outsider becomes gradually more open to his neighbors and a self-absorbed member of the gentry learns to appreciate how his decisions affect the emotional lives of all those around him. On the other hand, the village characters are never reformed in their belief in the agency of the supernatural; their faith that Silas's condition consists of a marvelous wandering of the soul from the body is paired at the end of the story with their confidence that his "strange history" is infused with "blessing" (171). Silas assumes he has witnessed a miracle when his lost gold apparently returns in the form of a little girl. Even when the thief is discovered and the gold restored, he attributes its reappearance to a "wonderful" (157) divine agency. Each instance demonstrates the kind of perceptual error that, in *Daniel Deronda*, the narrator attributes to an ignorance of the scale of organic growth: "[T]he true bond between events and false conceit of means whereby sequences may be compelled—like that falsity of eyesight which overlooks the gradations of distance, seeing that which is afar off as if it were within a step or a grasp" (*DD*, 227). The narrator of *Silas Marner*, who remains steadily skeptical of miracles, does not commit this error. She understands and brings to narrative light the multitude of psychological and circumstantial events that deliver Eppie to Silas's door, as well as the power of sympathetic love to restore an all but dead man to active social life. Yet she has no explanation for Silas's catalepsy that can substitute for that of divine or satanic agency. Whatever it is that causes Silas's catalepsy remains a mystery, and that mystery is as arresting of narrative realism and the evolutionary progress it projects as it is of physical and mental activity.

The novel describes a human being who is forced to live without either the nourishing influence of sympathy or any more autocratic guide. Unlike Dinah, Silas is not called away by God to village life from the intensely isolated religious community of Lantern Yard, but rather banished from the latter by the apparent evidence of God's disfavor. Once his fellow members, directed by the deceitful William Dane, interpret his cataleptic attacks as a "visitation of Satan" rather than a sign of God's favor, Silas loses what little capacity he had for independent thought and spontaneous sympathy (11). His "old narrow pathway" (17) of thought is unable to distinguish human passions from divine action, so that instead of blaming Dane for his misfortunes, objecting to the archaic system of drawing lots as an instrument of justice, or speculating more generally that the forms of religion might be manipulated to human advantage, he loses trust in both God and man and blames an "unpropitious deity" even as he withdraws from society altogether (16). Unable to sever religious form from feeling by "an act of reflection" (13), he is as empty of the evolved capacities for reason and independent judgment as the "spinning insect" whose unquestioning life his resembles (17). The primitive condition of his mind before his exile, shaped as it was by the primitive life of an isolated community, is now further reduced to "utter bewilderment" (17).

Silas's cataleptic attacks bear no particular relationship to this change. They are apparently as frequent at Lantern Yard as they are at Raveloe, and so they cannot be identified as a natural consequence of increased isolation any more than they can be attributed to supernatural agency. The effect of this almost complete severance of sympathetic attachment to any other living being does, however, create another kind of deanimation, as solitude makes Silas increasingly less like a human being and more like a thing. His "face and figure shrank and bent themselves into a constant mechanical relation to the objects of his life, so that he produced the same sort of impression as a handle or a crooked tube, which has no meaning standing apart" (20). What seems like fetishism is in fact reduction to an even more primitive state: to the nonorganic thing itself. In the love of objects, on the other hand, the fetishistic investing of them with animate qualities, he shows "that the sap of affection was not all gone." He sees in the favorite pot that he breaks "an expression of willing helpfulness" (20) and in the coins that he is yet to earn "the unborn children" that he longs for (21). Yet excepting these expressions of primitive feeling, Silas is at the very lowest place in hierarchy of sensibilities that the novel sets up, from "the subtle and varied pains" (29) of the highly cultured, to the simple egotistic preoccupations of ruder minds, to the "unresenting" dog who will bear its masters blows because it sees no alternative, to the unquestioning insect, and finally to the inanimate object itself (31). Once his human affection is reduced to its smallest dimensions in fetishism, he himself becomes deanimated and his gold, "gather[s] his power of loving together into a hard isolation like its own" (40).

This metaphorical link to catalepsy is perhaps the closest the narrative gets to an explanation of the latter's strange manifestations. The almost total arrest of the nervous system and the reduction of mental activity to the point that even the breath is virtually undetectable are like the way that isolation and the disappearance of the affections cause the organism to shrivel into something that is barely alive. The story itself refuses to provide an adequate source for the attacks. The grown Eppie continues to be on the watch in case "one of her father's strange attacks should come on," the only clue being that emotional strain may be a precipitating factor (169). Other than providing William Dane with an opportunity to betray Silas at the beginning of the novel, the attacks do little to serve the plot, which could easily substitute Silas's near-sightedness as the cause of his obliviousness to Eppie's arrival. If, on the other hand, Silas's catalepsy is a physiological metaphor for arrested social growth, then the mental dissolution that characterizes it has leaked into narrative as another kind of deanimation. Catalepsy is not, in this case, an organic metaphor; it is not a figure that advances readerly understanding of the relationship between psychological and social phenomena. The cataleptic trance does not appear to have any formal relationship to those conditions of mind and social states shaped either by compassion, in the case of Silas's integration into the Raveloe community, or by moral cowardice, as in the case of Cass. The best function it can serve in the novel is in the much older literary mode of allegory. Yet allegory is what elsewhere the novel gently dismisses along with revealed religion, as the narrator observes that it is only in the "old days [that] there were angels who came and took men by the hand and led them away from the city of destruction" (123). The novel is no more a *Pilgrims' Progress* for modern times than it is a positivist account of the origins of unusual mental or spiritual phenomena. In Eliot's understanding of realism, it might be said that this story about catalepsy is itself barely a living thing.

Catalepsy thus represents the same anomaly for realist narrative that it does for medical science. This is particularly striking given the naturalization of miracle and mystery that the novel otherwise achieves. Even in the opening paragraph, we anticipate an intellectual gap between narrator and characters as we learn the story is to be set in "old times" and in a world limited to the contrast between direct experience and "a region of vagueness and mystery" (*S*, 5). The fairy-tale frame could not be more different from the opening narrative plunge into the complex psychologies of *Daniel Deronda*, where the question "was she beautiful or not beautiful?" (*DD*, 3), with all that it suggests about the relationship of form to the activity of the mind, belongs to both Daniel's and the narrator's consciousness. In *Silas Marner*, on the other hand, the narrator knows what most of the characters do not, namely, that natural causes can be assigned to extraordinary events. She knows that Silas's confusion of Eppie's hair with the lost gold is an effect of his lingering mental bent toward the objects of his miserly passion and that the miraculous transformation of inanimate object into living child is only the effect of a mind so disinherited from reason that it is capable of only the most primitive thoughts and feelings. And she sides with the skeptical farrier, who refuses to accept the existence of ghostly phenomena, as she ironically describes the apparition of Silas at the Rainbow. In addition, spectral phenomena are psychologically naturalized in Godfrey, as the sudden appearance of Silas and Eppie at the Red House, again described as an "apparition from the dead" (108), to the audience of dancers who witness it becomes for Godfrey "an apparition from that hidden life which lies, like a dark by-street, behind the goodly ornamented façade" (108). Godfrey's

willed forgetting and Silas's involuntary disconnection from his past provide tangible psychological causes for the apparent mysteries in the Raveloe
world. However much the causes of strange events may be dark to the characters, the property of the mind's vagueness and mystery, to the narrator they
can be explained in the context of natural laws, for they demonstrate the
"orderly sequence by which the seed brings forth a crop after its own kind"
(70).

In *Daniel Deronda,* suspended animation can be seen as a physiological
expression of prophetic vision that has collapsed back into the manifold—the
mind is frozen by the force of impressions it must contain. In *Silas Marner,*
on the other hand, nervous arrest is tied to a loss of historical consciousness,
a confidence that "the world's the same as it used to be," and the assigning
of difference to the dark and unknown (171). The ordering consciousness
of the narrative does not penetrate the mind of the cataleptic Silas or record
in his character what Richard Menke, describing how Lewes's physiological
psychology influences Eliot's prose, has described as "the hidden flows and
pulses of the body . . . [and] subtle possibilities of feeling."[70] Yet it is not just
that psychological narrative balks at the anomaly of catalepsy and its dissolving of the interior state. For indeed no characters represent "the subtle and
varied pains springing from the higher sensibility that accompanies higher
culture" (29). Instead, the narrator describes "ruder minds" (29) condemned
to absorption in their own private suffering. Among these characters, even
those who experience remorse do not do so with Gwendolen's intensity. Nor
do they experience, as she does, a sudden awareness of an evolving universe
of events indifferent to her needs and the resulting near-destruction of the
organizing relationship of self to world. Godfrey Cass is so dulled by the
monotony of his environment that his potential for finer thoughts is reduced
to self-absorbed reflections on his own petty history. Such stagnancy then
seems to be reinforced by the narrator herself who resists invading the "privacy of Godfrey's bitter memory" (29). To do this would be to dissect the
fluid emotions of entrapment and guilt that are so important to the psychological development of characters like Gwendolen or Arthur Donnithorne in
Adam Bede.

For both Lewes and Eliot, the distinction between higher and ruder
minds is nowhere more pronounced than in the history of religion. In a
discussion of the developmental conditions under which supernatural causes
are invoked to explain the unknown, Lewes uses the term "primitive mental
state" to describe the refusal to admit scientific methodology into inquiry
about the world or to set aside the authority of sacred texts in favor of
verification through experience.[71] Such ignorance, he argues, also perpetu-

ates an imperfect Christian ethics, since the latter continues to be rooted in superstition and tradition.[72] In Eliot's 1855 essay "Evangelical Teaching," which asserts the moral dangers of both ecclesiastical dogma and a belief in direct inspiration, she asserts a hierarchy of mental processes and an alliance between intellect and feeling that is central to her moral philosophy: We must allow religious impulses to be guided by intellect rather than an enthusiastic exaltation of feeling. Hence the "highest moral habit, the constant preference of truth, both theoretically and practically, pre-eminently demands the co-operation of the intellect with the impulses . . . [something which] is indicated by the fact that it is only found in anything like completeness in the highest class of minds."[73] This concept of moral "completeness" matches the broader developmental prediction Lewes makes about the eventual triumph of science over theology and superstition:

> Nowadays, among the cultivated minds of Europe, it is only in the less-explored regions of research, where argument is made to do duty for observation that the supernatural and metempirical explanations hold their ground. When science has fairly mastered the principles of moral relations as it has mastered the principles of physical relations, all Knowledge will be incorporated in a homogenous doctrine rivaling that of the old theologies in its comprehensiveness, and surpassing it in the authority of its credentials.[74]

Lewes's Comtean dream of universal scientific knowledge expanding into all realms of human experience, moral as well as physical, relies on both the exhaustion of unexplored phenomena and the extinction of uncultivated minds. In *Problems of Life and Mind,* this historicized and teleological model of knowledge is more aggressively united with imperialist ideology as "the intellect of the explorer distinguishes and classifies" where the "axe of the colonist clears the way."[75] Together they illuminate the ancestral landscape inhabited by the superstitious, idolatrous "savages and semi-cultivated nations" of the current day.[76] Yet Lewes's primitive is also figured in the excessively religious or fanciful minds of those who fail to test the intuitions and conclusions that the rational and abstracting mind always generates beyond the data of sense perception. Once again linking the work of the scientific observer with that of the artist and critic, he uses the example of a spectator at the theater who should properly recognize at once the idealizing nature of the play and its capacity to avoid falsifications that are inconsistent with that ideal. This critic figure thus recognizes that reality is partly reflected through and partly symbolized in the mind. The test of true knowledge is to verify symbolic and abstract thought by testing its correspondence to the presentation of feeling, which is all that the mind directly experiences of external reality. Hence, despite the physical basis of mind, which exists in reality, the work of that mind, and the symbolic power that it must muster in order to grasp any piece of reality larger than the fragments delivered by the senses, suggests that any knowledge of it can be acquired only through the higher processes of the intellect and the symbolic forms it produces. This is also the relationship between art and reality. Art promises access to the real, but only through a representative, not an actual, world. The veracity of the representation is then tested aesthetically in the emotions it is capable of stimulating.[77]

In *Silas Marner*, this higher capacity of the mind to unite thought and feeling is everywhere lost: Evidence for its disappearance shows in the superstition of the Raveloe villagers, in Silas's catalepsy and analogous social withdrawal, and in Godfrey's excessive attention to his own needs and subsequent suffering. In other early writings, Eliot identifies genuine sympathy, like genuine mysticism, as an expression of an advanced state in which truth is discernible through forms that demonstrate piety "towards the present and the visible" rather than in "the remote, the vague, and the unknown."[78] Not only are the characters in *Silas Marner* incapable of such sympathy, but the narrator too finds herself so intellectually remote from her subjects that she cannot provide them with a future true to human potential in the way that other parts of the story are true to human suffering. Gwendolen's nervous collapse is offset by her probable reformation under the influence of the greater narratives she has resisted, suggesting that present and visible sympathy can be linked to national spiritual destiny and the prophesied future. Where there is contraction rather than growth of the organism, however, there is less to be seen and said. In *Silas Marner*, the narrator's sympathetic access to the conscious and unconscious minds of her characters and their possible futures is so reduced that she is effectively drawn back into the primitive world from which she seemed at first so removed. And there she wanders through the territory of the unknown, where she encounters only the shrinking of human nature and the cavities of a primitive mind.

Daniel Deronda exempts neither the scientist's eye nor the raw gatherings of the imagination from the influences that can bring about cataleptic arrest. Loosened from the guiding forces of ego or vision, consciousness recoils from recognizing the vast organic and historical networks within which it is implicated. The way that Eliot's realism recognizes the proximity of narrow to visionary minds ties it to the subject of the next chapter: the otherwise very different genre of the detective novel. Victorian detective fiction, whose generic roots are in the sensation novel, combines nervously generated insight with the patient documentation of observable facts. Where the prophetic gifts of Eliot's characters grasp the fortunes of nations, the dreamy talents of Wilkie Collins's and Arthur Conan Doyle's detectives allow them to discern the sequence of events behind a crime. Doyle, in particular, is interesting to read after Eliot because his stories overcome the awkward kinship between dreamy discernment and nervous degeneration by invoking the figure of atavism. In his fiction, the primitive mind becomes the source of ancestral talents obscured in intervening generations and in this way offers a sort of evolutionary-scientific prelude to his subsequent spiritualist conversion.

DREAMY INTUITION AND DETECTIVE GENIUS

Ezra Jennings and Sherlock Holmes

*I*nspector Bucket's "high tower of the mind" in *Bleak House* is in many ways the cerebral model for the detective figure of later-century crime fiction. The enormous intellect and keen observational talent that characterize *The Moonstone*'s Sergeant Cuff repeat Bucket's high mental exercise, as do the extraordinary deductions of Sherlock Holmes. Yet it is not only the higher faculties that become activated in the service of crime solving. Cuff himself is rivaled by another and very different kind of investigative thinker—a medical man and devotee of John Elliotson who unlocks the real mystery of the novel with the help of mesmerism. Holmes, who solves many of the most obscure elements of his cases under the influence of drugs or while absorbed in art or music, effectively combines the rational command of a Cuff with the power of unconscious cerebration explored by an Ezra Jennings. Such recourse to the "lower" or more automatic mental functions in criminal detection compromises the figure of the robust intellectual hero by invoking its more nervous alter ego. The character of the detective becomes enfeebled in this way even as it merges with the figure of the mental alienist, who digs beneath the surfaces of conscious motive and reasoned behavior to uncover the psychological origins of criminal events.[1]

At the same time, these intuitive or dreamy elements of crime detection raise questions about medical science's mastery of the human mind, whose most primitive recesses contain mysterious powers that can appear supernatural rather than nervous in origin. Even as the detective decodes some puzzles of the mind—prevision, apparitions, or remote influence—exposing these either as criminal fraud or as nervous phenomena, others spring up or remain unsolved. In particular, clairvoyant powers associated with primitive human types—from the ancient worlds of the "barbarous East" or from prehistoric civilizations whose traits remain dormant in modern man—maintain an unexplained influence over the narrative above and beyond their significance for highly imaginative or superstitious characters. Indeed, manifesting in the irresistible gaze of the mesmerizer or in the mental magic of the detective sleuth, these imperfectly explained powers become instruments of the investigating mind as much or more as they become objects of its rigorous inquiry.

Perhaps because of its flirtation with Eastern mysticism, detective fiction engages, sometimes critically, with the science of degeneration. Although the concept of degeneration originated in eighteenth-century monogenetic accounts of human origins and the decline from an original type, the medicalization of "*dégénérescence*" begins properly in 1857 with Bénédict Augustine Morel's account of pervasive and progressive cross-generational decline. It therefore embraces what Daniel Pick describes as a "kaleidoscope" of medical conditions in the second half of the nineteenth century.[2] For Morel, degeneration combined hereditary and environmental factors: Traits acquired by an individual during its lifetime (particularly through modern overindulgence in toxic substances like alcohol) could be communicated in amplified form to subsequent generations.[3] Morel's concept of degeneracy offers a negative imprint of the Lamarckian principle of acquired, heritable, and advantageous characteristics; degenerative symptoms are cumulative, so that each generation becomes weaker than the last. In subsequent accounts of the phenomenon, such as Eugene Talbot's *Degeneracy: Its Causes, Signs and Results* (1898), Henry Maudsley's *The Pathology of Mind* (1890), E. Ray Lankester's *Degeneration: A Chapter in Darwinism* (1880), and Max Nordau's *Degeneration* (1892), the degenerate human body is further mapped onto a landscape of broad cultural and moral decline, often combining the biologically inherited characteristics of physical and mental decline with the poisonous environmental influence of industrial modernity.[4] Degeneration theory could therefore either predict, as Morel did, that degenerate types are headed for extinction, or else propose that under the influence of environmental factors, imbeciles and congenital criminals may thrive.[5]

The stress on acquired, negative characteristics in the context of social change turns the cultural signs of moral decline into biologically inherited, nervous dispositions that in turn determine perception and taste. For Nordau especially, the ill-disciplined, decaying bodies and brains of urbanized, morally decentered human beings find expression in the art, music, and literature of the fin de siècle and in the enervation and weak-mindedness of its connoisseurs. These "degenerates" and "hysterics"[6] are at the mercy of representations brought forth from an "unrestricted play of association" (56) and are "aroused and extinguished automatically" (56) while the will is mute and judgment is distorted. Mysticism, he argues, is also a symptom of the age, similarly arising from an incapacity to control the association of ideas by the attention and thus by weakness of will (46). Maudsley, who stressed that insanity was primarily a social problem that must be studied from a social point of view,[7] nonetheless took a similar view of spiritualism, linking it with the inherited and acquired nervous susceptibility, indeed even the "neurotic temperament" that characterizes delusions of the insane.[8]

While mysticism points to degeneration, the most vigorous and cultivated kind of thinking is represented by positive science. For Nordau, the mystic is the evolutionary inverse of the scientist, since the former is guilty of feeble observation: "He brings all the forms that he seems to discern into connection with the principal presentation which has aroused them" and "fancies that he perceives inexplicable relations between distinct phenomena" (*Degeneration*, 57). In future centuries, when nervous, mystical degenerates have perished along with the "aberrations of art," science and its observational methods will introduce "the uniformity of civilized life" (550). Science becomes a form of psychological therapy; those degenerates who have not yet reached an irreversible state of mental derangement may yet learn to interpret sense impressions properly and systematically (553). Maudsley too contrasted the degenerate mystic with the scientist, arguing that the former's obsession with evidence of prophesy, clairvoyance, and thought-reading represents the neurotic's defective power of observation, since the mind is so possessed by a single idea that its ability to discern facts is suspended.[9] Even for Lankester, a professed advocate of the theory of natural selection, the Lamarckian model of inheritance allows for self-cultivation or progressive adaptation in the individual's response to environmental influences, and hence the practice of rigorous thinking can reverse nervous and cultural deterioration. Lankester closed his *Degeneration* with a call to the "full and earnest cultivation of science—the knowledge of causes—. . . to which we have to look for the protection of our race—even of the English branch of it—from relapse and degeneration."[10]

Where crime solving depends on dreamy intuition even as it employs what Nordau lauds as "method[s] of observation and registration" (*Degeneration*, 106), the distinction between the degenerate and the rigorous empiricist comes under considerable pressure. The mental labors of the detective-hero therefore point to an evolutionist understanding of the human mind that emphasizes atavism, or the resurgence of ancestral forms, rather than progressive degeneration. Although Victorian writers themselves sometimes collapsed the terms, particularly when, following Morel and Cesare Lombroso, they identified atavistic features as the "stigmata" of degeneration, the Holmes stories, by blending the muscular, systematizing intellect of a Bucketlike man of science with the dreamy talents of a Bohemian art lover, recognize a subtle but crucial distinction between those terms. In so doing, the stories position the detective simultaneously in the modern metropolitan centers of scientific inquiry and in the worlds of primitive past and savage periphery invoked through the activity of the dreamy mind.[11] Rather than the pervasive decline of modern civilization, his character and his genius suggest that modern science itself is entangled with mystical forms of knowledge that rise up from a remote past as well as from earlier expressions of human physiology.

I. MESMERISM, DREAMY DEGENERACY, AND LITERARY FORM

With the arrival of table turning and table rapping in Britain in the early 1850s, mesmeric science was increasingly linked to investigations of spirit agency.[12] W. B. Carpenter's *Mesmerism, Spiritualism, &c, Historically and Scientifically Considered* (1877) highlighted the preposterous claims of mesmerism in its title, and dismissed the testimonies of mesmeric lucidity and supernormal intelligence as evidence of the mind's "extraordinary tendency to self-deception."[13] Carpenter proposed that the apparently clairvoyant perception of entranced subjects should be interpreted as the effect of the subject's liberation from his or her own controlling will and the consequently preternaturally acute and impressible senses.[14] In the case of artificially induced trance states, it was not the passes of the mesmerizer but rather the feeble will of his subject that brought on mesmeric sleep.[15] This physiological explanation for the strange results achieved by mesmerists followed in the path of numerous earlier efforts to rid animal magnetism of its occultist associations, including James Braid's hypnosis, which emphasized the power of suggestion, including autosuggestion over the manipulative power of the mesmerizer.[16] Hypnotic or "nervous sleep," Braid asserted, is "a peculiar condition of the nervous system, induced by a fixed and abstracted attention of the mental and visual eye, on one object, not of an exciting nature."[17] Even those physiologists who ignored Braid's studies and continued to focus on mesmeric influence downplayed the principles of magnetism. Although Elliotson enjoyed a renewed medical respectability in the 1840s, he emphasized the practice and practical benefits of mesmerism over the theory of magnetic fluid, while his colleague Chauncy Townshend remarked in *Facts in Mesmerism* that "we have asked whether such a *power* as mesmerism exists, when we should have demanded whether there is a *state* so denominated."[18]

However, efforts to minimize mesmerism's occult associations had been compromised by Elliotson's recording of somnambulistic marvels in *The Zoist*, as well as by the keen interest in paranormal mental phenomena maintained in studies on mesmerism, such as J. C. Calquhoun's *Isis Revelata* (1836), which went through three editions by 1844, or George Sandby's *Mesmerism and Its Opponents* (1848). Such works ignored Townshend's caution that mesmerism's advocates should refrain from emphasizing its inexplicable products. They also seemed to anticipate Elliotson's conversion to spiritualism by D. D. Home in 1868, an event apparently confirming that the "science" of mesmerism had always favored the occult.[19] When the preternatural events of artificial somnambulism became the subject of systematic investigation by the Society for Psychical Research (SPR) in the 1880s, both mesmerism and hypnosis became formally associated with efforts to establish the truth or otherwise of a noncorporeal intelligence. In particular, in *Human Personality and Its Survival of Bodily Death* (1903), Frederick Myers respiritualized the therapeutic science of hypnotism by proposing that the power of suggestion comes not from external but from internal sources and those are the property of a subliminal mind shaped by spiritually influenced "lower organic centers." [20] Animal magnetism and phreno-mesmerism proposed materialist accounts of altered mental states, yet their investigations were often approximations of the séance room and exalted in the exotic phenomena of trance states, including telepathy, clairvoyance, and the apparent existence of spirit visitors.[21]

To a large extent, mesmerism and hypnosis owed their occultist associations to their affiliations with ancient and Eastern medicine. Alison Winter has shown that British medicine in colonial India linked mesmerism rhetorically with indigenous magic and Eastern mysticism, even as it established the authority of Western knowledge over local, native practice.[22] In his *Mesmerism in India* (1847), the Scottish surgeon James Esdaile observed of the indigenous population of Bengal that the people in "this part of the world are peculiarly sensitive to the mesmeric power."[23] He attributed this susceptibility to their ill-nourishment and deficient nervous energy, yet he also observed that is was probable that the technique has been practiced in India since remote antiquity.[24] Indeed most influential books on the subject of artificial somnambulism refer to Oriental traditions: In *Isis Revelata*, Calquhoun stressed the ancient history of mesmeric practice and refers to magnetic marvels from numerous remote traditions, including those of physicians in India "who cure diseases merely from the breath":[25] Braid's research on cases of suspended animation, we have seen, was focused on the traditional practice of the Indian fakirs; while in his account of mesmerism in *Human Physiology*, Elliotson refers to the medical practice of the "imposition of hands" in India and China.[26]

Given these mystical and Oriental associations, it is scarcely surprising that mesmeric investigations of double consciousness, telepathy, and clairvoyance provide raw material for the neo-Gothic forms of the later-century British novel. Double consciousness and medical "pseudo-science" in Stevenson's *Dr Jekyll and Mr Hyde* (1886) and telepathy and mesmerism in Stoker's *Dracula* (1897), for example, take on grotesque, supernatural forms. Dracula's mesmeric powers, like those of Svengali in George Du Maurier's *Trilby* (1894), represent the malevolent influence of the East. Yet these novels are as much engaged with the aesthetics of realism as they are with the tropes of the Gothic, since in each case they draw attention to narrative exactness and the careful documentation of experience and events whether by a journalistic, legal, medical, or artistic eye. In the literary context, degeneracy conflates realists and mystics, naturalism and Gothic sensation, and contemporary urban excess with "the primitive chaos of human nature" (*Degeneration*, 73). Novels that present the figure of the degenerate in a modern setting show the contemporary psyche corrupted by a failure of will and a surrender to lower and more automatic nervous activity.[27]

Gothic-realist hybrids that blend modern scenes and characters with the monsters and mysteries of the premodern imagination give form to such pervasive mental deterioration, illustrating both the retreat of the organism into its primitive nervous pathways and the sensation-driven, mystically minded culture to which they give rise. In *Dracula,* the modern technologies of the West that enable up-to-the-moment recording of events—the typewriter and the phonograph—merge with the ancient practices of the East as the documenting of Mina's mesmeric visions becomes the means by which Dracula is pursued and destroyed. In *Dr. Jekyll and Mr. Hyde* the rational men of the professional classes in industrialized London are disturbed by evidence of demonic possession in one of their own. The degenerative proximity of monstrous to modern is quite pronounced in *Trilby,* whose hostility to aestheticism rivals Nordau's and which self-consciously describes the contamination of realist "truths" by the nervous influence of primitive, mystical forces. Bohemian Paris nurtures both the mysteries of "the poisonous East,"[28] figured in Svengali's mesmeric abduction of Trilby, and the genius of the realist artist, Little Billee, who is mentally and physically fragile and pointedly inferior to the other specimens of British manhood with whom he associates. Despite his moral repugnance at the grosser spectacles of Parisian decadence and despite his improving reading choices of *Silas Marner* and *On the Origin of Species,* he is overwhelmed by his passion for Trilby and his loathing of Svengali, and finds himself as nervously depleted as Trilby herself or as Jonathan or Mina Harker are when unable to resist their captors' marvelous powers. The protagonists in these novels lose their ability to "re-evoke . . . the essence of things . . . by a mere effort of the will,"[29] becoming Nordau's fin-de-siècle artists: "weaklings in will, unfitted for any activity requiring regular uniform habits" (*Degeneration,* 337).

Such spectacles of moral and physical attenuation implicate late-century narrative fashion in the degeneration of the civilized world, as bodily weakness and nervous susceptibility contaminate even the sturdiest protagonist. For Nordau, realism elevates sensation over moral content, triggering pleasure or excitement through the sensory organs rather than through the intellectual faculties, thus "exciting the nerves and dazzling the senses" (*Degeneration,* 11). The artistic representation of nature is thus only another form of nervous encounter with the world and the surrender to associative habits of mind that characterize mental weakness. Hence, artistic realism is at best a poor substitute for a systematic investigation of natural forms and at worst a malicious and invalid claim on the reality that can be properly captured only by science. With the mid-century emergence of the detective hero, however, this nervous susceptibility itself promised illuminatory talents that, in combination with careful documentation, could expose and expel rather than exacerbate the criminal and degenerative influences of civilized modernity.

II. MEDICAL SCIENCE AND MYSTICISM IN
THE MOONSTONE

In a series of letters titled "Magnetic Evenings at Home," written to G. H. Lewes and published in *The Leader* in February and March of 1852, Wilkie Collins recorded scenes of mesmeric clairvoyance that he witnessed while visiting friends in Somersetshire. His belief in the genuineness of the phenomena he observed, notwithstanding Lewes's skepticism, is joined to an enthusiasm for the practical benefits of mesmerism, which include enabling artists' models to maintain a single position without discomfort over an extended period of time. He also confesses to an admiration for the secret powers of the mind, whose origins might be understood as something more than physical:

> I have a thinking machine about me, normally called a "brain"—by what process is it set working? What power, when I am asleep, and my will is entirely inactive, sets this thinking machine going?—going as I cannot make it go, when my will is active, and I am awake? I know that I have a soul—what is it? Where is it? When and how was it breathed into the breath of my life?[30]

Collins's conception of the soul as the force that puts unconscious mind into motion and that acts more powerfully than the will—or engine of conscious thought—is the metaphysical account of a process that Carpenter would describe two years later in *Principles of Mental Physiology* as the reflex actions of the cerebrum. What for Collins suggests the imprint of spiritual force is for Carpenter the "lower" or automatic activity of a nervous center that undergoes modifications below the threshold of consciousness. When the sensorium, Carpenter argues, is unreceptive to these modifications owing to its absorption in other impressions (which may occur during sleep or during states of preoccupation), they affect the organism as unconscious cerebration rather than influential intellectual products (*Principles*, 517–19). For this reason, a great part of the creative genius of a writer like Wordsworth, he argues, must be attributed to "an inborn gift, the working of which is entirely automatic" (510), even while that imaginative faculty must be "directed and . . . cultivated" by the "chastening activity of the will" (513). Collins's fascination with the apparently spiritual dimensions of dreamy phenomena does not dissuade him of their nervous origins. Rather, he combines a scientific focus on automatic mental activity with narrative attention to the metaphysical content of dreamy episodes, whose mystery raises spiritual questions even as it proposes nervous explanations.

Collins's fiction converts the signs of Morel's *dégénérescence,* as Nordau would later do, into symptoms of pervasive cultural decline. His characters, like his implied readers, are so exaggeratedly, even morbidly, nervous and susceptible to developing a lopsided attachment to an idea that they fail to discern the proper arrangement of things in physical reality; his sensationalist narratives are replete with Gothic tropes that elevate suspense, supernaturalism, and gruesome spectacles over the kind of patient observation of detail that in Dickens's novels, for example, counterbalance mystery and melodrama. They draw on contemporary mental science to represent the physiology of thought and feelings, but they do so in order to heighten the nervous experience of the reader by delivering strange and horrifying scenes to familiar and domestic settings and stimulate the kind of associative thrills that Nordau would censure. This "pathology of the real" or "morbid naturalism,"[31] as Jenny Bourne Taylor describes it, brings the cult of spiritualism to what is in other ways an extremely "scientific" form of writing, observing at the most minute level how human physiology shapes experience. When, for instance, Walter Hartright first encounters Anne Catherick in *The Woman in White,* he is absorbed in the idea of his future life at Limmeridge. This state of reverie combines with the nervous shock caused by her sudden appearance to create the impression of an "apparition," while also affecting him with a dreamy unreality so that the familiar road they walk on, the recently departed domestic environment of his mother's cottage, and his very identity seem estranged and uncertain to him.[32] The "supernatural" event of Anne's appearance is not supernatural at all; yet it appears so under the influence of nervous automata that occur as Hartright's attention is drawn away from his physical surroundings, and it takes on a premonitory significance in the larger narrative that unfolds around the mystery of Anne's identity. Collins's narratives draw force from the marvelous productions of the mind—like the presentiments of Hartright and Marian Halcombe in *The Woman in White* or the "supernatural movements"[33] of *The Haunted Hotel*—and at the same time recognize these as the likely epiphenomena of cerebral reflexes or involuntary nervous movement. They at once lay claim to the existence of spiritualist phenomena and also identify exotic mental phenomena as the nervous productions of "lower" faculties.

This confluence of spiritual manifestation and exquisite nervous physiology explains both the ambiguous representation of science in Collins's novels and the poor physical condition of the nervous hero, who in both *The Woman in White* and *Heart and Science* contrasts with a villainous and more vigorous antagonist. The experimental chemist, Count Fosco, and the physiologist and vivisectionist, Benjuila, are both extremely large as well as emotionally powerful men, whose physical strength is exaggeratedly opposed to the weakness of Hartright and Ovid Vere.[34] Both too are students of nervous automata: Fosco is skilled at mesmerism; Benjuila experiments with spinal reflexes in order to isolate specific nervous pathways. In the detective novel, on the other hand, the man of science himself is often a nervous subject. Ezra Jennings of *The Moonstone* is so frail as to be on the point of death; his practicing of mesmerism situates him on the fringes of medical practice; and his "science" is dangerously close to the mesmeric "magic" performed by a group of Indians who are likewise endeavoring to recover the mysterious stone. Although he shares the disturbing gypsy features of Benjuila, and although he remains a mysterious and less-than-respectable figure in the novel, he transforms the figure of the mental alienist from villain to hero and endows him with the frail physique that signifies "heart" over "science" in the later novel so titled.[35]

The Moonstone describes both an unwitting robbery and its exposure in an opium-induced trance, thus overlapping the dreamy and the scientific minds as it links the nature of the crime to the process of its detection. Both scrupulous observation and dreamy intuition, it emerges, have a role to play in uncovering the mystery. Even before the novel introduces the unlikely nervous profile of its true detective, leading us instead to imagine the self-possessed Sergeant Cuff will properly assemble all the forensic clues, it introduces another disorienting and thrillingly unfamiliar element that brings "primitive" and modern minds into contact: Indian conjurers appear incongruously in the English countryside. To decipher their role in a mystery that turns on the agency of a subliminal consciousness demands recognizing the proximity of ancient, Eastern "magic" to the most up-to-date inquiries in mental science. Extraordinary events in the unconscious that drive unpredicted events in the English country home thus become associated with Oriental mysticism, even as they are studied and accounted for by Jennings and Dr. Candy, the representatives of Occidental medicine.

This proximity of East to West and of mysticism to science is embodied in the physician-detective himself.[36] Jennings has eyes that are "dreamy and mournful." Although this can be attributed to his failing health and his opium addiction, his accompanying "complexion of gypsy darkness" and a nose that recalls those "found among the ancient people of the East, so seldom visible among the newer races of the West"[37] imply a hereditary tendency to the degenerative disease that has prematurely aged and enfeebled him. When he is excited, his eyes become "wild and glittering" (373), just as Rachel described Franklin Blake's eyes as unusually bright when she saw him take the Moonstone from her cabinet in his opium-induced sleepwalk. Indeed, although he is the carefully observing physician who understands mesmerism physiologically—he is writing a book on the brain and the nervous system—his own nervous susceptibility and his manifestation of the symptoms of trance align him with all the other characters in the novel who experience these symptoms: with Blake himself as he twice walks unconsciously through the house; with Rosanna Spearman who is bewitched by the shivering sands; with Rachel, who, despite her repulsion at Blake, acts "under some influence independent of her own will" (338) and then "willingly open[s] her whole mind to [him]" (342); with Miss Clack's erotic fascination with Godfrey Ablewhite, which she represents as a state of religious ecstasy; and with everyone who gazes at the "unfathomable" (61) Moonstone itself, whose hypnotic properties even the skeptical amateur-detective Betteredge confesses, contained "a yellow deep that drew your eyes into it so that they saw nothing else"—so that it "laid a hold" on you (62). Where "the great" (109) Sergeant Cuff is set apart from and intellectually above all these other characters by his exceptional scientific ability to "look about" him (97), Jennings is as much a victim of the nervous contagion set loose by the stone and its Indian guardians as the English characters whom he has directly and indirectly taken under his care. He is a detective who assembles evidence like the pieces of a "puzzle" (370) and who, by drawing such data from Blake's subliminal consciousness rather than exclusively from forensic and circumstantial evidence, is more successful than Cuff. Yet he is also himself a dreamy, nervous subject who suffers from opium-induced visions. And when Blake finds himself so much under the physician's influence that he covers the paper on which he intends to write notes to Betteredge with images of the "irrepressible Ezra Jennings" (354), readers might be reminded of the involuntary and irrepressible preoccupation of the members of a "quiet English house" with "a devilish Indian diamond." This in turn reminds us of mysterious forces that the novel never exposes as natural—that of the jewel whose influence is set loose supernaturally by "the vengeance of a dead man" (33) and the legend of the special protection of the stone by Vishnu.

Indeed, scientific method struggles through much of the novel to preserve respectability as much as epistemological sovereignty. Jennings's dubious, possibly gypsy origins, combined with the mysterious, scandalous event that has destroyed his career, make him a less-than-reputable representative of the medical profession. Moreover, his hypotheses about Blake's unconscious cerebration and about the probable duplication of his actions on the night of the robbery according to the principles of double consciousness are, as critics have noted, based on the contradictory authorities of Carpenter and Elliotson.[38] Although it is set in 1848, *The Moonstone* postdates Elliotson's conversion to spiritualism in 1863, as its readers would have been aware and although Carpenter's *Mesmerism, Spiritualism, &c., Historically and Scientifically Considered* was not published until 1877, his assault on spiritualism was anticipated in his papers and articles published in the 1850s.[39] Carpenter's position is broadly represented in the account of Indian clairvoyance provided by the gentleman-explorer Murthwaite, who claims that such power is nothing more than nervous sensitivity and that strange events , must be traced "by rational means to natural causes" (282–83). Yet the novel reaches no firm conclusion about the scene Penelope witnesses in which the Indians force their captive clairvoyant child to read the whereabouts of the Moonstone in an ink-stained palm. Nor does it, in Murthwaite's closing account, entirely dismiss a supernatural explanation for the eventual return of the stone to the Temple of Brahma. Occult possibilities linger, if only to titillate readerly nerves.

Moreover supernatural explanations and scientific investigations of the unconscious are conflated in one narrative point of view that dismisses both as disreputable: that of solid English skepticism. Betteredge dismisses Jennings's experiment as a "conjuring trick" (398), while also identifying belief in "the ability to see persons and things beyond the reach of human vision," as the effect "in our country, as well as in the East . . . [of a] curious hocus-pocus . . ." Above all, he is contemptuous of what he sees as a quintessentially un-English interest in the special powers of the mind, something which accounts perhaps for his instinctive distrust of Jennings and his natural liking for Cuff, despite the latter having insulted the family with his suspicion of Rachel. Cuff himself speaks only teasingly of the prophetic powers of the detective, when he informs Betteredge of three significant events that will expose both the hiding place and thief of the diamond, but these are happenings whose likelihood Cuff has determined through his professional skill at interpreting events via experience rather than through any special intuition (129). In this respect, Cuff manifests the same mental talents as Betteredge's English literary hero, Robinson Crusoe, whose physical and psychological survival of the castaway ordeal was achieved in large part by the careful recording of his daily experiences in a diary. In Defoe's novel, the diary form is in itself a sort of stand-in for realist narrative, as it binds together the day-to-day material realities of Crusoe's life—finding food, domesticating animals, protecting his enclosure, and so forth—with the internal experience of these realities, the first-person account of the feelings of triumph, comfort, or despair that characterized his religious and emotional development. Cuff himself, reciprocating Betteredge's sentiment, often indicates his liking and approval of the latter, whom he describes in terms that seem to applaud his veracious narrative mode as much as the man himself: Betteredge is, Cuff praises, as "transparent as a child" (177).

But *The Moonstone* has little formally in common with *Robinson Crusoe*. Murthwaite and Jennings dismiss the possibility of supernatural agency in the disappearance of the stone; yet their grasp of the way that nervous automata affect knowledge suggest that the mystery cannot be resolved through the systematic approach of Defoean realism, where truth is secured by consulting the conscious mind's record of events and thoughts as they have occurred over time. Too much is stored in the subliminal mind to make this "child-like" transparency possible. If the sequence of events and the subjective states that precipitate them (not to mention the thrill of their revelation) are rooted in nervous activity that takes place beneath the conscious threshold, then the investigation of a crime must be simultaneously the interrogation of the "lowest" mental activity. *The Moonstone* stresses that this very form of inquiry engages the primitive, dreamy movements of the mind. The investigator must be more than a careful and exact observer; it is the opium-addicted "Easterner," traveling in dreams with "the phantoms of the dead" (392), who can fully reconstruct the sequence of events and the reasons for their occurrence. Jennings's success suggests that the scientific mind should not be sequestered from the visions associated with weakness and nervousness.

Doyle's detective stories deliver very similar conclusions. However, in his characterization of Holmes, scientific observation and dreamy intuition converge specifically in the resurgence of savage traits, or atavism. Like *The Moonstone,* the Holmes stories resist the plots of degeneracy in which only the sanitizing influence of the ordered, reasoning mind can restore nervous and social health to a corrupted physiology and a degraded culture. Instead, criminal and immoral acts are uncovered by the more obscure workings of genius. Understood as a resurgence of peculiar ancestral talents, genius invokes the figure of the savage to suggest not contemporary moral decline but rather the recovery of mental riches stored in the subliminal mind and therefore normally unavailable to conscious thought. In this way, detective genius anticipates the spiritualist focus of Doyle's later work. Holmes's genius is intuitive rather than rational and, it turns out, as worthy an object of scientific and psychical investigation as are the strangest phenomena of the séance room.

III. THE SAVAGE GENIUS OF SHERLOCK HOLMES

Like the story of the moonstone, the history of Sherlock Holmes and Dr. Watson begins in the East. When they first meet in *A Study in Scarlet*, Watson is an itinerant medical veteran of the Second Afghan War who, sick and rootless, without "kith or kin" in England, is naturally drawn to London, "that great cesspool into which all the loungers and idlers of the empire are irreversibly drained."[40] Lacking emotional ties, physical strength, and purpose of any real kind, Watson seems to illustrate the "feverish restlessness" and "blunted discouragement" that Nordau describes as symptoms of the age (*Degeneration*, 2). Watson's identification with urban refuse of the empire, together with his metaphor of the metropolitan landscape as cultural sewer, suggests Nordau's degenerative "feeling[s] of immanent perdition and extinction" (2), and emphasizes both the pervasiveness of modern social decay and the destructive potential of insalubrious influences that lurk within the civilized world as much as they do on its remote peripheries. Although, in his association with Holmes, Watson will not only remove himself from these influences but also actively help to cleanse late Victorian England of its morally most unsavory and dangerous elements, the threat of contagious degeneration is apparently never very far away even in the business of criminal detective work. The dandyish Holmes himself is subject to depression, has a taste for the Romantic composers, and has an addiction to cocaine that compromises a lifestyle otherwise remarkable for its "temperance and cleanliness" (*Study*, 1).

Yet once Watson meets Holmes and agrees to share accommodation with him, he begins to recover respectability and civility. Suddenly the "lowest portions of the city" (13) have nothing to do with him and the attention that had been dangerously "objectless" becomes focused on the character and methods of his companion. Watson then becomes healthier in mind as well as body, and he transmutes into the practical-minded Englishman whose personality provides a narrative counterweight to Holmes's own often dreamy eccentricity.[41] Despite his peculiar character, there is much Cufflike intelligence in Holmes, and it is no surprise that he has a healing effect on Watson. The detective's extraordinary powers of ratiocination, his skill at interpreting evidence, and his ability to empty his memory of superfluous cultural knowledge so as to retain only a perfectly ordered collection of facts provide an antidotal influence to the aimlessness and excessiveness of Nordau's fin de siècle. For Holmes, burdening the mind with "small matters" like Copernican theory jumbles thought so much as to risk mental torpor (15). He is thus the antithesis of Nordau's degenerate, who, like the formerly dissolute Watson, is unable "to fix his attention long, or indeed at all, on any subject, and [is thus] equally incapable of correctly grasping, ordering, or elaborating into ideas and judgments the impressions of the external world" (*Degeneration,* 21).

The healing of Watson has its counterpart in the healing of the city, whose criminal underworld is exposed and frustrated by the penetrating detective mind.[42] In narrative form, correspondingly, the stories themselves conduct a kind of self-purging of sinister or barbarous elements. The realism of detective fiction, refusing to shy away from the most brutal elements of modern life and truthfully recording what it sees, encounters and overcomes that fiction's own attraction to the Gothic—to the horrific, the concealed, and the (often) apparently supernatural. The dark alleyways and subterranean passages of criminal London, hidden behind and beneath the houses of the respectable and well-to-do as well as in the poorest and most desperate parts of the city, are exposed to the light of discovery that shines from 221B Baker Street. Yet the stories do not fully expel the Gothic. For one thing, the miraculous findings of deductive reasoning seem sometimes so improbably achieved that the work of ratiocination blurs with mysticism; Holmes may have a superbly logical mind, but he also has a divinatory gift, and the stories intrude primitive nervous activity into the most evolutionarily advanced nervous and social networks—intellectual inquiry and civilized modernity. As Srdjan Smajic puts it, Holmes's ratiocination "has something oddly intuitive about it."[43] Moreover, the stories tend to linger distractingly on Gothic tropes: *A Study in Scarlet* opens with the spectacle of writing in blood; "The Man with the Twisted Lip," centers on disguise and the double life; "The Speckled Band" is set in a haunted mansion; and so on. Although Holmes brings these mysteries to light, he does so through his own mysterious disappearances and reappearances in the murky criminal underworlds or other sinister settings that give these mysteries life. Illuminatory realism struggles against the sensational attractions of the Gothic.[44]

Given that this realist–Gothic hybrid promises to exacerbate the attenuated nervous state associated with thrill and superstition, the Holmes stories might be seen to manifest behavioral and aesthetic signs of degeneracy. Yet if they depict the peculiar recesses of the mind on which Holmes draws as an atavistic throwback to primitive mental talents rather than morbid deviation from a higher form, then they in fact challenge the principles of *dégénérescence.* Morel declared that evidence of degeneration could be found in the abnormal features or "stigmata" of inheritable physical, mental, and moral disease that are carried, often invisibly, through succeeding generations. These features, he argues, are sometimes brought into prominence by particular environmental circumstances, but they often remain concealed for long periods of time, surfacing as a variety of individual ailments that collectively promise to undermine social order and the health of the nation as a whole.[45] Atavism, on the other hand, which was central to the Italian school of positivist criminology, describes the unexpected reappearance in a single organism of ancestral characteristics, often very remote ones. Unlike degeneration, atavism, which Darwin emphasized is represented in the "astonishing" appearance of traits from a distant ancestor,[46] defies neo-Lamarckian principles, since atavistic features are not the directly inherited modifications determined by an organism's relationship with its environment as vestigial or degenerated forms might be. Moreover, although atavism, particularly Lombroso's taxonomy of criminal stigmata, was appropriated by the language of degeneration, it does not in itself carry any implications of pervasive biological and social decline since, on the contrary, it highlights the anomalous status of the throwback.

That atavism does not imply degeneracy was a subject of debate in the last decades of the century. In *The Criminal* (1890), which he wrote in order to bring England up-to-date with continental developments in criminal anthropology, Havelock Ellis defends the use of the term "atavism" to describe the progressive degeneration within families and the "rising flood of criminality" that occurs as a consequence.[47] The argument that "degenerescence and atavism are two absolutely distinct facts," he objects, is disproved when we consider that reversion to older and lower physical, mental, and social states—all of which are increasingly visible conditions in the diseased modern nation—can very probably be said to have a pathological cause and that pathology itself "is the science of anomalies."[48] For Maudsley, reversion to savage or even lower animal characteristics reveals the "evil ancestral influences"[49] latent within civilization, but he stresses with Morel that these are expressed in degeneration, as the "germs of a morbid variety" are passed down "from generation to generation" culminating in "the extreme degeneracy of idiocy."[50] Talbot's *Degeneracy*, on the other hand, identifies atavism as the feature of heredity that determines diversity within a species. Degeneracy, like Spencer's dissolution, is the effect of a "gradual change of structures by which the organism becomes adapted to less varied and less complex conditions of life"[51] and determined by the principle of the inheritance of such acquired modifications. Atavism, by contrast, "tends to preserve the type and offsets the influence of degeneracy."[52]

For Doyle, as a member of the SPR and an increasingly committed spiritualist, the difference between degeneracy and atavism was crucial. His stories demonstrate what could be called the persistence of a primitive mind that cannot be collapsed into the symptoms of moral and social degeneration that characterize the metropolitan underworld. The mysterious powers that this mind reveals testify to human evolutionary potential as much as to our savage past and that past's lasting expression in a crime-infested present. The instances of atavism in these stories, we shall see, encourage his fin-de-siècle audience less to read the tendencies of prehistoric man into the social problems of late nineteenth-century England than to take the scientific study of human faculties into a primitive past in which ancient mental talents recognize otherworldly dimensions of knowledge and experience.

Despite the healthier state of mind it encourages in him, Watson's life with Holmes and his involvement in the detective's work is not without its moments of doubt and distress. In the early days, he retains the suspicion of a séance-room skeptic, as "there still remained some lurking suspicion in my mind . . . that the whole thing was a prearranged episode, intended to dazzle me" (*Study*, 23). Later in their career together, this uncertainly about Holmes's genuineness develops into ambivalence about the moral safety of crime-solving work itself. In "A Case of Identity," Watson observes that the stories of criminal violence, often domestic, reported in the papers are "rude, bald, and vulgar," thus suggesting "realism pushed to its extreme limits."[53] His fear is that the work of criminal detection is procedurally allied with the lowest forms of realist narrative—sensation fiction and naturalism—both of which satisfy the contemporary appetite for representations of the morally ugliest and most brutal symptoms of modern life. Where he had once doubted the authenticity of Holmes's methods, speculating that such arch positivism could only be rehearsed and pretended observation, he now feels corrupted by his own involvement in a business that is so readily commoditized for a sensation-hungry public. In either case, realism, the narrative method that (like Holmes's strategies of detection) creates a true picture by recording and ordering a multitude of facts, risks degenerating into mere spectacle. Holmes, however, calms Watson by insisting that "there is nothing so unnatural as the commonplace," thus distinguishing the true job of criminal detection from the sham realism of sensation fiction. Police reports and newspaper stories lay more stress "upon the platitudes of the magistrate than upon the details, which to an observer contain the vital essence of the whole matter" ("Case," 75). In its true incarnation (as detective fiction), then, realism is a bulwark against the degenerate literary forms and appetites that affect the age.

Although it was published four years before the English edition of *Degeneration*, Doyle's story thus seems to anticipate and answer Nordau's assault on realism as the literary manifestation of pervasive nervous and cultural decay in the late nineteenth century. Realism's impressionistic sacrificing of the concept to mere sensory stimulation, Nordau accuses, fails to engage the higher centers of the brain in which true knowledge of phenomena is produced through reason and judgment. Moreover, through the vehicle of "milieu," realist novelists have the arrogance to theorize about and experiment with the impact of environment on character without any of the systematic assembling of facts that has been undertaken in biological science and criminal anthropology. The result, he claims, is not only an erroneous but also a decadent portrait of the social world in which sexual pathologies, brutal behavior toward one's fellow creatures, and hysteric disorders become the norm. "The would-be 'realist,'" he pronounces, who "sees the sober reality as little as a superstitiously timid savage," manifests the primitive mental activity and intellectual and moral laziness of a generation that is witnessing the end of civilization (495). For Doyle's detective hero, on the other hand, the careful assembling of facts without selection or discretion, facts that ultimately announce the truth on their own, is precisely the means by which criminal and moral insanity can be exposed and punished.

But of course this is not really how Holmes finds his man, nor does it accurately describe his character. Holmes could not be less like his fact-loving literary forefather, Thomas Gradgrind. For one thing he has a dreamy appreciation of art and music. Music, in particular, he proposes, citing Darwin, calls up not exact knowledge but rather "vague memories in our souls of those misty centuries when the world was in its childhood" (*Study*, 42). Second, the bare facts alone do not lead to his divining of the meaning behind the mystery. Indeed, Watson admires the way in which Holmes can unravel a detective puzzle without leaving his room, where other men who have seen every detail surrounding it remain baffled, and Holmes describes the rules of deduction that enable him to do so as "intuitive" (*Study*, 20). Apparently having intuited Watson's earlier skepticism about his methods (along with the probable story behind the murder), he then jokingly compares his mysterious deductive powers to the "conjurer's trick." Hence while Watson praises Holmes for bestowing the status of "exact science" (36) on criminal detection, the latter betrays how his methods employ something of the psychically supernormal, even if, perhaps, like even the most genuine séance room, they inevitably also contain something of the theatrical.

"A Case of Identity" opens with Holmes suggesting that the supernormal interpretative powers of the detective, if properly realized, would generate knowledge and appreciation of the marvels of nature in ways that far outstrip any awareness of the world that either ordinary perception or existing literary conventions are capable of producing. To really grasp criminal goings-on in London, he proposes, he and Watson would need to

> fly out of that window hand in hand, hover over this great city, gently remove the roofs, and peep in at the queer things which are going on, the strange coincidences, the plannings, the cross-purposes, the wonderful chains of events, working through generations, and leading to the most *outré* results, it would make all fiction with its conventionalities and foreseen conclusions most stale and unprofitable. (75)

Doyle draws on a convention that Peter Brooks recognizes in realism of dollhouse play: The artificial device of Alain-René Le Sage's *Le Diable boîteux* (1707), wherein a supernatural figure reveals the private lives of the city by removing all the rooftops, becomes the figure for panoramic and penetrative narrative vision in novels by Balzac and Dickens.[54] Here, the fantastic ability to see events not only from the bird's eye but from the perspective of an airborne voyeur would, in turn, expose not the moral bleakness of a city awash in criminal activity but the marvelous and the extraordinary realities whose existence it is beyond the capacity of the ordinary senses to grasp. Such "a wonderful chain of events" seems to invoke the complexity of Darwin's "entangled bank" where "elaborately constructed forms, so different from each other, and dependent on each other in so complex a manner, have all been produced by laws acting around us.[55] Yet these realities are also psychologically *outré*: excessive, improbable, beyond the pale of what can be known empirically to the mind. Although detectives, unlike benevolent devils, cannot fly or lift off rooftops, the best of them are gifted with a form of intuition that analogously enables them to see more than the human faculties normally make possible.[56]

Such vision might belong to the class of remarkable psychological phenomena examined by members of the SPR, including clairvoyance, spirit materializations, and thought transference. The society was formed in 1882 in order to investigate "amid much delusion and deception, an important body of remarkable phenomena, which are prima facie inexplicable on any generally recognized hypothesis, and which, if incontestably established, would be of the highest possible value."[57] Despite the findings of some key members in its early decades that the empirical evidence of human immortality remained inconclusive at best,[58] the society endeavored to lift investigations of spiritualism beyond the simple testimony of believers, on the one hand, and the prosecuting actions of the law on the other, so as to make the study of occult phenomena genuinely scientific. This was particularly the case when, after 1886, many disaffected spiritualists abandoned the organization, leaving it largely in the hands of its intellectual founders. Although the attitudes of these and later prominent members ranged from steady skepticism, like that of Henry Sidgwick and Frank Podmore, to profound spiritualist faith, like that of Alfred Russel Wallace, Fredrick Myers, and Doyle himself, the members shared a frustration with the limiting of natural-scientific inquiry to the material world and sought to expand its framework to include nonmaterial objects and events.[59]

Doyle himself became a member of the society in 1891, although his interest in spiritualism developed a good decade earlier. Despite his reservations about the antisensationalism of the society's investigative work, which, he said, sometimes undermined its effectiveness, and although he later resigned his membership over what he considered to be the organization's betrayal of the spiritualist cause, he maintained even in his later life that the society did "splendid work" that "helped me to shape my thoughts."[60] Such work provides the intellectual complement to the ideological struggles of spiritualism itself, since the latter, he proposes in *The History of Spiritualism*, challenges the nearsightedness of conventional nineteenth-century scientific intelligence, both because spiritualism represents "a survival of savagery" and because it demands rethinking of the parameters of scientific investigation.[61] Doyle's spiritualist writings postdate nearly all of the Holmes stories. However, his emphases on legitimating the study of supernormal phenomena in mainstream science and on the primitive character of mystical experience suggest the interpretive preoccupations and atavistic mental talents of his detective hero as much as they advocate for spiritualist faith.

In the decade that Holmes became a celebrity, Myers was exploring the notion of a subliminal self whose powers might include thought transference, precognition, and the ability to communicate with disembodied spirits. Its more mundane task, he suggested, was to preserve all the sensory experiences that an organism expels from primary consciousness in a subliminal memory. When data from the subliminal self leaks into the supraliminal mind or conscious threshold, he proposed, it can introduce either retrocognition, the "knowledge of the past extending back beyond the reach of our ordinary memory," or precognition, "knowledge of the future, extending onwards beyond the scope of our ordinary inference."[62] Such knowledge may be manifest in dreams, telepathy, or clairvoyant perception, and it may include information that extends back beyond that recorded by a single life, in which case it is communicated to the subliminal mind either directly by departed spirits or by objects that retain the trace of those departed souls. These objects are thereby rendered, in language that seems to echo Charles Lyell's reading of the fossil, "luminescent with the age-long story of the past."[63] When we explore the action of the subliminal self, Myers suggests in *Human Personality and Its Survival after Bodily Death,* we discover both the childish weakness and the profound hidden powers of the human organism. The subliminal mind demonstrates both a readiness to "obey the whims of the hypnotist," or to succumb to its own self-suggestions in the case of hysteria, on the one hand, and a capacity for fantastic cognition, on the other (1:45). Curiously then, this dimension of mind is the source of both the most primitive and the most expansive elements of mental life.

Myers's critics included other members of the society like Podmore, who was incredulous of much of the supernatural phenomena recorded by his colleagues. Yet in 1895, Podmore defended Myers's theory of the subliminal self against Arthur Pierce's claim that this supposed secondary consciousness was merely a symptom of physiological disorders (such as hysteria) wherein memories and sensations may be suppressed from and then restored to consciousness. We infer as much about physical activity in the brain as we do about mental states, Podmore points out, and therefore the observed facts do not compel us to reduce all mental phenomena to cerebral events. "Subliminal consciousness" may be as useful a way of explaining unusual events in the mind as Pierce's account of overtaxed nerve channels is useful for thinking about what happens in the brain. Podmore then inquires whether abnormal mental states might reveal something about the psychological evolution of human beings. In the subliminal consciousness, he suggests,

> We come across memories of childhood and many old forgotten things; we [also] come across traces of long lost but once serviceable faculties—telepathy, sense of time, of direction, of weight; we acquire partial control over our bodily functions—digestion, circulation, and the like—which civilized man has learned to acquiesce in as beyond his guidance. . . . [The subliminal consciousness] show[s] us what we have once had, and have not yet wholly lost.[64]

This conjecture is not so very different from Doyle's proposal in *The History of Spiritualism;* that is, those who are capable of spirit communion may be the few members of the "complex races"[65] who grasp the primitive secrets of our species, thereby explaining why they are often to be found in ruder communities like those of the American provinces. [66] Wallace, too, observed that the powers of second sight are more frequent and energetic in remote, mountainous terrain and among uncivilized races.[67]

In *Human Personality and Its Survival of Bodily Death,* Myers speculates that the subliminal consciousness might give us the kind of mental access to automatic functions in our bodies that humans achieved more readily at an earlier evolutionary stage. When inspiration bursts into the mind, he proposes, we come "one step nearer to primitive reality than in that specialized consensus of faculties which natural selection has lifted above the threshold for the purposes of working-day existence" (1:97). In other words, human evolution has suppressed the agency of the primitive mind by limiting the size and number of portals through which it can penetrate the conscious threshold. Subliminal modes of perception direct us to the "unguessed potentialities from the primal germ" (1:98). These may take the form of profound inspiration or genius, or they may manifest in hysterical disintegrations of personality, where the ordinary flow of thoughts is paralyzed by an *idée fixe,* a terror that reaches back not only to childhood fears but to "a prehistoric past" and "the vanished perils of primitive man" (1:41). Natural selection has repressed these primitive emotions and perceptions, he argues, in order that we can keep the ideas we need for ordinary working, waking life easily within reach. Yet we have glimpses of their power in the form of nervous collapse as well as in that of inspired genius.

Myers thus conceives of genius as a form of automatic mental performance as well as a "flash of the supernormal" onto the supraliminal consciousness (1:107). The man who is guided solely by ratiocination, the complex work of the supraliminal mind alone, is destined to mediocrity. In linking genius so closely with nervous pathologies like hysteria, he seems to echo Nordau's claim that the inspiration of genius belongs to the same category of nervous pathologies as the inspiration of the mystic. For Nordau, such "hallucinations" are the product of a disturbed mind in which the imagination responds to memory-images rather than sense perceptions, thus permitting the association of ideas to predominate over the higher activities of judgment and reasoning, which, in a healthy organism, receive and order these sense perceptions. Epilepsy, hysterical delirium, and the degeneration manifest in mystics—so-called realists, aesthetes, egomaniacs, and the morally insane—are all heritable, morbid consequences of this nervous and mental disorganization in which a train of associations leads the mind away from the true realities of the external world toward disturbed and "ghostly presentations" (56). Myers too links genius to mysticism, since he attributes both to the psychical work that goes on beneath the conscious threshold. Yet he argues that supernormal perceptions, rather than being symptoms of nervous exhaustion and moral and cultural decline, are the stuff of currently unimaginable truths accessible only to the subliminal mind.

Myers's emphasis on the atavistic event of genius, the moment of inspiration as an explosion of primitive knowledge into the evolved, civilized psyche, in fact brings him closer to Lombroso than to Nordau, for whom genius represents only one of so many morbid erosions of a healthier type. In his review of *Degeneration*, Lombroso praises Nordau for identifying how genius is a form of degenerative neurosis, yet cautions him not to dismiss the extraordinary productions of artistic genius as merely symptoms of mental disease.[68] In *The Man of Genius* Lombroso, like Nordau, links such gifts of the mind to criminal insanity and mysticism, and he suggests that all three tend to run together in families, thus indicating progressive degeneration of the line. Yet he also argues that both genius and insanity are expressed in an atavistic resurgence of the ancestral mind—whether that of the prophets or occultists of ancient times or to the strange precocious brilliance of present-day savages. The powerful, divinatory conceptions of modern-day genius, like the impulsive acts of the insane, "suddenly burst forth" as they did out of the premodern minds of prophets, saints, and demoniacs.[69] Hence the shared isolation and "hypnotic condition"[70] of the genius and the madman, neither of whom can "be restrained within the bounds of common sense" or made to respect immediate realities.[71] Lombroso's genius, like Myers's, has a power of divination "which precede[s] all common observation."[72] Given that Lombroso does not miss the opportunity to comment on Nordau's own genius and the "gaps and errors"[73] that inevitably accompany it (in this case his overzealous condemnation of so many great artists), it is hard to imagine that he would not look wryly back on his own account of the revelatory moment in which he became convinced that the anatomy of delinquent criminals, their "stigmata," expressed traces of our remote ancestry:

> "This was not merely an idea, but a revelation. At the sight of that skull, I seemed to see all of a sudden, lighted up as a vast plain under a flaming sky, the problem of the nature of the criminal—an atavistic being who reproduces in his person the ferocious instincts of primitive humanity and the inferior animals. Thus were explained anatomically the enormous jaws, high cheek bones, prominent superciliary arches, solitary lines in the palms, extreme size of the orbits, handle-shaped ears found in criminals, savages and apes, insensibility to pain . . . and the irresponsible craving of evil for its own sake, the desire not only to extinguish life in the victim, but to mutilate the corpse, tear its flesh, and drink its blood."[74]

Lombroso's discovery is nothing short of a revelation of genius. Given the proximity of intellectual inspiration to criminal insanity and present-day savagery that he identifies in *The Man of Genius,* this account suggests his not-so-distant relation to the blood-drinking criminal lunatics who revive the violent instincts of primitive humankind.

The risk of embarrassment by this association perhaps explains why Henry Maudsley endeavors to distinguish between the genius, whose organic variation is "evolutional," and the madman, whose is "pathological and degenerative."[75] Nonetheless, in arguing for atavism as a principle of variation in breeding contesting that of simple heredity, Maudsley too is forced to link manifestations of genius to primitive ancestry. Atavism, he argues, the "latency or dormancy of ancestral qualities that afterwards wake again to open activity," is the principle at work in the individuation in the species, whereas the law of heredity determines the preservation of that species' character.[76] If one child in a family should manifest symptoms of insanity and another of genius, this has less to do with their shared "pathology," than with the "deep-lying potentialities of the family stock."[77] There is scant evidence, he corrects the eugenicist Francis Galton, that genius is hereditary; rather its rarity suggests that it represents an unstable variation which is corrected by the normalizing and stabilizing influence of heredity.

Any late-century account of heredity and atavism is of course indebted to Darwin's use of instances of anomalous primitive physiology in some humans as evidence of our descent from a lower primate. What he describes in *The Origin* as the "well-known principle of reversion to ancestral characteristics" enables us to reconstruct how our early progenitors looked and behaved.[78] Ellis identifies Darwin as the father of criminal anthropology, highlighting the latter's observations in *The Descent of Man* about the phenomenon of the "black sheep," as well as his suggestion that some of humankind's "worst dispositions . . . may perhaps be reversions to a primitive state."[79] Much more useful to Darwin's account of human social development than the relatively rare incidents of reversion, however, is the living evidence of our past in the form of present-day savage societies. The amazement that he describes in *The Voyage of the Beagle* at the "wide difference between savage and civilized man," highlights at once the proximity and the enormous distance between them.[80] "Savages," as Cannon Schmitt has put it, are "living mnemonic devices" for Darwin, enabling him to recover the early history of humankind and its subsequent development (the myriad of tiny events that Holmes deems essential to any true understanding of life) while marveling at the fantastic power of natural selection to create civilized scientific observers out of primitive, unreflecting animals.[81] If atavism seems disturbingly to create a bridge across this enormous evolutionary gulf, such disturbance can be neutralized, for Darwin, by invoking the absolute alterity of existing savage communities.

However, once savage man is interpolated more aggressively into the civilized world (becoming visible either in the form of the pervasive cultural influence of degeneracy or in the aberrant tendencies of the criminally insane and the intellectually *outré*), this distance cannot be so easily maintained. The reincarnation of primitive man, hitherto encountered primarily in the figure of the colonial savage, occurs in the late nineteenth-century discourses of degeneration and atavism as a socially destructive influence *within* the civilized world, displayed on the bodies of European criminals in the form of stigmata that in turn link those bodies to those of the non-European savage.[82] Late nineteenth-century criminal anthropology thus not only directed scientific investigation to humankind's greater history; it also indicated the enduring human potential for violence and madness as well as for exceptional acts of perception.

Crime fiction, like the technologies of fingerprinting and anthropometric analysis that were introduced to police work in the late nineteenth-century, can perhaps be seen to endorse Lombroso's insistently positivist approach to the study of human behavior.[83] Holmes, after all, claims that one can know almost anything about a man "by his fingernails, by his coat sleeve, by his boots, by his trouser-knees, by the callosities of his forefinger and thumb, by his expression, [and] by his shirt-cuffs" (*Study*, 28). Yet the maturing of the detective novel is contemporary, not only with the development of criminal anthropology but also with theories of the unconscious mind or subliminal awareness. In *The Hound of the Baskervilles*, Doyle at once references the interpretive techniques of criminal anthropology and pointedly links the activity of the subliminal mind with atavism. While the supposed agency of some otherworldly diabolical force is exposed as fraud, the man who discovers it is mentally and physically associated with the exceptional mental powers of his criminal opponents.

The Holmes of this story—part stand-in omniscient narrator, part scientific experimenter who sets much of the action in motion and then removes himself to watch the results—has "the power of detaching his mind at will" and removes himself mentally from the world of crime when he is not focused on a case.[84] Here this detachment takes the form of art appreciation rather than an apparently narcotic-induced catalepsy of earlier stories in which he "lie[s] upon the sofa . . . hardly uttering a word or moving a muscle from morning to night" (*Study*, 24). Nonetheless, as the earlier stories have already shown, this apparent split in Holmes between the dreamy bohemian and the "reasoning and observing machine" barely disguises the way in which his subliminal mind also becomes part of the apparatus of detection.[85] One of the qualities that Watson admires about Holmes is that his deductions, while rooted in logical reasoning, are so rapid as to be "swift as intuitions."[86] What turns reason into intuition, Holmes himself has explained to a client in *A Study in Scarlet*, is "the train of thoughts [that] run so swiftly through my mind that I [arrive] at the conclusion without being conscious of intermediate steps" (20). His description of the work done by subliminal consciousness seems to challenge a distinction that William Benjamin Carpenter makes between, on the one hand, the withdrawal from external reality and the surrender of will to automatic activity and, on the other hand, the volitional "vigorous mind"[87] (640). Holmes's extraordinary reasoning powers are intuitive because they belong to the subliminal mind as much, if not more, than they do to conscious thoughts.

In *The Hound of the Baskervilles*, such mental magic becomes quite explicitly linked with the theme of reversion. Doyle transports his detective hero from Baker Street to the Devonshire moor, where, unbeknownst to Watson, he hides out to observe the goings on of the various suspects in the murder of Sir Charles Baskerville. Here, in the company of at least one criminal savage—the escaped convict—he is also camping amid the ruined monuments of prehistoric human culture. The Neolithic wigwams out of which Watson expects to see crawl a "skin-clad, hairy man," instead house Holmes (77–78). This discovery is especially peculiar because it substitutes the detective for the animallike criminal who himself seems a throwback to the "old savages" of the Moor: The convict has "an evil yellow face, a terrible animal face, all seamed and scored with vile passions. Foul with mire, with a bristling beard, and hung with matted hair, it might well have belonged to one of those old savages who dwelt in the burrows on the hillsides" (97). Ironically, in the opening chapter of the novel, Dr. Mortimer expresses his astonishment at the shape of Holmes's skull, which is oddly "dolichocephalic" and which exhibits "well-marked, superorbital development" (8). A follower of the French criminologist, Alphonse Bertillon, who developed the anthropometric system for criminal identification, Mortimer cannot help linking cranial morphology to individual development and disposition. He is so struck by the Neolithic characteristics of the detective's skull, features that seem remarkable in a man with such mental accomplishments, that he remarks that a cast of it would provide a valuable addition to an anthropological museum.[88]

Despite this possibility that, in Holmes's skull, science might find evidence for the atavistic physiology of genius as compelling as that for the stigmata of criminal violence, we are initially more inclined to pair the detective with Mortimer so as to, as Holmes himself puts it, join the methods of the "man of science" with those of the "specialist in crime" (7). Together they are capable of deducing the whereabouts of the convict and any link he might have with the Baskerville murder. Indeed, Mortimer's reputation as a medical scientist provides the first clue to the mystery. We have been expecting the convict to emerge from one of these burrows, not only because Watson and Sir Henry have seen his light on the moor but also because we were alerted to the theme of ancestral throwback early in the story. Dr. Mortimer, we are told even before we meet him, is the author of essays on comparative pathology titled, "Is Disease a Reversion?" "Do We Progress?" and "Some Freaks of Atavism" (6). His professional résumé will prove more significant than even Holmes suspects, since the fact eventually emerges that Sir Charles's killer is himself a Baskerville descendent, marvelously identical in all his facial features as well as his brutal character to the seventeenth-century Sir Hugo Baskerville, whose crime against a local beauty and subsequent terrible death is the source of the strange legend of the murderous hound. It turns out, then, that the biological fact of ancestral reversion reveals the truth of the Baskerville curse even while it empties that legend of supernatural content. But strangely (and in plot terms, rather superfluously) Holmes must set up camp in the ancient landscape and live like prehistoric man in order to discover this uncanny truth.

When he exposes the villain, Holmes declares that the study of atavism in old family portraits might convert him to a belief in reincarnation. The improbability that he would turn spiritualist perhaps suggests that his appearance, magicianlike, in place of the criminal savage, is merely a conjuring trick on Doyle's part to enhance narrative suspense rather than a genuine effort to link the fantastic mind of the detective with the activity of our Neolithic forebears. In the opening pages of the story, after all, Holmes reveals to the astounded Watson that he observed what the latter was studying, without looking at it and with the help of a "well-polished silver-plated coffee-pot" (3). He also teases Watson by telling him that, while his body has been in an armchair, he has been "in spirit" to Devonshire, when in fact he has merely been reading an ordnance map of the moor (27). Yet these revelations about the material truth behind apparently spiritual phenomena, a prelude to Holmes's exposure of the murderer's "trick" of using phosphorous to create his hell hound, do not entirely represent Holmes's methods any more than the ordnance map captures the spirit of the moor. The "primitive" Holmes seems to be a mysterious creation of the moor itself, which appears "like some fantastic landscape in a dream" (5) and which restores ancient forms to life. It is a place where, Watson observes, one is so mentally transported into the prehistoric age that one would not be surprised to see "a skin-clad, hairy man crawl out from the low door" (77). When Sir Henry first catches sight of the country where his forefathers have left their mark, his attention is so powerfully drawn to it that he ceases to look to Watson like a tweed-coated American in "the corner of a prosaic railway carriage," and becomes instead a "true descendent . . . of that long line of high-blooded, fiery, and masterful men" (56). This sudden appearance of the family likeness is of course the prelude to the climactic moment when Stapleton's face will step out of the portrait of Sir Hugh.

Fixed on the object of enquiry as Sir Henry is fixed in rapt gaze upon this landscape, Holmes also undergoes a physical transformation. When he is working on a case, his "intense mental concentration" has the effect of blotting out the memories that influence ordinary perception (160). This gift of self-hypnosis equips him with the marvelous vision that penetrates the secrets of the criminal mind. In Watson's narrative, however, such vision also lends Holmes a supernatural stature. Before he reveals himself in the Neolithic ruins, Holmes appears to Watson one evening "outlined as black as an ebony statue on [the] shining background" of the moon (98). Too tall to be the convict, he becomes the mysterious figure on the moor, the rival specter to the hound and the "the unseen watcher, the man of darkness" (105). In his report to the Holmes he believes to be at home in Baker Street, Watson insists it was not a delusion. Yet the explanation that emerges when Holmes reveals himself seems scarcely more credible than the possibility that the moor is inhabited by multiple phantoms and that the danger to its living inhabitants does not come from flesh-and-blood villains alone. Human and mundane as it is revealed to be, the apparently supernatural knowledge and command of the moor expressed in the stature of the "spirit" Holmes is neutralized neither by the natural, yet extraordinary, explanation for his appearance nor by the teasing exhibitions and debunking of "clairvoyance" with which Holmes taunts Watson earlier in the novel.

With his invention of a new kind of detective—a scientific investigator who also possesses the primitive gifts of supernormal vision—Doyle thus creates characters and scenes that at once suggest something comic or preposterous and yet at the same time genuinely attract us to the heroic and the miraculous. Holmes's prodigious appearance on the moor, strangely contrasting with his jibes about clairvoyance and superstition, embodies something of Doyle's claims for spiritualism in his *History* that "laughed at, it laughs back; scorned, it gives back scorn for scorn."[89] Holmes's subtle mocking of his own mysterious powers, however, also anticipates a combining of the absurd and the illuminatory that will characterize the rather more eccentric scientific character of Professor Challenger. Challenger is the truly atavistic genius, at once an intellectual marvel who can discover truth in the naturally impossible and a man of violent and intolerant temperament. In "When the World Screamed," he is a "cave-man in a lounge suit . . . born out of his millennium";[90] like the moor-residing Holmes of "The Hounds of the Baskervilles," Challenger rightly belongs "to the early Neolithic."[91] In *The Lost World*, he represents an even more radical form of reversion. Here the principle of atavism drives the entire plot: A team of scientists and adventurers discover a plateau in South America where human beings coexist with all the vertebrate animals that have preceded them in evolutionary history. Challenger's squat, heavy figure, beard, and hairy chest pair him, bizarrely, with the king of a species of bloodthirsty anthropoid apes. Unlike Holmes, however, who seems to be aware of the ironic links Doyle's stories make between savage intuition and scientific discovery, Challenger is the last to admit the comic truth that the king appears to be an "absurd parody" of him.[92] Similarly, in "The Land of Mist," where he reluctantly learns, finally, to admit spiritual phenomena into the arena of scientific facts and possibilities, he remains quite unconscious of the irony of his earlier remark that the séance is best suited to "the stone cabin of a Neolithic savage."[93]

If the last laugh on Challenger comes from the spiritualist narrator of "The Land of Mist," Holmes can be outwitted only by his invented intellectual match: the evil genius Professor Moriarty. Their encounter, in "The Final Problem," brings Holmes's career to a narrative close, not only because he and the professor plunge over the falls of Reichenbach together but also because the communication between two such men is so purely telepathic that words become unnecessary: Moriarty observes to Holmes that "all I have to say has already crossed your mind," and the detective replies that then "possibly my answer has crossed yours." [94] Doyle brings his detective hero back to life in 1901 in *The Hound of the Baskervilles*, with the implication that this story takes place chronologically before the tragedy at the falls. Yet however wry and eloquent, he returns as the yet-living master crime solver, he also seems to have come back as a ghost, with the supernatural vision that he had forecast through the image of the flying detective that introduces "A Case of Identity." Silhouetted on the moor, Holmes has literally transcended ordinary perception and moment-to-moment observation. He has positioned himself, narratorlike, over and above the goings on of ordinary mortals, so as to witness "the chain of events" as it "work[s] through generations" ("Case," 75).

In so doing, Holmes elevates the events of the story above the sordid realism of family feuds and sensational scandal revealed in its closing pages and invokes instead the marvels of the subliminal mind. In the attitude of intense concentration, he is transformed in Watson's eyes into the spirit of the moor, breathing the ancient talents of his forebears into the mysteries of the present, even as he decodes these mysteries through the physical evidence of reversion. That which is primitive about the detective hero, linking the lower nervous organization of the addicted Jennings to the dreamy inspirations that fuel Holmes's discoveries, is not the expression of degenerative traits that counteract the patient accumulation of physical data but rather the deeper illumination of empirical facts by the agency of the subliminal or unconscious mind. Both Collins and Doyle introduce the spiritual talents of atavistic genius to the definite, commonplace truths of literary realism, so giving narrative life to Myers's prophecy of "making for a vaster future, by inheritance from a remoter past" (1:655).

THE END OF THE NOVEL

Naturalism and Reverie in
Tess of the d'Urbervilles and *The Return of the Native*

In some respects it is odd to think of Arthur Conan Doyle and Thomas Hardy as contemporaries. Hardy's narratives center on the anguished and disoriented subjects of industrial modernity while the Holmes stories uncover and defuse threats to collective order. Moreover, where Doyle's career reflects an increasingly confident belief in the spiritual afterlife, Hardy scrutinizes the "primitive believer in his man-shaped tribal god"[1] and endorses the agnosticism of Spencer and Darwin over the idea of an omnipotent and beneficent deity.[2] What they do share, however, is a shift in emphasis from Lamarckian evolutionism, with its stress on the purposive striving of the individual to bring about the improvement of the species, to a more Darwinian interest in transformations that are neither predictable nor necessarily progressive. Both also respond to this recognition with a turn to the automatic, or "lower," activity of the mind, although for Hardy this automatism provides, at best, temporary psychic relief from the conscious suffering of his protagonists, where for Doyle it promises to unlock great human potential. Also, in a very different way from Doyle, these states in Hardy's fiction produce spectral and mystical forms in place of a force for omnipotent goodness in the universe. These forms exert so much pressure on the realist narratives that they perhaps explain why Hardy abandons the novel and turns to poetry, recognizing it as a medium that can better represent the automatic motions of the mind and the faint hope such motions hold out against what he famously described in *Tess of the d'Urbervilles* as "the ache of modernism."

Hardy's novels struggle to retrieve forms of spirituality, especially pagan mysticism and animism, from the secular and scientific modernity embedded in the realist novel's very form as well as in its subject matter.[3] They do so both formally, through the dreamy and magical perceptions of a narrative voice that paradoxically remains agnostic, evolutionist, and antihumanist and in the novels' content, where ancient and primitive objects and rituals continue to affect the characters, providing some narrative counterweight to the stories of human nature and social disintegration that otherwise promise to dominate and destroy them. The "gift" of the novelist, Hardy proposed in an 1891 essay on realism, is not the naturalist's ability to "count the dishes at a feast" but rather to "see written on the wall" Prospero's vision that "'we are such stuff / As dreams are made of.'"[4] Although Hardy's narratives, which position their characters at the mercy of circumstance, could not be more different than Shakespeare's story of the magician-duke who tames the elements, both acknowledge that productions of the dreamy mind are consolations as much as curiosities, for they partly mitigate human suffering at the hands of nature and history.

I. THE NOVEL AND THE MODERN ACHE

Darwinian readings of Hardy's novels show that their stories of individual lives are dwarfed by the great plots of geological history, natural and sexual selection, and the accidents, interdependencies, and contingencies of a world that John Glendening has identified with Darwin's entangled bank.[5] The indifference of these larger stories to the fates of their individual human actors can determine the undue suffering of those, like Tess d'Urberville, who are driven by the pulse of nature yet neither cradled nor redeemed by it. At other times, nature and its rhythms may be a source of refuge from the discomforts of social life, as characters ranging from farm laborers and milkmaids to those who have risen in the metropolitan world, experience something like a oneness with the natural world as they seek to forget the dislocation, want, or emotional pain inflicted on them by human institutions and systems.[6] Even as they diminish individual experience in relation to these greater narratives, the novels thus intrude the cruelties and attractions of culture into the stories of humans and nature—whether in the form of the lure of high culture represented by Christminster in *Jude the Obscure,* or the glamour of the commercial world in *The Return of the Native,* or the exploitation of rural laborers at the hands of industrial modernity as in *Tess.* Natural and cultural forces are further entwined by the contradictions and constraints nature and culture exercise on each other,[7] and within such entanglements, Hardy's characters seem to lose all power of self-determination.

Such themes are quintessentially novelistic. In *The Origins of the English Novel,* Michael McKeon divides the historical analysis of the novel into two mutually informing categories: questions of truth and questions of virtue. Responding at once to the discoveries of empirical science and the upheavals of secularization and social reform in the seventeenth and eighteenth centuries, he argues, the novel wrestles with how to present the world given by nature and, at the same time, how to navigate its changing moral shape. As a literary form that responds to and records both social uncertainty and epistemological instability, the novel is therefore robustly modern.[8] Hardy might be said to have formulated a late nineteenth-century response to precisely these questions of "truth" and "virtue" in two essays that express his views on the responsibilities and limits of fictional forms—views that are informed by the findings of evolutionary biology as well as by his attitudes to the literary public sphere and middle-class prudery. Cautioning against the censoring of fiction by magazine editors and publishers, he argues:

> in representations of the world, the passions ought to be proportioned as the world itself. This is the interest which was excited in the minds of the Athenians by their immortal tragedies, and in the minds of Londoners at the first performance of the finer plays of three hundred years ago. They reflected life, revealed life, criticized life. Life being a physiological fact, its honest portrayal must be largely concerned with, for one thing, the relations of the sexes and . . . of catastrophes based upon sexual relations as it is.[9]

Hardy emphasizes the biological fact of sexual desire that, like other facts of human instinct, underwrites even as it threatens to destroy the most fundamental units of social organization; he insists that the writer's allegiance must be to those realities that go beyond "social expedients by humanity" to Nature's essential laws—realities that urge "the triumph of the crowd over the hero, of the commonplace majority over the exceptional few."[10] This biologism also drives the structure of fiction itself, with human nature determining not only the subject matter of novels but the very form of that subject's delivery. To adopt the "false colouring" of the happy ending in which estranged lovers are reunited and remain happy ever after is to fly romantic-comically in the face of the tragic reality that we are biologically driven by passions that easily outmaneuver the social forms devised to contain them.

Yet even this account does not quite capture the full degree of his characters' entrapment, which is determined by "social expedients" as well as by natural laws. In a much-discussed passage from *Tess*, Angel Clare observes how strange it is that a simple milkmaid should suffer from the melancholy spirit of the age, or what he calls the "ache of modernism" (*Tess*, 124). Some time ago, David de Laura showed how this phrase captures not only the broad themes of modernist aesthetics—rootlessness, isolation, spiritual emptiness—but also Hardy's skepticism toward Matthew Arnold's secular-humanist promise to retrieve a rational, creedless faith from the ruins of Christian mysticism. In the frustrated idealism, neo-Hellenism, and intellectual liberalism of characters like *Tess*'s Angel Clare and Clym Yeobright in *The Return*, de Laura proposed, Hardy projects the failure of these modern forms of faith *either* truly to overcome "custom and conventionality" *or* to relieve human beings from the painful awareness that all experience is the product, not of benevolent design, but of blind natural laws.[11] He creates modern, intellectual characters like Angel and Clym, who, while they may be, as J. Hillis Miller has put it, "separated from the universe by the detached clarity of . . . mind" also "participate in the motion of nature through . . . body."[12] Their active resistance to the cultural traditions or social conditions that limit human potential can find its reference point only in fantasies of a pristine, premodern world untouched by the corrupting influence of modernity. Meanwhile, their female counterparts, Tess d'Urbeyfield and Eustacia Vye, who are at once the desired and desiring figures in the dance of sexual selection and at the same time the outcast victims of moral conventions and laws, are likewise tormented by both the power of social forms and the indifference of natural laws. Whatever longings the characters may have, either for the full, liberating realization of the modern spirit or for a world uncontaminated by its ills, none is able to fully retreat from the social environments that oppress them or to successfully integrate their longings with the natural forces that shape their lives. Indeed, in their very efforts to do so, they usually precipitate their own or others' suffering.

In this respect, they demonstrate the melancholy underside of what Bruno Latour has identified as the triumphant critical posture of the modern subject, who moves back and forth between the ideas of a transcendent nature, "out there," beyond the control of human beings, and notions of a human-constructed reality that conditions our understanding of all phenomena. Modernity, Latour argues in *We Have Never Been Modern*, is a historical construction that announces the separation of human-made and nonhuman worlds, or the transcendence of both "a Nature that is not our doing" and Society as something "we create through and through."[13] However, at the same time as they declare this separation of the human from the nonhuman, moderns are able to mobilize "critical possibilities" that invert and overlap these realms while appearing to keep them in place:

> Nature remains mobilizable, humanizable, socializable. Every day, laboratories, collections, centers of calculation and of profit, research bureaus and scientific institutions blend it with the multiple destinies of social groups. Conversely, even though we construct Society through and through, it lasts, it surpasses us, it dominates us, it has its own laws, it is as transcendent as Nature. . . . The critical power of the moderns lies in this double language: they can mobilize Nature at the heart of social relationships, even as they leave Nature infinitely remote from human beings; they are free to make and unmake their society, even as they render its laws ineluctable, necessary and absolute.[14]

Using the examples originally twinned by Steven Shapin and Simon Schaffer of Boyle's air pump and Hobbes's Leviathan, Latour argues that moderns simultaneously liberate themselves socially through ideology critique, which exposes the fusion of power and knowledge at the origin of society, and acknowledge their natural limits by raising scientific reasoning above the human-made procedural and social world, then appealing to the certainty of nature's laws to emphasize what is inevitable. Yet they are also able to maneuver within these categories, binding social and natural relations so as to render themselves less impotent as natural beings and less anchorless as social actors. As they assert the absolute separation of natural and social worlds while concealing and repressing the hybrid forms, Latour suggests, the moderns "purify" the categories of Nature and Society. In so doing, they banish to the premodern any pretensions to "science" that combine spiritual knowledge with the investigation of nature, such as alchemy or astrology.

Hardy's "ache" transforms the self-assurance of Latour's moderns into helplessness and paralysis. His characters struggle against forces of social domination only to find that their power of choice is profoundly limited by desire or physical want or both; in answering their raw bodily needs they risk entrapment or disgrace at the hands of those who exercise social power over them. Even as their struggles against social limitations reveal heredity and desire as the determining force in their lives, the unyielding influence of these natural forces joins with persistent tyrannical social forms. Jude's defiant relationship with Sue does not liberate him from the condition of his birth or from the domestic traps woven by sexual desire; Eustacia's modern rebelliousness leaves her in nature's clutches as she pursues her material ambitions in "the secret recesses of sensusousness," while at the same time she has "hardly crossed the threshold of conventionality" (86); Angel's sexual fascination with Tess is what drives his need to identify her with a unspoiled Arcadia, and his subsequent rejection of her once he learns the story of her past exposes the morally conventional heart of the intellectual rebel. All three struggle uselessly against a confluence of natural and cultural forces that confirms the fatalism of the folk expression "'It was to be'" (*Tess,* 74) but that, as a hybrid, has more tragic power than purely natural oppressiveness like that of the milkmaids' futile passion for Angel or purely cultural oppression like the Evangelist preaching Tess learns to despise.

Angel's treatment of Tess demonstrates how the denial of these hybrid forms contributes to the disempowerment and alienation of those most vulnerable to them. Until her revelation, Tess remains for him "a genuine daughter of nature," embodying both the premodern wholeness that he experiences in rural life and the unburdened joy of his own past. His physical separation from the other dairy hands and his ignorance about the real toil and suffering of rural laborers prevent him from ever immersing himself in the particulars of Tess's world. He can no more perceive the confluence of modern historical forces that have brought Tess to Crick's dairy—the industrialization of agriculture and the ascendancy of a new merchant class represented by the Stoke-d'Urbervilles—than he can recognize "the particulars of an outward scene" over the "general impression" (119). Such romanticism shapes his encounter with nature and "the voices of inanimate things" (118), even as an unyielding Evangelical background drives him to revile Tess after he learns about her seduction. By refusing to recognize that Tess is as much a child of history as of nature, he exposes her to greater punishment from the elements and, as a consequence, to further human exploitation.

On the other hand, as an intellectual who is nonetheless more conventional than he knows, Angel himself is able both to disparage social rules that forbid him to marry a woman of a lower station and to resist the creaturely yearning for joy when it conflicts with his rather traditional moral sympathies. Once he condemns Tess, desire has no hold on him and "propensities, tendencies, habits, are as dead leaves upon the tyrannous wind of [his] imaginative ascendancy" (245). Angel's combination of determined resistance to the voices of nature and his critical stance on the artificial obstacles to union with the woman he loves suggest his immunity to the ache. His life is shaped by will rather than by necessity, and his position as a younger son of a clergyman allows him the freedom to choose both a profession and a mate. Despite his romanticism about rural life, he never has any illusions about his own relationship to it, determining on a future as a gentleman farmer because it will afford him financial independence while allowing for intellectual liberty and because "something had to be done" (117). He is therefore "wonderfully free from the chronic melancholy . . . taking hold of the civilized races with the decline of belief in a beneficent Power" (118). In these ways, he is very different from Clym Yeobright, who turns his back on Paris and the glamorous life of a diamond merchant in the hope of recovering the organic community that he associates with his childhood on Egdon Heath. Clym finds that he cannot return; and although he works as a furze cutter, he never ceases to be the Rousseau-like modern, looking longingly back from this side of modernity on a lost world.

Angel, however, is no less modern than Clym. His relationship with Tess highlights his modern's way of thinking even as it positions him within a cluster of natural and cultural forces to which he remains oblivious. This is true even as he analyzes the effect of modernity on others. With the kind of insight that is usually reserved for the narrative voice, Angel attributes Tess's sadness to an ache arising from the place of human beings in an animate yet cruelly indifferent nature. Tess has described this nature as a place where human and nonhuman exchange looks that seem to communicate only the inevitability of anguish and death. "The trees have inquisitive eyes," she says, "And the river says 'why do you trouble me with your looks?'" (124). At first Angel interprets her words in the context of modern alienation. He then reflects that this very act of interpretation is taking place within the human-made context that gives new names to old sensations. In this self-correction, he suggests the need to distinguish between the laws of nature and the social lenses through which they are interpreted and, with true modern flair, exchanges the transcendence of the natural world for that of the social. After he condemns Tess, however, he becomes the object of narrative analysis rather than the analyzer. The narrator shows the hybrid forms that Angel represses: social forces in the form of moral conservatism exert pressure on him outside the sphere of his own awareness, determining the lovers' separation; but these are compounded by the organic consequences of that separation, whereby, the narrator tells us, "new growths insensibly bud upward to fill each vacated place [and] unforeseen accidents hinder intentions" (246). Here nature absorbs the effects of social life into the larger story of change under the pressures of growth and circumstance. In Latour's account of the teleologies and elitisms of modernity, the segregation of science and the social world results in the triumphant demystification of both as curious objects and knowing subjects are both divested of their premodern power. For Hardy, however, such segregation and the recombinations of social oppression and natural cruelty that it permits create mental suffering at all levels of human experience. In his misery, Angel blames first Tess's peasant woman's ignorance of social proportions and in the next breath her aristocratic heritage whose "exhausted seedling" points to the inevitable decline of the narrow breed through natural selection. Limited by his modern relationship both to nature and to culture, Angel punishes the characteristically passive Tess, who then becomes doubly victim to the ache.

II. AUTOMATISM AND ESCAPE FROM THE MODERN

Yet there is some relief from this bleakness. Although there is no return from the modern, Clym's rejection of metropolitan luxury in favor of helping the folk of his childhood to withstand the destructive effects of a commercially upward-bound civilization immerses him in the folk culture of rural Wessex. Like Angel's Hellenism, his return to the traditional world of his childhood and his "barbarous satisfaction" in the failure of new farming methods to tame the Heath may ultimately fail to alleviate the pains of modernity, but they earn him the respect of the narrator, who allows him a provisional return, associating him with that very landscape, as "he might be said to be its product" (148). This association in turn ties him to the evidence of premodern human activity that decorates the Heath: the Druidical monument he points out to Eustacia, and the "jumbled Druidical rites and Saxon ceremonies" that Egdon waste hosts. Correspondingly, *Tess* holds out the hope that the miseries inflicted by Darwinian nature might be overcome through pagan spirituality. The narrator tells us that "women whose chief companions are the forms and forces of outdoor Nature retain in their souls far more of the Pagan fantasy of their remote forefathers than of the systematized religion taught their race at a later date" (104). This passage follows closely from one in which we learn that Tess, although burdened by disgrace and grief following Alec's seduction and the death of her child, is nonetheless led by "the irresistible, universal, automatic tendency to find sweet pleasure somewhere, which pervades all life from the meanest to the highest" (103). Alone this account links joyful nature with the evolutionary force or "deep time" that has no care for the individual life.[15] Yet the narrator ties the experience of natural release from the prejudices of social convention and "systematized religion" to Tess's pagan worship of the "Sun and Moon . . . [and] Green Things upon the Earth" (104). This tension between the indifference of Darwinian nature and the comfort or joy of pagan animism is repeated at the end of the novel. Here Angel's pairing with Tess's sister, Liza Lu, negates the value of an individual life by positioning it in the greater story of descent. Yet this undramatic ending, in which the couple simply "join hands and [go] on" (398) after Tess is executed, is narratively speaking much less powerful than the preceding scene at the pagan temple of Stonehenge in which Tess tragic-heroically announces her "glad" (396) resignation to her death.

Creatures of the premodern mind—preternatural forms, ancient "ghosts," and pagan spirits that blend human and nonhuman worlds—do not disturb the daylight realities of industrialization, social injustice, and the struggles of the rural poor as these are depicted in the novels. Instead, they appear in Hardy's depiction of the peculiar mental states of trance, dream, and reverie. Tess's "fetishistic utterance" is part of a "half-conscious rhapsody" (104); the days before Tess's capture belong to the lovers' dream world in which "all that's sweet and lovely" defies the "inexorable" (390). In the Flintcombe-Ash swede field, where the conditions of industrialized farming reach their most brutal, she is indifferent to the injustice of her lot so long as "it was possible to exist in a dream" (285). At one level, dreaminess is associated throughout the novel with her self-destructive passivity, most obviously in her feeling of separateness from her surroundings and "dream-like fixity"(151) when she is raped by Alec d'Urberville and in the "drooping eyelids" that express her shame and submissiveness when she tells Angel about her past. Yet dreams and other states of automatic mental activity also free her from creaturely suffering. Having confessed to Angel how she experiences the cold gaze of nature, she adds, "but *you* can raise up dreams with your music, and drive all such horrid fancies away" (124). Angel first notices her when he hears her state to the dairyman how "our souls can be made to go outside our bodies when we are alive" (120). She describes how by self-hypnotically fixing her mind upon a star, she can travel hundreds of miles from an unwanted physical body. She feels relief only when her mind is removed from its natural surroundings to fix upon some creature of its own making and consequently when it does not meet the gaze of nature.[16]

Like Tess's reverie, Angel's somnambulism briefly offers hope against the inexorable forces that direct the narrative through separation and suffering toward death. When Angel comes into her room the night before he leaves her, Tess recognizes immediately by his vacant stare that he is sleepwalking, and despite the physical danger to both of them when he carries her across the river and into a graveyard, she experiences this somnambulistic episode as a "beatific interval" (249). Angel's state is clearly the effect of his mental exhaustion. Yet it endows him with unconscious prevision: As he carries his wife to a graveyard he prefigures the scene in the d'Urberville family tomb when Alec entraps her, and as he weeps over her "dead" body, he anticipates the final scenes of the novel. The narrator faults Angel for not being insightful enough to recognize his wife's real virtue, because the "shade of his own limitations" blinds him to her goodness. Only in sleep does he know her as "sweet, good, and true" (247).

Such foresight links his somnambulism to the local legends and superstitions that likewise forecast the tragic events to come. Although these are far from beatific, they stress the hybrid human-nature forms of the premodern, and in that respect they echo the episodes of dreamy release from the burdens of modernity. When the newly wed Tess and Angel step into the coach to travel to the former d'Urberville manor house, Tess's feelings of foreboding express themselves in a strange and sudden recognition of the vehicle itself: She says she "must have seen it in a dream" (213). Angel then partially reveals the legend of the d'Urberville coach, explaining that a crime was committed in it by some sixteenth- or seventeenth-century d'Urberville but refusing to finish telling her the gloomy legend since it presumably forecasts murder. Tess ignores his subsequent naturalistic explanation, for some dim knowledge of the story has come to her mind by association and prophesies that it signifies either crime or death. Her intuition is then reinforced by the call of an afternoon crow, which the dairyman observes bodes an unhappy union, notwithstanding his wife's anxious, naturalizing assurance that "it only means a change in the weather" (216). Later in the story, the legend of the coach echoes ironically in Tess's fancy that she hears it again, followed by the appearance of Alec, the sham d'Urberville, who comes as false redeemer to save her family from destitution. Although Tess is delivered from the oppressive voices of Evangelism by Angel's heterodox rejection of the word of scripture, her modern's skepticism is only ever for her a temporary keeping at bay of the folkish "gloomy specters" (195) that the plot will reveal to be rightfully foreboding.

Although Tess's dreamy presentiments are borne out by the plot of her own life, as we have seen, the narrator persists in the story of nature's indifference to individual beings in its relentless push toward generation. Despite its significance in the lives of Tess and Angel, Dairyman Crick's household belongs only to "another year's installment of flowers, leaves, nightingales, finches, and such ephemeral creatures [who take] up their place where only a year ago others had stood in their place when these were nothing more than germs and inorganic particles" (128). The narrator of *The Return of the Native*, on the other hand, appears torn between evolutionary awareness and a susceptibility to reverie. In his tribute to "the particular glory of the Egdon [heath]"[17] labored personification draws the landscape into the human world, animated by "sympathy" and "fraternization" to merge with the darkening sky at dusk and then "appear[s] slowly to awake and listen" (9). The heath, for him, is a reminder of Lyell's expanse of geological time, remaining unchanged while all who occupy it continually change and disappear. And yet it is also one and the same with its human inhabitants who, in sped-up evolution, "appear upon the scene" in the title of chapter 2, "Humanity Appears Upon the Scene, Hand in Hand with Trouble." Their celebration of Guy Fawkes, which evokes Druid and Saxon rites, provokes "muttering articulations of the wind" in the hollows of the surrounding hills (18). He describes these figures in the landscape as indistinct, grotesque bodies, whose exaggerated features in the firelight suggest something "extreme" and "preternatural" belonging again to the peculiar magic of the heath at sundown but also to the Christian prehistory of that landscape, so that "the first instinct of an imaginative stranger might have been to suppose it the person of one of the Celts . . . so far had all of modern date withdrawn from the scene" (15). Similarly, in his first description of Eustacia, he emphasizes the "material minutiae" that create the effect of the heath coming to life as "the united products of infinitesimal vegetable causes" (50). Yet again, as an "imaginative stranger" he hears the sounds announcing the appearance of a woman whom he describes as a reincarnated Sappho and whose ritual nighttime wandering on the heath emphasizes its otherworldly character. Ghostly and pagan visions float across his awareness of actual evolutionary time.[18] Despite his attunement to the gulf between geological and human time as well as of the "intelligible [historical] facts" (10) that belong to the heathland, the narrator experiences its apparently unchanging forms as a "ballast to the mind adrift on change and harassed by the irrepressible New" (11). In this state of reverie, time stands still: These scenes "exhibit the inertness of the desert"; they suggest a cataleptic "condition of healthy life . . . nearly resembling the torpor of death" (14–15).

This tension in the narrative voice between modern knowing and the reverie brought on by the strange visual effects of the heath at dusk introduces a broader pattern in the novel whereby the mind's painful awareness of circumstances is suspended and the intellectual gap between the separate, observing modern and the unreflecting "native" driven by forces outside his control collapses. Eustacia's longing to escape from the stifling rural environment and her painful sense of being isolated and out of place in relation to the villagers is relieved at several key moments. The first is on the Heath when her voice mingles with the sounds of the scene in a "spasmodic abandonment . . . as if, in allowing herself to utter the sound, the woman's brain had authorized what it could not regulate" (51). The second is in the illicit dance with Wildeve when her "reason become[s] sleepy" and "her face rapt" as "her soul . . . passed away from and forgot her features, which were left empty and quiescent" (219–20). Her trance state, like Clym's blindness and resulting social regression, temporarily relieves her feelings of separateness from the people and countryside around her, but again, like him, she suspends her suffering at the cost of nervous and mental superiority to all that surrounds her. "The fantastic nature of her Passion," the narrator observes, "which lowered her as an intellect, raised her as a soul" (104). Such passion withdraws her attention from her surroundings as she becomes so absorbed in daydream that she mentally erases both her own history and that of the countryside she lives in. She longs for the cosmopolitan pleasures of a Paris that exists only in her imagination, but that she feels is much more native to her than rural England, a longing so powerful that it sometimes overwhelms awareness of her surroundings and she sees "nothing of human life now" (63). When Clym draws her attention to an ancient Druidical landmark, she replies "I was not even aware that there existed any such curious Druidical stone. I am aware that there are Boulevards in Paris" (160). Although it is the urban heart of modernity that she longs for and the pagan landmarks that she ignores, the dreamy non sequitur removes her mentally from both the scene of sexual desire and the constraints of convention that cluster in a changing social landscape, thereby offering release from her own, very modern pain.

While Eustacia attempts to escape the constricting life of Edgon in reverie, Clym tries to find some alternative to "the grimness of the human situation" (161) in his return. Abandoning not only his commercial position in the world but eventually even his aspirations to pass along high knowledge to those who have been denied it, he endeavors to discover "a bare equality with, and no superiority to, a single living thing under the sun" (177). To his mother, watching him cut furze on the Heath, he becomes one with the landscape and, like an insect, so primitive as to have "no knowledge of anything in the world but fern, lichens and moss" (231). Yet such absorption in nature brings him not comfort but the pain of jealousy and loss. Following Eustacia's death, Clym is able to forget his grief only when he walks on the heath alone and his imagination fills the landscape with ancient figures.[19] Neither character can overcome social and intellectual separateness from those around them except by retreating from the world delivered by the senses. This propensity to dreaminess is thrown into relief by the contrasting example of Thomasin, who is able to renounce the snobbish ambition that kept her from loving Diggory when she begins to "[lay] her heart open to external influences of every kind" (316).

As in *Tess,* dreamy states of mind often intersect with folklore and magical thinking in *The Return of the Native.* The revelation that the haunted Christian Cantle is "the man that no woman will marry" (26), partly, it is thought, because he was born on a moonless night, is followed by Fairway's warning that ghosts show themselves to unmarried sleepers. Susan Nunsuch accuses Eustacia of practicing witchcraft, and although the more educated Mrs. Yeobright declares such superstition absurd, Eustacia's mysterious rituals on the heath initially suggest sinister magic. At the very least she has a powerful mesmeric influence over her male "subjects": Susan's son, Johnny Nunsuch "seem[s] a mere automaton, galvanized into moving and speaking by the wayward Eustacia's will" (55) as he helps her to light the fire; Wildeve, who next appears on the scene, comes "in obedience to [her] call" (58). Although the informed reader knows that it is the power of sexual selection, not witchcraft, operating here, the narrative does not entirely reject the possibility of psychic and malevolent influence at a distance. Coincidences between Susan's burning of the wax effigy, Clym's prescient sense, while he waits in hope that his wife will come back, that "invisible shapes of the dead were passing in on their way to meet him" (297), and Eustacia's death are never explained away. Moreover, the half-mesmerized narrator, who becomes so lost in his description of her queenly carriage and "Pagan eyes" (61) that he cannot deliver any precise information about her history or parentage until well after he first introduces her, describes Wildeve's unrequited passion as the product of a "spell" (305).

If there is something witchlike about Eustacia, there is plenty ghost-like in the character of Diggory Venn, the reddleman. Christian, whose fear of ghosts gives him a horror of the reddleman's coloring, encounters the latter in "strange places, particularly dreams" (262). Diggory himself is a figure of the old rural world destined for extinction, the narrator muses, like the dodo in the world of animals. His career is the inverse of Clym's, since he begins life beneath his potential but sheds his red skin at the end of the novel to revive his courtship of Thomasin and advance himself as a farmer and husband. Despite the narrator's pointed identification of his fortunes with the natural and commercial forces of transformation in the novel, however, we experience him at least as much through the haunted minds of other characters as through the descriptions of his own suffering and cynicism. Our first introduction to him is as the specter of Christian's terrified imagination, and he preserves this ghostlike quality throughout most of the novel, materializing as if out of nowhere at key moments in the emotional lives of the other characters or as if he were the embodiment of Eustacia's conscience, appearing suddenly on the heath to remind her of the illegitimacy of her relations with Wildeve. A sort of spirit of the heath, he belongs to the dreamscapes of the other characters even as he gives voice to the rural culture of Mosaic censorship that seeks to quiet Eustacia's rebellious passions. Diggory is thus at once a key figure in the realist description of how human potential is liberated or constrained by circumstance, and in another the creature of primitive superstition conjured up by the superstitious or guilty fears of other characters. It is not surprising then, that it is to Diggory that Clym expresses his spiritualist longings following Eustacia's death, lamenting that "we, who remain alive, [are not] allowed to hold conversation with the dead" (265).

While reverie and dreamy clairvoyance temporarily liberate the characters from the painful conditions of their lives, Hardy's later fiction recognizes the cruelties of nature and history as being themselves the creations of automatic or unconscious mind on a cosmic scale. According to an evolutionary principle called the "Immanent Will," which he assembled from his reading of Schopenhauer and Von Hartmann in the late 1880s and 1890s, life is animated evolutionarily by an unconscious force that has no awareness of and hence no compassion for its actors. The blind indifference of this Will is the primitive root from whose reflex acts branch ever ascending creations, culminating in the powerful intellect and complex sensibilities of modern human beings. This means humans are afflicted with a painful awareness of natural and social constraints on any attempt at self-determination, an awareness that itself represents an evolutionary achievement unforeseen by the purposeless energy of the original creative force. Although Hardy would later soften this philosophical pessimism with the idea of "evolutionary meliorism" or the gradual coming to consciousness of this automatic creative force, his novels show little anticipatory evidence of this concept.[20] Instead they propose that refuge from the pain of conscious reflection on the indifference of the Will is to be found in a more primitive mental state, which mimics the Will's automatism, reversing the exquisite mental talents that human beings have acquired to their own detriment.

Hardy's lengthy, three-part play, *The Dynasts* (1904–8) gives the Will dramatic realization as it is repeatedly described and apostrophized by an allegorical cast of spirit intelligences. Driven only by the patterns of "rapt aesthetic rote,"[21] Will is "like a knitter drowsed / Whose fingers play in skilled unmindfulness."[22] The historical events of the play, which center on the Napoleonic wars, reveal the deterministic forces in the universe against which human beings vainly assert purpose and deliberate change. The Spirit of the Years insists on the futility of such endeavor when "Thus does the Great Foresightless mechanize / In blank entrancement now as evermore / Its ceaseless artistries in Circumstance."[23] Although the play concludes with the hope that the Will may eventually become self-aware, this possibility of "kindly eyed benevolence"[24] is both faint and remote. However, the unwieldy form of the play to some extent offsets its modern subject matter: the failure of human ambition to overcome the power of an indifferent creative universe. In his Preface, Hardy emphasizes that while the play's material stagery, wherein the Spirits look down upon and discuss events in human history, did not suit it to the traditional theatre, it might be performed with

> A monotonic delivery of speeches with dreamy conventional gestures, something in the manner traditionally maintained by the Christian mummers, the curiously hypnotizing impressiveness of whose automatic style—that of persons who spoke by no will of their own—may be remembered by all who ever experienced it.[25]

In place of a naturalistic "closely-webbed development of character and motive," this automatism would bring dramatic life to the motiveless, dreamy forces that dwarf human intentions. In thus linking mental automatism with premodern dramatic form, the play promises to forge an imaginative reconciliation between the Will and the historical world that *The Dynasts* portrays.

In the novels, on the other hand, the pressure of the realist form to respect history and nature separates the alert minds of the characters from the undesigned natural world in which events play out with cruel indifference to their desires and ideals. In an early scene from *The Return,* Eustacia disguises her gender and acts in a Mummer play in order to spy on Clym, the object of her romantic fantasies and the key, she believes, to escape from the dreary rural life from which she, as a woman, has no possibility of delivery other than through marriage. Yet as dutifully as she learns the part, Eustacia remains agonizingly self-conscious throughout the performance, terrified of exposure, and so inhibited that she makes a "preternaturally inadequate thrust" (117) of her sword and delivers her lines too faintly to appear convincingly absorbed in the part. Her awkwardness derives at once from a discomfort at her too-bold transgression of social convention, which however exhilarating also brings her uneasiness and shame and from the shuttle of seductions to which her performance is linked: It requires that she give the original player her bare hand to kiss in return for taking his part, and conceal her passionate interest in a man she has never met as the motive for her actions. Within the novel, then, Hardy embeds the Mummer play in a web of social and libidinal forces that transform it from an automatic to a highly self-conscious event.

III. HALLUCINATION AND INSIGHT

Physiologically speaking, sleepwalking and reverie represent the escape from circumstance that Hardy's characters pursue. Macnish had argued that reverie was similar to dreaming in that it represented a want of balance in the faculties arising from excessive application and solitude (*PS* 249). Although in reverie there is no disturbance of the external senses and the dreamer can see and hear everything in the external environment, he or she is attached to ideas that bear no relationship to this environment (248). Later accounts of the nervous origins of dreamy states (on both sides of the Atlantic) recast Macnish's phrenology in a cerebral map according to which the higher faculties that help navigate environment—volition, judgment, and moral sense—are suspended during dreamy episodes and the mind abandons the moderating guidance of the senses and the will. Henry Lyman's *Insomnia and Other Disorders of Sleep* (1885) argues that, in somnambulism, the active faculties are coordinated on an even lower plane than that of ordinary dreaming, so that the ideas and actions they produce are less capable of rising into consciousness and thus into relation with external circumstance.[26] Similarly, Hack Tuke links reverie and somnambulism to hypnosis as states in which reflex cerebral acts, liberated from the higher work of consciousness, enable ideation to take place independently of the external conditions that ordinarily moderate that ideational activity.[27] Such unrestrained movement, he argues, may produce hallucinations. At the same time, the exaltation of certain faculties in combination with the depression of others may enable the kind of extraordinary physical coordination demonstrated in sleepwalking, as the mind limits awareness to only those impressions that relate to its preoccupations.[28] In either case, the mental events that take place bear little or no relation to the circumstances of the dreamer, for they are "entirely outside the individual's conscious personal existence."[29]

Tess confidently identifies the nervous origin of her husband's somnambulism in "continued mental distress" (246). Following Tuke, she recognizes somnambulism as the exhaustion of the will by prolonged attention to ideas that then continue to flow automatically.[30] In Lyman's account, clairvoyance is one possible product of the dreamy withdrawal from the external world and acute focus of the mind on particular ideations:

> The wonderful exaltation of certain faculties during the unequal sleep of the different organs of the mind is usually to be considered as something relative rather than absolute. But there is little reason to doubt that sometimes the excitement of the waking portions of the brain does really transcend the ordinary functional capacity of the structure. The undivided concentration of attention upon the comparatively limited circle of ideas which are thus produced, greatly increases the intensity of the resulting impressions upon the mind in consciousness—. Hence the grandeur of the visions which may arise; hence also, the possibility of their construction in accordance with fact rather than with fancy. As the darkness of the night, by shutting out the earth from sight, opens our eyes to the glory of the starry sky, so in like manner sleep, by closing the senses against the distractions of the external world, may sometimes afford the conditions enabling a richly gifted intellect to comprehend the course and the destination of those deep and silent streams of thought which move on unnoticed during the hours of wakeful life.[31]

These are the "obscure recesses" of the mind that in the mid-century William Hamilton argued were recognized by consciousness in "extraordinary exaltations of mental power"[32] and that Carpenter described as "unconscious cerebration" or the process by which hidden ideas or reservoirs of knowledge are delivered to consciousness, appearing miraculous (*Principles,* 515–43). Such "mental latency"[33] explains, for example, the remarkable cases in which someone suddenly acquires a whole language or a talent in some art in which the person has had no training. In Lyman's account the latent knowledge is that of sequenced events, whose minute gradations offer a pattern that is too subtle for the conscious mind to detect. In this way the dreamy withdrawal from circumstance may entail episodes of clairvoyance whose origin in the attention makes it akin to the astral voyaging that Tess describes as a release from the sorrows of waking life.

Mental science pathologized visions and previsions as "hallucination" and evidence of madness. Esquirol identified the "visionary" as "one who is said to labor under a hallucination" and who gives substance to images reproduced by memory without the senses intervening.[34] At the end of the century, such symptoms pointed not only to the insanity of the individual subject but generally to a pervasive pathological condition of modern life: Maudsley attributed telepathic phenomena and clairvoyance resulting from the alleged communication of spirits to the nervous disorganization that caused hallucination and identified these as morbid evidence of degenerative nervous stock.[35] Yet the "hallucinatory" visionary was not universally recognized as insane or even as the victim of inherited nervous weakness or overextension. In mid-century France, in particular, debate about the compatibility of hallucinations with reason was energetic, taking up no less than eight meetings of the *Société medico psychologique* in 1855 and 1856. The leading figure in this debate, a respected alienist and secretary of the Society, was Alexandre Brière de Boismont, whose *Hallucinations, or the Rational History of Apparitions* (1852), the first full published study of hallucinations, had precipitated the society's discussions.[36] *Hallucinations* maintains that medical observations of the mind should not intrude upon sacred knowledge and that divine inspiration and "the ecstatic character which the struggles of the soul impart to ideas" cannot be reduced to hallucinatory madness.[37]

De Boismont's etiology of hallucinations is compatible with Tuke's and Carpenter's claims that clairvoyant phenomena can be explained as the sudden gift of cerebral activity to sensations stored in the memory that have previously been dormant (*Hallucinations*, 257). He argued that certain kinds of epileptic seizure, apoplexy, and hysterical fit, somnambulism, magnetism, and ecstatic states involve hallucinations, including prevision, whereby "the mind, as in dreams, is fixed upon certain impressions which it takes for so many real and actual external sensations" (245). Hallucinatory previsions, he cautions, must be "subjected to severe examination . . . [and] their occurrence guaranteed by men of intelligence and integrity"(243). However, he stresses that these ideations may coincide with the full rational activity of the mind. Having proposed that they are not necessarily the product of a diseased mind, he then asks why the rational species of hallucination recognized as vision or prophecy has disappeared from modern culture. He then traces the loss of visionaries to the spiritual impoverishment of modern culture:

No serious comparison can be made between the hallucinations of those famous men [of past ages] and those of the visionaries of our day. There, enterprises conceived, carried out, consummated with all the powers of reason, the train of facts, the force of genius, and with whom the hallucination was but an auxiliary; here, projects without connection, without aim, without fact, and always stamped with insanity.

But it may be said, how does it happen that this species of hallucination has disappeared in our day? Here is a reply to the query: to be hallucinated in this manner needs profound conviction, intense belief, extreme love of humanity; to live in the midst of a society partaking of the same belief and willing, in case of necessity, to die for it. Then, they walked with the age. Where are the new creeds? Where are the martyrs? What voice governs the world? Everyone lives for himself and in himself. Skepticism has gained all classes. Generous devotedness excites a smile. Material happiness is the motto. It will be allowed that such a disposition of mind is little favourable to enthusiasm and great enterprises. (xi)

Despite the distancing voice of the alienist who classifies hallucinatory episodes as "enthusiastic" in his closing remarks, he also reclaims them as genuine spiritual phenomena of a precommercial and presecular culture. In this respect he inverts Maudsley's identification of hallucinations as stigmata of degeneracy. He then suggests that there *is* a contemporary analogue for the rational hallucination of past ages in the form of a certain kind of reverie, where the prolonged mediation on an object or an idea can generate impressions of things we have never seen, "phantoms that our imagination, by its sole power, gathers around us . . . beneath the charm of its sorcery" (42). While reverie is "a state of mind that everyone has experienced and which shows with what facility hallucination can be produced," and while it may delude us with "waking dreams" or "castles in the air" that release us from "the sad realities of life" (43), it may also be the prelude to extraordinary productions of mind like those of prophets, poets, and philosophers, for whom "reverie is force, power, health, and often even longevity" (42). The creative power of reverie can be distinguished from that which is slavishly obedient to the image it produces and is thus a symptom of, at best, mental weakness and, at worst, madness (42). Likewise, the hallucinations produced by religious ecstasy may still be categorized as visionary where they "spring from an enlarged faculty of perception [or] a supernatural intuition" (259). For this reason, he asserts, although we cannot admit theology into a book of medical science, we must remain respectful of "the creeds which have thrown so bright a refulgence on the world, to which humanity owes its greatest conquests, and which can alone save it from the abyss, [and] we cannot keep silence when we hear them loudly proclaimed as the lucubrations of diseased brains" (ix).

Among members of the SPR, the question of whether hallucination constituted a pathological symptom or evidence of a spirit personality also turned on the relationship of modern minds to ancient creeds. In *Modern Spiritualism* (1902), Frank Podmore argued that the presence of psychic phenomena in premodern societies is precisely what should alert us to the way in which the mind itself produces these phenomena. The susceptibility of spiritual mediums and séance audiences to hallucinatory encounters with the dead, he proposed, represents "a striking recrudescence in civilised countries of the old-time belief in agencies working outside and beyond physical nature."[38] Indeed, spiritualist activation of the primitive, automatic regions of the mind revives in modern lives the group automata seen in traditional societies where, for instance, "spontaneous outbreaks of bell-ringing and stone-throwing . . . from time to time perplex a country village."[39] For Podmore, the spirit contact does suggest madness as it occurs in

> a person of unstable mental equilibrium in whom the control normally exercised by the higher brain centres is liable, in slight provocation, to be abrogated, leaving the organism, as in dream or somnambulism, to the guidance of impulses which, in a state of unimpaired consciousness would have been suppressed before they could have resulted in action.[40]

More spiritualist Society members, however, insisted that evolutionary and mental science needed to be sensitive to possibilities categorically dismissed as the products of cerebral malfunction and the primitive superstition that can provoke it. Darwin's one-time rival and fellow-discoverer of natural selection, Alfred Russell Wallace, advocated that spiritual phenomena be incorporated into evolutionary conjecture, meaning that "the existence of sentient beings unrecognizable by our senses would no more contravene [natural laws] than did the discovery of . . . those structureless, gelatinous organisms which exhibit so many of the higher phenomena of animal life without any of that differentiation of parts or specialization of organs."[41] Myers proposed that beyond our modern, scientific fetishizing of reason and consciousness in which we encounter only "shrunken and shadowed souls," we might explore deeper levels of awareness that recapture our power of "higher vision" (*HP* 1: 67). In *Science and a Future Life,* he argued that the empirical study of the phenomena that we still perceive to be contradicting the laws of nature in fact opens evolutionary science to our spiritual future where it has hitherto been limited to our animal origin. Clairvoyance, telepathy, or communication from a departed personality all work beneath the threshold of awareness to point to a self much greater than that represented by the superficial consciousness with which we habitually associate our intellectual existence. This greater Self is recognized in the Gospels and by Plato and Socrates; the continuity between the deep past and the greater future of the mind discovered in the Self is, however, beyond the grasp of current scientific observation.[42]

In another essay, Myers suggests that this recognition of the greater Self is available to poetry, and, like de Boismont, he distinguishes between true prophets and the more superficial "self-inspired mystic."[43] In Tennyson's poems, he argued, the radically secularizing discoveries of evolutionary science are allowed to provoke "the worldly discovery" that the soul has no "immutable destiny" ("Science and the Future Life," 148–49). Yet by powerfully expressing "flashes of a strange delight" or ecstatic episodes in which the self dissolves into the cosmic whole, Tennyson respiritualizes the universe and exalts the human presence within it (163). The great mind that suffers from "nerve storms" may reveal "a deep lying capacity in us that otherwise would not come to light" (159) and its genius therefore may "have as much to teach us of the mind's evolution as the study of insanity has to teach us of its decay." The greatest truths of evolution may thus "rise into consciousness" before they are confirmed by empirical science (160).

Hardy had no affiliation with the SPR. He did, however, summarize several passages from Myers's essays on poetry in his notebooks. One from "Essays Classical" described the task of the poet to combine "reality and sense" with "magical and suggestive power."[44] Another, from "Modern Poets and the Meaning of Life," published in the January 1893 issue of *The Nineteenth Century*, asked whether the law of conservation condemned mind to extinction with the death of the body, or whether consciousness might itself constitute a form of transformable energy, and whether evolution might apply to the moral as well as the material world.[45] Such speculations in the context of Hardy's aesthetics certainly do not testify to any shared sympathies with Myers concerning the existence of a greater Self or an afterlife. However, they do suggest that spiritualist belief provides a point of access to the premodern social and spiritual psyche that Hardy invokes in his characters to relieve their otherwise unmitigated sorrow. Defending himself against the accusation of inflexible rationalism, he declared that he "believe[d] (in the modern sense of the word) in specters, mysterious voices, intuitions, omens, dreams, haunted places, etc."[46] This rather ironic "spiritualism" recognizes the shaping power of the human mind in place of divine agency. Yet his remark also seems to imply that, through suspension of disbelief, something other than alienation and despair might greet the subjective negotiation of modern experience.

The trance states into which Hardy's characters fall temporarily belie the novels' naturalism. While other aspects of the stories invoke Émile Zola's detached narrative "experiments," abandoning individual lives to the natural forces that shape them, these episodes replicate the kind of altered consciousness represented in neo-Gothic and later in spiritualist literature, where mystical experience offers a refuge from oppressive social conventions and institutions as well as from nature.[47] Tess's self-hypnotic contemplation of the stars and a mental journey Clym takes across the surface of the moon remind us of how, in her desolate and outcast state, Jane Eyre looks up from her hovel on the heath into the milky way and feels "the might and strength of God" (*JE*, 364). Lucy Snowe too escapes to "the sky . . . amidst circling stars" (*Villette*, 215). In Marie Corelli's popular *A Romance of Two Worlds* (1886) the narrator is initiated into full union with Christ when, by drinking an electrical liquid, she is able to travel not only out of her body but also out of the world to "gaze upon countless solar systems."[48] The stresses and burdens of the physical life are relieved when her terrestrial bonds are broken and she is released into outer space.[49] Similarly, the Geneva psychologist Theodore Flourney's biography of the medium Mlle. Hélène Smith, *From India to the Planet Mars* (1900), includes a lengthy section on the descriptions of Mars and the Martians provided by her "spirit guide" and encountered, whether by clairvoyant perception or truly by means of an astral body, when the soul is permitted to "leave momentarily its terrestrial prison."[50] Flourney's Hélène, like Hardy's Eustacia, has an "instinctive revolt against the modest environment in which it was her lot to be born, [and] a profound feeling of dread and opposition, of inexplicable *malaise,* of bitter antagonism against the whole of her material and intellectual environment."[51]

Although they have little to say about the nervous and even less about the spiritual origins of such episodes, Hardy's stories do position somnambulist experiences, including "astral travel" at key moments in the romantic plot. Tess describes her escape to the stars at an early moment during hers and Angel's courtship; as Clym waits for the newly won Eustacia, he stares at the ancient landscape of the moon and "feels himself to be voyaging bodily through its wild scenes" (166). These dreamy events thus mark the point at which each set of histories disastrously merges with the other, yet they momentarily resist the inevitable tragedy of that confluence. Rather than trampling individual stories under the march of events, they entertain, however briefly, a counternarrative in which human stories unfold in a universe animated by human needs and values—one in which the individual history then has some meaning and significance. It is when Tess speaks of traveling out to the stars that Angel notices her voice and distinguishes its tones from those of the other milkmaids. Clym declares that Eustacia's "moonlit face" and sees the "hairbreadth . . . [that makes] the difference between everything and nothing at all" (167).

However, neither reverie nor the transcendent or otherworldly experience it hosts gains much narrative traction in these novels. If ghosts, witches, and mediums are allowed to roam across Egdon heath and ghostly presentiments to forecast tragic events in *Tess,* the stories nonetheless deliver their characters into the fates powerfully determined for them not by spirits or pagan deities, but by the conditions of their modern lives. *Tess* concludes with the anticipation of a union between Angel and Tess's sister, suggesting that individual suffering will be swallowed up in the larger story of reproductive life and its unquenchable energies. *The Return of the Native* ends with Clym's moderately content life as an itinerant, open-air preacher, in which role he can appear either as native or as cosmopolitan, using simple language in Rainbarrow and the neighboring hamlets or more cultivated speech in larger towns. Reconciled to the inevitable fissures of identity that inflict him and to his permanent homelessness, Clym is clearly resigned to the modern, and his vocation seems more like a trade, for "it was well enough for a man to take to preaching who could not see to do anything else" (336). The narrator's closing words tell us that "everywhere he was well received, for the story of his life had become generally known." At the end then, his modern's story of desire and loss, passion and suffering is more compelling and truer than any tale he has to tell of return.

IV. VISION IN POETRY

In 1898, Hardy announced in a letter to William Archer that he no longer intended to write novels, complaining that "by printing a novel which attempts to deal honestly and artistically with the facts of life one stands up to be abused by any scamp who thinks he can advance the sale of his paper by lying about one."[52] However, his shift to poetry suggested more than his irritation at prudish reviewers and censoring publishers; it reflected the hope that "the checked tendency in prose may . . . be resumed in verse."[53] The novel was, he observed "gradually losing artistic form . . . and becoming a spasmodic inventory of items."[54] Although such dreary naturalism might currently be ascendant, he observed, poetry would again see its day, and "in divine poesy there is no such thing as old fashion or new. What made poetry 2000 years ago makes poetry now."[55] This claim that poetry outlasts fashion (perhaps somewhat revised in his later baffled responses to Pound's modernism[56]) and resists the ravages of the modern raises the possibility that his fiction writing had become unbearably strained by its responsibilities to the material truths of modern life, on the one hand, and its pursuit of the ghostly creations of the intuitive mind, on the other.

In lyric poetry, on the other hand, spectral voices can take over from the exhausted living speaker and its weary recognition of circumstance. Such ghostly voices are a feature of what Susan Miller has called Hardy's "impersonal lyric," as they help separate awareness of an *idea* about the inevitably painful nature of human experience from the lived experience itself.[57] In "The Self-Unseeing," from *Poems of the Past and the Present* (1902), for example, the speaker describes a time before the unanticipated death of the beloved when the floor on which she walked and the door through which she entered carried no painful associations: "Here was the former door / [w]here the dead feet walked in" (11.3–4), while "[e]verything glowed with a gleam / [y]et we were looking away" (11.11–12).[58] This "gleam" was no more available to living consciousness than the "dead feet" that walked through the door belong to the lost past, since they were then, of course, part of a living body. The poem thus dramatizes a structurally impossible form of human awareness.[59] Sensation and experience are here separated from thought and meaning.[60] The latter are therefore liberated in hallucinatory fashion in the form of pure ideation.

At times this liberation takes the form of an astral journey. In an early poem from the *Wessex* (1898) collection, "In Vision I Roamed," the speaker describes a mental voyage to a stellar region so remote that it cannot be spotted from earth. His surrendering of mind to vision as he is freed from the restraining influence of sense perception initially seems to restore him to terrestrial longing: he is reminded that although separated from him, his beloved is nonetheless within his sensible grasp:

And the sick grief that you were far away
Grew pleasant thankfulness that you were near,
Who might have been, set on some outstep sphere,
Less than a want to me, as day by day
I lived unaware, uncaring all that lay
Locked in that Universe taciturn and drear. (11.9–14)

Yet the last four lines change the meaning dramatically. The journey has reminded him that in space too vast to be navigated by the senses, the beloved might become "less than a want." The vision raises the possibility of escape from yearning, of "unawareness." At the same time, it becomes unclear what or who is "uncaring" in line 13. This may be the Universe which, like the "mother nature" of "The Sleep Worker," from *Poems of Past and Present* is entranced and indifferent, to its own creations. Or it may describe the speaker, who is no longer tormented by longing and separation. In this ambiguity then, the latter becomes united with an indifferent universe or, in Hardy's terms, "immanent will." In that Universe, oblivious to the suffering of its creatures, living beings experience release from their sense-inflicted pain, as the speaker does, through hallucination.

In his letter to the editor of the *Daily Chronicle* concerning the poem "A Christmas Ghost Story" (1899), Hardy invokes the figure of the interterrestrial voyager to account for the poem's unheroic portrait of war. The point of view of the Boer War soldier's ghost is he says,

> no longer local; nations are all one to him; his country is not bounded by seas, but is co-extensive with the globe itself, if it does not even include all the inhabited planets of the sky. He has put off the substance, and has put on, in part at any rate, the essence of the Universal.[61]

This ghost's combined worldliness and otherworldliness make it the most articulate critic of national prejudice and the unnecessary suffering that it produces in the form of war. In this respect, it concurs with the speaker of "The Sick Battle God" (*Poems of Past and Present*), who announces the absence of both the war-mongering, Old Testament "Battle-god" and of a benevolent creator who might oversee the lives of his creatures and who suggests there remains only the comfort of human "souls [who] have grown seers" (1.29) with an evolved a capacity for sympathy in the face of the overwhelming suffering to which they have become attuned. This evolutionary divide between creator and creatures, putting the most highly sensitized organisms at the mercy of an indifferent primitive force, revives the merciless determinism of the novels. Yet the Christmas ghost in Hardy's account of the poem is not simply a stand-in for the exquisitely sensitive consciousness that can perceive the uselessness of its own strivings; it is also a specter or hallucination, a "creature[] of the imagination . . . uncertain, fleeting and quivering, like winds, mists, gossamer-webs, and fallen autumn leaves."[62] In the poem itself, the ghost of the fallen soldier is less a supernatural character than a heavy-handed literary device to present the cruelties of war and the continued deafness of its actors to Christ's teachings. Yet it is summoned up by a speaker who himself travels mentally "South of the line inland from far Durban" (1.1), where "A mouldering soldier lies—your countryman" (1.2) and who, having found that corpse, then acts as ventriloquist to the soldier's phantom.

In many of the later poems, reverie and vision are provisionally depicted as the condition of a troubled mind that cannot quite manage the material and emotional realities with which it is presented. In "The Ghost of the Past," from *Satires of Circumstance* (1914), the allegorical figure of the past—a "spectral housekeep[er]"—defends the order and comfort of the speaker's mind against the turmoil of "gaunt griefs." In "Self-Unconscious," from the same collection, the speaker is so absorbed in "specious plans" that he is incapable of recognizing the transient details of "earth's artistry" until it is too late to do so. "The Phantom Horsewoman" (*Poems of 1912–1913*) describes a man who compulsively hallucinates the figure of a perpetually young woman on horseback while he himself continues to "wither daily" (1.29). Yet in each case the dreamy structure of the poem distracts us from its ostensible attention to the fraught emotional circumstances it presents. "The Ghost of the Past" describes the fading echo and shape of the speaker's spectral companion, yet because the formal arrangement of the poem is so strict—each stanza carefully repeats the final word or phrase from the first line in the second and the fifth line in the seventh—it produces a mesmerizing chant that itself appears undaunted by the message of change. "Self-Unconscious" has a similarly hypnotic structure as the rhyme and meter remain consistent within each stanza, a form that must be seen as deliberate and pointed for a poet who emphasized the "enormous worth" of the Gothic principle of "cunning irregularity." [63] The *regular* form reminds us that the "focused distance" (1.39) on nature that the speaker sacrificed to self- preoccupation is, in the present tense of the poem, elevated to a higher level of reverie in which "he is aware / a thing was there / that loomed with an immortal mien" (11.46–48). The past fluttering of yellowhammers and "metal shine" (1.20) of the sea are not "moments that encompass him" (1.6) but rather ideas whose immortal shapes transcend the sensible natural origins that have "passed away" (1.33).

In the same way, the dreamer of "The Phantom Horsewoman" is released from the diagnosis of mental strain when his perception merges with that of the speaker. The "thing" that, in the second stanza, he is said to conjure up out of his grief is

> Warm, real, and keen,
> What his back years bring—
> A phantom of his own figuring. (11.16–18)

Yet the hallucination that the speaker describes here, and which in the third stanza is still located "everywhere / In his brain," (11.24–25), steps out from the space of his distressed imagination to assume a three-dimensional presence in the poem, as she whose form has hitherto been withheld because she

was a mere figment of the disordered brain takes firm shape and becomes the
subject rather than the object of feelings and actions:

> But she still rides gaily
> In his rapt thought
> On that shagged and shaly
> Atlantic spot,
> And as when first eyed
> Draws rein and swings to the tide. (11.31–36)

Not only the lover's "rapt thought" but also the now-entranced speaker experiences the girl as a palpable presence. This joining of dreamy minds is in
striking contrast to the opening of the poem, when the speaker begins with a
distancing "Queer are the ways of a man I know" (1.1) and asks, "And what
does he see when he gazes so?" (1.9). Where he sees only "sands" (1.5) and
"seaward haze" (1.6) in the first stanza, he watches the specter herself in the
final lines, as she emerges in the present tense of the poem itself. That utterance now expresses not the thoughts of an observing, kindly speaker, but the
mind of the mourner and the specter it has created.

Like "The Phantom Horsewoman," "The Voice" also explores the possible natural origin of the phantom in romantic longing, describing both the
loss of passion in the past relationship between the lovers and its restoration
in the spectral form conjured up through the force of the speaker's grief:

> Woman much missed, how you call to me, call to me,
> Saying that now you are not as you were
> When you had changed from the one who was all to me,
> But as at first, when our day was fair.

In the second half of the poem, the speaker acknowledges that what he hears
as the woman calling is created by his longing and explains the natural origin
of the sounds he has hallucinated as voice:

> Or is it only the breeze, in its listlessness
> Travelling across the wet mead to me here,
> You being ever dissolved to wan wistlessness,
> Heard no more again far or near?

The last stanza then describes the autumn landscape whose sounds are so
sympathetic to the speaker's loss:

> Thus I; faltering forward,
> Leaves around me falling,
> Wind oozing thin through the thorn from norward,
> And the woman calling.

Yet there is more happening here. Unlike "Self-Unconscious" or "The Phantom Horsewoman," the structure of this poem is irregular. Not only is the final stanza metrically different from the preceding three, but where the latter consists of grammatically complete, complex sentences, the last lines take the form of an elaborate sentence fragment or a series of abandoned subordinate clauses. This stanza is clearly distinguished from the others, as we move out of the speaker's mind and away from the internal dialogue he is conducting with the ghost to the external scene in which he appears in a cold, wooded landscape. Yet the formal boundary between internal reverie and external reality is undermined by the final line, which reintroduces the figure of the ghost, only this time directly into the sensible, natural world where she earlier existed merely as the fantasized addressee of the speaker's distraught questioning. Although she has been naturalized as the sound of the breeze and the falling leaves, she achieves substance in defiance of her disappearance even from yearning in the previous stanza: the "wan wist*less*ness" that has apparently silenced her in the speaker's thoughts. Her non-human voice becomes audible at the end of the poem even as the speaker's carefully articulated study of his own mind becomes less so.

Such apparitions are harder to find in Hardy's fiction. In his novels, he explained, plot arises "from the gradual closing in of a situation that comes of ordinary human passions, prejudices and ambitions."[64] The novel recognizes that "this planet does not supply the materials for happiness to higher existences,"[65] and those spiritual visions and moments of dreamy relief from circumstance that his characters sometimes experience are in great part naturalized as the productions of a mind driven by the modern ache into hallucinatory escape. Tess's dreamy fascination with the other worlds she imagines in the stars is a response to the miseries that convince her that she lives in "a blighted one" (*TD*, 31); Eustacia's daydreams of cosmopolitan glamour are the phantoms of modern want; while Clym's pagan ghosts people a landscape in which he hopes to retreat from commercial corruption and romantic loss. Yet even as latter-day visions, they preserve an enclave for the spiritualization of nature and the melioration of human relationships that are otherwise shaped by suffering and skepticism. Despite her knowing caution about the way the world has treated and will treat her, and despite the novel's larger anticipation that her life will be shaped and finally destroyed by the twin forces of desire and descent, Tess can allow her wonder at Angel to dissolve all other aspects of her life into a "luminous mist," showing, the narrator suggests, that "she was a sort of celestial person, who owed her being to poetry" (212). The surrender to poetry, in this way, offers a little primitive hope against the gloom of fiction's modern facts.

ONCLUSION

onsciousness occurs, Antonio Damasio explains, when "self comes to mind," or when the self bears witness to events in the mind. This self, he echoes William James, is two-sided. It is an objective, material something, generated by feelings, or somatic markers, that establish the difference between "me" and "not me." And it is also subjective—the self-aware knowing "I," which sometimes constructs erroneous intuitions about its relationship to the world but which, situated at the origin of inquiry, also ultimately "makes reason and scientific observation possible."[1] For Damasio, consciousness occurs when we have the "feeling of knowing"; that is, we do not just create a stream of images that represent the objects we encounter internally, but we have a feeling accompanying the making of that image in which we mark that image as somehow our own.[2] As an increasingly differentiated and coordinated flow of images is triggered by objects in the environment, this embodied mind unfolds in a "normal" sequence of proto, core, and finally autobiographical selves. Eventually it delivers a higher-order awareness that sweeps beyond the "here and now" of core consciousness into both the past and the future.[3]

"Power outages" that occur with certain brain dysfunctions can, however, obliterate this magnificent architecture, depriving the mind of its self.[4] As Damasio puts it:

> When selves do not occur within minds, those minds are not conscious in the proper sense. This is a predicament faced by humans whose self process is suspended by dreamless sleep, anesthesia, or brain disease.[5]

If we Victorianize this list to include the conditions of hypochondriasis, hysterical epilepsy and catalepsy, mesmeric sleep, spiritual trance, and reverie, then the episodes of dissolving selfhood in the novels I have written about in this book might be seen to challenge Damasio's implicit linking of mental health with a deep grasp of reality. In the novels, it is not the highest form of self but rather a dreamy, disorganized mind that moves simultaneously into the past and the future or that discovers the invisible influences and suppressed forms beneath the observable surface of things. In Brontë's fiction, this dreamy mind pulls back from the observing self to find ecstatic union with God, Nature, or another human spirit and in so doing recognizes and resists women's oppression. Dreamy intuition uncovers disguised connections linking disparate characters and events in *Bleak House,* the organic bond between the living and the dead in *Our Mutual Friend,* and hidden criminal motives in Victorian detective fiction. In *Silas Marner,* the collapse of the functional self obliterates both personal history and medical knowledge, yet it also points to the dilatory awareness of a longer novel where self-loss allows for deeper forms of knowing, unhampered by the narrowing influence of the ego: in *Daniel Deronda* the mind discerns evolutionary threads intersecting in even the most subtle events of feeling and recognizes in these the origins of precognitive dread and prophecy. Finally, in *Tess* and *The Return of the Native* the haze of reverie provides the protagonists relief from their psychic suffering as it infuses modern landscapes with spiritual forms from the deep pagan past.

If, as Kay Young argues, we are aware when reading nineteenth-century novels that we are in the presence of other minds, those minds do not always or consistently house a functional self.[6] In Damasio's *The Feeling of What Happens,* many of the examples of self-loss are acute and tragic, such as coma, advanced Alzheimer's disease, and stroke-induced akinesia (in which a patient loses almost all power of animation), although he also discusses temporary loss of or impaired consciousness in absence seizures and automatisms. The "cases" in the novels I have talked about here represent not so much a lost as a reduced self or, as James put it, a shrinking of that aspect of self that enables us to "think ourselves as thinkers."[7] James describes some spiritualized states—alternating selves and mediumship—as "abnormal alterations in the present self."[8] The "(often deplorably unintelligent) rudimentary utterances" produced in trance and automatic writings "are the works of an inferior fraction of the subject's own natural mind."[9] Victorian novelists broadly agreed. The attenuations of consciousness that belong both to characters and to the organizing narrative minds in their stories represent evolutionarily lower states of mind. Yet in each case, the novel values this primitive mind for its reach into the otherwise imperceptible regions of the objective world it depicts.

The title of my last chapter, "The End of the Novel," is of course disingenuous. The novel did not disappear, not even the realist novel. Nonetheless, what Hardy experienced as the strain of animating ghostly half-selves under the pressure of naturalism might have something to do with the twentieth-century shift to a much more Jamesian, self-aware narrative mode, where inward movement is to some extent independent of external environment. One way of characterizing modernist fiction is through its representations of the palpitating consciousness, as James described it, "in a constant play of furtherances and hindrances"[10] magnifying the felt movements of thought or sequenced "cephalic adjustments"[11] that produce the self. Victorian novels, more interested in the inherited and environmentally wrought nervous changes that determine what the embodied psyche makes of the world and how much it sees, instead direct us to exotic, otherworldly dimensions of the real. They do so by showing us minds in which both the self and the certain forms it make possible slide dreamily away.

OTES

INTRODUCTION

1. See especially John Bender, "Enlightenment and the Scientific Hypothesis," *Representations* 60 (Winter 1997): 1–23; Lennard J. Davis, *Factual Fictions: The Origins of the English Novel* (New York: Columbia University Press, 1983); J. Paul Hunter, *Before Novels: The Cultural Contexts of Eighteenth-Century English Fiction* (New York: W. W. Norton & Co., 1992); Michael McKeon, *The Origins of the English Novel 1600–1740* (Baltimore: The Johns Hopkins University Press, 1987); Ian Watt, *The Rise of the Novel: Studies in Defoe, Richardson and Fielding* (Berkeley: University of California Press, 1957).

2. N. Katherine Hayles, "Constrained Constructivism: Locating Scientific Inquiry in the Theater of Representation," in *Realism and Representation: Essays on the Problem of Realism in Relation to Science, Literature, and Culture,* edited by George Levine (Madison: University of Wisconsin Press, 1993), 27–43 (29–30).

3. György Lukács, "Realism in the Balance," in *Aesthetics and Politics,* edited by Ernst Bloch (London: Verso, 1977), 28–59 (56).

4. Harry E. Shaw, *Narrating Reality: Austen, Scott, Eliot* (Ithaca, NY: Cornell University Press, 1999), xii–xiii.

5. Jason Daniel Tougaw, *Strange Cases: The Medical Case History and the British Novel* (New York: Routledge, 2006), 122.

6. George Levine, *Dying to Know: Scientific Epistemology and Narrative in Victorian England* (Chicago: University of Chicago Press, 2002), 1–43.

7. Vanessa Ryan has shown how Victorian novels highlight the role of nondeliberative thought in everyday mental processing, producing knowledge and insight that conscious thought cannot deliver as efficiently. Novels recognize the value of this "thinking without thinking" because they alert the reader to cognitive events that are usually invisible. See Ryan, "Fictions of Medical Minds: Victorian Novels and Medical Epistemology," *Literature and Medicine* 25 (Fall 2006): 277–97; "Reading the Mind: From George Eliot's Fiction to James Sully's Psychology," *Journal of the History of Ideas* 70.4 (October 2009): 615–35.

8. Mary Poovey, *A History of the Modern Fact: Problems of Knowledge in the Sciences of Wealth and Society* (Chicago: University of Chicago Press, 1998), 1–28.

9. Thomas Nagel, *The View from Nowhere* (Oxford: Oxford University Press, 1986).

10. Lorraine Daston, "Objectivity and the Escape from Perspective," in *The Science Studies Reader*, edited by Mario Biagiolli (New York: Routledge, 1999), 110–23.

11. Caroline Levine, *The Serious Pleasures of Suspense: Victorian Realism and Narrative Doubt* (Charlottesville: University of Virginia Press, 2003); Elizabeth Deeds Ermarth, *Realism and Consensus in the English Novel* (Princeton, NJ: Princeton University Press, 1983).

12. Amanda Anderson, *Powers of Distance: Cosmopolitanism and the Cultivation of Detachment* (Princeton, NJ: Princeton University Press, 2001).

13. As referenced below and in the chapters that follow, the work of, in particular, Roger Luckhurst, Pamela Thurschwell, and Athena Vrettos has explored the fluid boundary between spiritualism and mental science in the Victorian period. See also Nicola Bown, "What Is the Stuff That Dreams Are Made Of?" in *The Victorian Supernatural*, edited by Nicola Bown, Carolyn Burdett, and Pamela Thurschwell (Cambridge: Cambridge University Press, 2004), 151–72.

14. John Tyndall, "Address Delivered Before the British Association Assembled at Belfast," in *Victorian Science: A Self-Portrait from the Presidential Addresses to the British Association for the Advancement of Science*, edited by George Basalla, William Coleman, and Robert H. Kargon (New York: Anchor Books, 1970), 436–78 (477). Hereafter referred to as "Belfast Address."

15. Tyndall, "'Materialism' and Its Opponents," *Fortnightly Review* 18 (1875): 579–99 (579).

16. Tyndall, "Belfast Address," 476–77.

17. For an extended discussion of Tyndall's recognition of the way aesthetics complements empirical science see Jason Lindquist, "'The Mightiest Instrument of the Physical Discoverer': The Visual 'Imagination' and the Victorian Observer," *Journal of Victorian Culture* 13.2 (2008): 171–99.

18. Ibid., 452–54. On late-Victorian efforts among professional scientists to reconcile religious values with scientific discoveries, see Peter J. Bowler, *Reconciling Science and Religion: The Debate in Early Twentieth-Century Britain* (Chicago: University of Chicago Press, 2001).

19. "Belfast Address," 475.

20. Ibid., 470.

21. Thomas Henry Huxley, *Evidence as to Man's Place in Nature* (New York: D. Appleton & Co., 1873), 72.

22. Charles Darwin, *The Descent of Man, and Selection in Relation to Sex* (London: Penguin, 2004), 17.

23. Ibid., 136. On the figure of the evolutionary scientist in *Descent,* see Misia Landau, *Narratives of Human Evolution* (New Haven, CT: Yale University Press, 1982), 39–60.

24. Hallam Tennyson, *Alfred, Lord Tennyson: A Memoir by his Son,* 4 vols. (Leipzig: Bernhard Tauchnitz, 1899), 2:85.

25. Sir Walter Scott, *Guy Mannering* (Edinburgh: T & A Constable, 1901), 151. Quoted in James Crichton-Browne, *Stray Leaves from a Physician's Portfolio* (London: Hodder and Stoughton, 1927), 1.

26. Oliver Wendell Holmes, *The Autocrat of the Breakfast Table* (Boston: Houghton, Mifflin & Co., 1894), 106–7.

27. Thomas Hardy, *A Pair of Blue Eyes* (New York: Henry Holt & Co., 1874), 168. Quoted in Crichton-Browne, *Stray Leaves,* 5. All further references to *Stray Leaves* cited in the text.

28. John Addington Symonds, *The Memoirs of John Addington Symonds,* edited by Phyllis Grosskurth (Chicago: University of Chicago Press, 1986), 57–58.

29. Ibid., 58.

30. N. G. Waller, B. A. Kojetin, T. J. Bouchard et al., "Genetic and Environmental Influences on Religious Interests, Attitudes, and Values: A Study of Twins Reared Apart and Together," *Psychological Science* 1 (1990): 138–42; Jeffrey L. Saver and John Rabin, "The Neural Substrate of Religious Experience," *Journal of Neuropsychiatry* 9.3 (Summer 1997): 498–510.

31. D. Kapogiannis, A. K. Barbey, M. Su et al., "Neuroanatomical Variability of Religiosity," *PLoS One* 4:9 (September 28 2009): e7180; F. Ng, "The Interface between Religion and Psychosis," *Australia and New Zealand Journal of Psychiatry* 15.1 (February 2007): 62–66; D. Chan et al., "The Clinical Profile of Right Temporal Lobe Atrophy," *Brain* 132.5 (2009): 1287–98; O. Dennsky and G. Lai, "Spiritualists and Religion in Epilepsy," *Epilepsy Behavior* 12.4 (May 2008): 636–43; M. A. Persinger, "Religious and Mystical Experiences as Artifacts of Temporal Lobe Function," *Perception Motor Skills* 53.3 (Part 2) (December 1983): 1255–62; J. I. Fleck, D. L. Green, J. L. Stevenson et al., "The Transliminal Brain at Rest: Baseline EEG, Unusual Experiences, and Access to Unconscious Mental Activity," *Cortex* 44.10 (November–December 2008): 1353–63.

32. Wilder Penfield and Herbert Henri Jasper, *Epilepsy and the Functional Anatomy of the Brain* (Boston: Little, Brown and Co., 1954). Cited in John Pearce, "Dreamy States," *ACNR* 3:2 (May–June 2003): 17–20 (19).

33. V. S. Ramachandran and Sandra Blakeslee, *Phantoms in the Brain: Probing the Mysteries of the Human Mind* (New York: HarperCollins, 1998), 174–98.

34. William James, *The Varieties of Religious Experience: A Study in Human Nature,* 1st ed. (Scotts Valley, CA: IAP, 2009), 8.

35. Marilynne Robinson, *Absence of Mind: The Dispelling of Inwardness from the Modern Myth of the Self* (New Haven, CT: Yale University Press, 2010).

36. James, *Varieties,* 13.

37. Sally Shuttleworth and Jenny Bourne Taylor, eds., *Embodied Selves: An Anthology of Psychological Texts 1830–1890* (Oxford: Clarendon Press, 1998); Jane Wood, *Passion and Pathology in Victorian Fiction* (Oxford: Oxford University Press, 2001); Athena

Vrettos, *Somatic Fictions: Imagining Illness in Victorian Culture* (Stanford, CA: Stanford University Press, 1995). See also Peter Melville Logan, *Nerves and Narratives: A Cultural History of Hysteria in Nineteenth-Century British Prose* (Berkeley: University of California Press, 1997).

38. Jenny Bourne Taylor, "Obscure Recesses: Locating the Victorian Unconscious," in *Writing and Victorianism,* edited by J. B. Bullen (London: Longman, 1997), 137–79 (158).

39. Laura Otis, *Networking: Communicating with Bodies and Machines in the Nineteenth Century* (Ann Arbor: University of Michigan Press, 2001), 226.

40. Henry Maudsley, *Natural Causes and Supernatural Seemings,* 2nd ed. (London: Kegan Paul, Trench & Co., 1887), 41.

41. Alison Winter, *Mesmerized: Powers of Mind in Victorian Britain* (Chicago: University of Chicago Press, 1998).

42. Roger Luckhurst, *The Invention of Telepathy* (Oxford: Oxford University Press, 2002), 10. On the networks of knowledge that surrounded spiritualism see also Luckhurst, "Passages in the Invention of the Psyche: Mind-Reading in London, 1881–84," in *Transactions and Encounters: Science and Culture in the Nineteenth Century,* edited by Roger Luckhurst and Josephine McDonagh (Manchester: Manchester University Press, 2002), 117–50.

43. Pamela Thurschwell, *Literature, Technology, and Magical Thinking* (Cambridge: Cambridge University Press, 2001); Richard Noakes, "Spiritualism, Science and the Supernatural in Mid-Victorian Britain," in *The Victorian Supernatural,* edited by Nicola Bown, Carolyn Burdett, and Pamela Thurschwell, 23–43. Other recent studies that link the spiritualist movement to shifting social formations in the late-Victorian period include Marlene Tromp, *Altered States: Sex, Nation, Drugs, and Self-Transformation in Victorian Spiritualism* (Albany, NY: SUNY Press, 2006); Jill Galvan, *The Sympathetic Medium: Feminine Channeling, the Occult, and Communication Technologies* (Ithaca, NY: Cornell University Press, 2010); Daniel Pick, *Svengali's Web: The Alien Enchanter in Modern Culture* (New Haven, CT: Yale University Press, 2000); Sarah Willburn, *Possessed Victorians: Extra Spheres in Nineteenth-Century Mystical Writings* (Aldershot, Hampshire: Ashgate, 2006).

44. See James R. Moore, *The Post-Darwinian Controversies: A Study of the Protestant Struggle to Come to Terms with Darwin in Great Britain and America 1870–1900* (Cambridge: Cambridge University Press, 1979).

45. Janis McLarren Caldwell, *Literature and Medicine in Nineteenth-Century Britain* (Cambridge: Cambridge University Press, 2004), 24.

46. Stephen J. Gould, *The Structure of Evolutionary Theory* (Cambridge, MA: Belknap Press of Harvard University Press, 2002), 193–95; 475–77; Joseph Carroll, "Introduction," *On the Origin of Species by Means of Natural Selection* by Charles Darwin (Peterborough, ON: Broadview Press, 2003), 30. Carroll argues (against Gould) that Darwin strips Lamarckism of all notion of evolutionary progress.

47. Gould identifies Cuvier's anti-evolutionist functionalism (the coordination of parts that cannot undergo change independently of one another, thereby rendering the transmutation of species practically impossible) and emphasis on extinction in the history of organic succession as influential in the development of paleobiology and his own theory of "punctuated equilibrium." See Gould, *Structure of Evolutionary Theory,* esp. 293–95.

48. Although Cuvier and Owen were both opponents of evolutionary adaptationism, neither unequivocally positioned species history within a Christian universe. Cuvier's functionalism, Gould stresses, privileged the material relationship between organism and environment over the formalist position that function followed only divinely created types. See Gould, *Structure*, 291–304. While Owen is often thought to have organized taxonomies around a set of Platonic archetypes, he did not see homologous organs representing a creator's functional "plan." See Ron Amundson, ed., *Richard Owen: On the Nature of Limbs* (Chicago: University of Chicago Press, 2007), xxxvi–vii.

49. Shuttleworth and Taylor give Freud no special prominence in the literature of Victorian mental science, referencing Freudian psychoanalysis only in relation to the science of hypnosis and nineteenth-century medical studies of dreams and hysteria. See *Embodied Selves*, 6, 68, 70, 166.

50. On Freud's spiritualism, see F. X. Charet, *Spiritualism and the Foundations of C. G. Jung's Psychology* (Albany, NY: SUNY Press, 1993), 171–227.

51. Edward Erwin, ed., *The Freud Encyclopedia: Theory, Therapy, and Culture* (New York: Routledge, 2001), 396–99. Pamela Thurschwell points out that despite his demystification of prophetic dreams, Freud "can't leave forecasting alone." See Thurschwell, "Forecasting Falls: Icarus from Freud to Auden to 9/11," *Oxford Literary Review* 30.2 (2008), 301–22 (209). In *Literature, Technology, and Magical Thinking*, Thurschwell shows how psychoanalysis emerges at the cultural juncture of new communications technology and psychical research, where newly imagined forms of intimacy carried a troublingly erotic charge.

52. Marilynne Robinson, *Absence of Mind*, 103–7.

53. See R. M. Young, *Mind, Brain and Adaptation in the Nineteenth Century: Cerebral Localization and Its Biological Context from Gall to Ferrier* (Oxford: Clarendon Press, 1970); Michael Davis, *George Eliot and Nineteenth-Century Psychology* (Aldershot, Hampshire: Ashgate Press, 2006), 1–9; Edward S. Reed, *From Soul to Mind: The Emergence of Psychology from Erasmus Darwin to William James* (New Haven, CT: Yale University Press, 1997); Rick Rylance, *Victorian Psychology and British Culture 1850–1880* (Oxford: Oxford University Press, 2000), 21–39.

54. Thomas Huxley, *Lessons in Elementary Physiology*, edited by Frederic S. Lee (New York: Macmillan & Co., 1900), 545.

55. Rylance, *Victorian Psychology*, 21–39.

56. Thomas Huxley, *Evolution and Ethics* (London: Macmillan & Co., 1893), 36.

57. Reed, *From Soul to Mind*, 5.

58. William B. Carpenter, "Physiology an Inductive Science," *British and Foreign Medical Review* 5 (April 1838): 317–42 (342).

59. See Sally Shuttleworth, *George Eliot and Victorian Science* (Cambridge: Cambridge University Press, 1984), 1–23.

60. Erasmus Darwin, *Zoonomia or the Laws of Organic Life*, 2 vols. (Dublin: P. Byrne, 1796–1800), 1: vii,1.21. For a discussion of Darwin's evolutionary understanding of mind, see Alan Richardson, *British Romanticism and the Science of the Mind* (Cambridge: Cambridge University Press, 2001), 12–16.

61. *Zoonomia* 1:1. Emphasis in original.

62. Ibid., 1: 20.

63. Robert Chambers, *Vestiges of the History of Natural Creation*, 10th ed. (London: John Churchill, 1853), 298.

64. Charles Darwin, *Descent,* 106.

65. On periodical publishing and the Victorian novel, see Linda K. Hughes and Michael Lund, *The Victorian Serial* (Charlottesville: University Press of Virginia, 1991); Graham Law, *Serializing Fiction in the Victorian Press* (New York: Palgrave Macmillan, 2000); Deborah Wynne, *The Sensation Novel and the Victorian Family Magazine* (Houndsmills, Basingstoke; Palgrave Macmillan, 2001).

66. George Croom Robertson, "Prefatory Words," *Mind* 1.1 (January 1876): 1–6 (1).

67. Debra Gettelman has also emphasized these interdisciplinary careers. See Gettelman, "Reverie, Reading, and the Victorian Novel" (Ph.D. diss., Harvard University, 2005), 21.

68. Charles Darwin, *Evolutionary Writings,* edited by James A. Secord (Oxford: Oxford University Press, 2008), 421.

69. Luckhurst, *Invention of Telepathy,* 17.

70. Henry G. Atkinson and Harriet Martineau, *Letters on the Laws of Man's Nature and Development* (Boston: Josiah P. Mendum, 1851), 9.

71. Huxley, *Lessons,* 544.

72. On this subject, see Davis, *George Eliot,* 122–34.

73. George Henry Lewes, *The Study of Psychology,* Problems of Life and Mind, 3rd series (London: Trübner & Co., 1879), 3–38. All further references cited in the text.

74. Herbert Spencer, *Essays: Scientific, Political, and Speculative,* 3 vols. (London: Williams and Norgate, 1891), 1:1–7. Originally published anonymously as "The Development Hypothesis," *The Leader* (March 20, 1852).

75. See Lorraine J. Daston, "British Reponses to Psycho-Physiology, 1860–1900," *Isis* 69 (1978): 192–208; Rylance, *Victorian Psychology,* 39, 69–70; J. Schiller, "Physiology's Struggle for Independence in the First Half of the Nineteenth Century," *History of Science* 7 (1968): 64–89; Young, *Mind, Brain and Adaptation,* 234.

76. Alexander Bain, *The Emotions and the Will,* 2nd ed. (London: Longman Green & Co., 1865), 603.

77. Ibid., 14.

78. Bain, "Review of 'Darwin on Expression,'" postscript to *The Senses and the Intellect* (London: Longman, Green & Co., 1873), 698.

79. On the limited influence of the theory of natural selection in the later nineteenth century see Peter J. Bowler, *The Eclipse of Darwinism: Anti-Darwinian Evolution Theories in the Decade around 1900* (Baltimore: The Johns Hopkins University Press, 1983); *The Non-Darwinian Revolution: Reinterpretation of a Historical Myth* (Baltimore: The Johns Hopkins University Press, 1992).

80. J. B. Lamarck, *Zoological Philosophy: An Exposition with Regard to the Natural History of Animals,* translated by Hugh Elliot (London: Hafner Publishing, 1963).

81. Ernst Haeckel, *Generelle Morphologie der Organismen,* 2 vols. (Berlin: G. Reiner, 1866).

82. Lamarck, *Zoological Philosophy,* 10.

83. See Thomas M. Dixon, *From Passions to Emotions: The Creation of a Secular Psychological Category* (Cambridge: Cambridge University Press, 2003), 137.

84. See Reed, *From Soul to Mind,* 100–101.

85. Lewes, *The Physical Basis of Mind,* Problems of Life and Mind, 2nd series (London: Trübner & Co., 1877), 107.

86. Ibid., 107, 109.

87. Herbert Spencer, *First Principles* (London: Williams and Norgate, 1862), 221.

88. See C. U. M. Smith, "Evolution and the Problem of Mind: Part II. John Hughlings Jackson," *Journal of the History of Biology* 15.2 (Summer 1982): 241–62.

89. Ibid., 245.

90. John Hughlings Jackson, "Remarks on the Evolution and Dissolution of the Nervous System," *Journal of Mental Science* 33 (1887): 24–48. Republished in *Selected Writings of John Hughlings Jackson,* edited by James Taylor, 2 vols. (New York: Basic Books, 1958), 2:45–118 (46).

91. Edwin Ray Lankester, *Degeneration: A Chapter in Darwinism* (London: Macmillan & Co., 1880), 32.

92. Henry Maudsley, *Natural Causes and Supernatural Seemings,* 2–3.

93. Max Nordau, *Degeneration* (translated from the 2nd ed. of the German work) (1895; reprint, New York: Howard Fertig, 1968), 56.

94. Ibid., 57.

95. Nicholas Royle, *Telepathy and Literature* (Oxford: Basil Blackwell, 1990), 91.

96. Huxley, "On the Physical Basis of Life," *Fortnightly Review* 11 (February 1868): 129–45 (137).

97. Huxley, *Evidence as to Man's Place in Nature* (New York: D. Appleton & Co., 1873), 131.

98. Maudsley, *The Physiology of Mind; Being the First Part of a 3rd Ed. Revised, Enlarged, and in Great Part Rewritten of "The Physiology and Pathology of Mind"* (London: Macmillan & Co., 1876), 445.

99. Maudsley, *Natural Causes and Supernatural Seemings,* 260.

100. Ibid., 225.

101. James, *Varieties,* 19.

102. For an extensive discussion of the implications of phrenology for self-advancement over disempowering determinism, see Sally Shuttleworth, *Charlotte Brontë and Victorian Psychology* (Cambridge: Cambridge University Press, 1996), 57–70.

103. Carpenter, *Principles of Mental Physiology,* 4th ed. (New York: D. Appleton & Co., 1894), 722. All further references cited in the text.

104. See also Davis, *George Eliot,* 123.

105. Carpenter, *Mesmerism, Spiritualism &c. Historically and Scientifically Considered* (New York: D. Appleton & Co., 1877), 4.

106. Carpenter, "Spiritualism and Its Recent Converts," *Quarterly Review* 131 (October 1871): 301–53.

107. Jean-Etienne Esquirol, *Mental Maladies: A Treatise on Insanity,* translated by E. K Hunt (Philadelphia: Lea and Blanchard, 1845), 244

108. James Cowles Prichard, *A Treatise on Insanity and Other Disorders Affecting the Mind* (New York: Arno Press, 1973), 287.

109. John Barlow, *On Man's Power over Himself to Prevent or Control Insanity* (London: William Pickering, 1843), 12.

110. Sir William Hamilton, *Lectures on Metaphysics and Logic,* edited by H. L Mansel and J. Veitch., 4 vols. (Boston: Gould and Lincoln, 1859), 1:236.

111. Thomas Laycock, "On the Reflex Function of the Brain," *British and Foreign Medical Review* 19 (1845): 298–311 (305).

112. Thomas Laycock, *Mind and Brain; or, the Correlations of Consciousness and Organization,* 2 vols. (Edinburgh: Sutherland and Knox, 1860), 2:465–80.

113. John Addington Symonds Sr., "Habit," in *Miscellanies by John Addington Symonds, M.D.,* edited by his son, John Addington Symonds (London: Macmillan & Co., 1873), 293–324; Daniel Hack Tuke, *Sleepwalking and Hypnotism,* (London: J. & A. Churchill, 1884); H. Maudsley, *Physiology,* 246; John Hughlings Jackson, "Remarks on the Evolution and Dissolution of the Nervous System,"; "Lectures on the Diagnosis of Epilepsy," *The Medical Times and Gazette,* February 8, 1879, 141–43.

114. Carpenter, *Mesmerism,* 4.

115. Ibid., 19.

116. Symonds, "Habit," 322.

117. Maudsley, *Physiology,* 208–14, 298.

118. Ibid., 160.

119. Ibid., 168.

120. Tuke, *Sleepwalking and Hypnotism,* 6.

121. Ibid., 7.

122. James Braid, *Observations on Trance and Human Hibernation* (London: John Churchill, 1850).

123. See, for example, J. Milne Bramwell, "Hypnotism: A Reply to Recent Critics," *Brain* 22.1 (1899): 141–56; J. Mitchell Clarke, "Hysteria and Neurasthenia: Papers on Hypnotism, Hysterical Somnambulism and Double Consciousness," *Brain* 17.2 (1894): 272–80; Hack Tuke, "On the Mental Condition in Hypnosis," *The Journal of Mental Science* (April 1883): 55–80; J. Mortimer Granville, "Hypnotism," *British Medical Journal* (August 1881): 305. Tuke, *Sleepwalking and Hypnotism;* Albert Moll, *Hypnotism,* 2nd ed. (London: Walter Scott, 1890).

124. James, *Varieties,* 6.

125. James Sully, "The Dream as a Revelation," *Fortnightly Review* 59 (March 1893): 354–65 (355).

126. Ibid., 357.

127. Ibid., 358.

128. F. W. H. Myers, *Human Personality and Its Survival of Bodily Death,* 2 vols. (New York: Longmans, Green & Co., 1903), 1:2.

129. G. H. Lewes, "Of Vision in Art" *Fortnightly Review* 1 (July 15, 1865): 572–89, (576). All further references cited in the text.

130. George Levine, *The Realistic Imagination: English Fiction from Frankenstein to Lady Chatterley* (Chicago: University of Chicago Press, 1981), 6–7.

131. Paisley Livingston, "Why Realism Matters: Literary Knowledge and the Philosophy of Science," in George Levine, ed., *Realism and Representation: Essays on the Problem of Realism in Relation to Science, Literature, and Culture* (Madison: University of Wisconsin Press, 1993), 134–54 (150).

132. Edward. O. Wilson, *Consilience: The Unity of Knowledge* (New York: Alfred A. Knopf, 1998), 64.

133. Peter Brooks, *Realist Vision* (New Haven, CT: Yale University Press, 2005), 62.

134. Ibid., 111.

135. Spencer, *The Principles of Psychology,* 3rd ed. 2 vols. (New York: D. Appleton & Co., 1883), 1: 627.

136. George Eliot, *Daniel Deronda* (London: Penguin Books, 1995), 803. All further references cited in the text.

137. Thomas Hardy, *Tess of the d'Urbervilles* (London: Penguin Books, 2003), 68. All further references cited in the text.

138. Nicholas Dames, *The Physiology of the Novel: Reading, Neural Science and the Form of Victorian Fiction* (Oxford: Oxford University Press, 2007), 11. In a related study, Debra Gettelman has traced how the states of reverie and rapt absorption are specifically associated with novel reading in the period, thus suggesting both the imaginative potential of and the proximity to mental disorder that novels offered to Victorian culture. See note 67.

139. Robert Macnish, *The Philosophy of Sleep* (New York: D. Appleton & Co., 1834), 98. All further references cited in the text.

140. E. S. Dallas, *The Gay Science*, 2 vols. (London: Chapman & Hall, 1866), 2:9. All further references cited in the text.

141. Gillian Beer, *Darwin's Plots: Evolutionary Narrative in Darwin, George Eliot, and Nineteenth-Century Fiction*, 2nd ed. (Cambridge: Cambridge University Press, 2000), 220–41.

142. George Levine, *Darwin and the Novelists: Patterns of Science in Victorian Fiction* (Cambridge, MA: Harvard University Press, 1988), 5–7. See also John Glendening's account of the epistemological importance of relativity and contingency as presented in Darwin's figure of the "entangled bank." Glendening, *The Evolutionary Imagination in Late-Victorian Novels: An Entangled Bank* (Aldershot, Hampshire: Ashgate Publishing, 2007).

143. Auguste Comte, *A General View of Positivism*, translated by J. H. Bridges (London: Trübner & Co., 1865).

144. Charles Dickens, *A Christmas Carol and Two Other Christmas Books* (London: Collector's Library, 2004), 9.

145. Sully, "The Dream as a Revelation," 354.

CHAPTER 1

1. In addition to those described below, recent studies of Brontë's use of Gothic, Romantic, and realist conventions include Toni Wein, "Gothic Desire in Charlotte Brontë's *Villette*," *Studies in English Literature* 39.4 (1999): 733–46; Robyn R. Warhol, "Double Gender, Double Genre in *Jane Eyre* and *Villette*," *Studies in English Literature* 36.4 (1996): 857–75; Emily W. Heady, "Must I Render an Account? Genre and Self-Narration in Charlotte Brontë's *Villette*," *Journal of Narrative Theory* 36.3 (2006): 341–64; Heta Pyrohönen, *Bluebeard Gothic: Jane Eyre and Its Progeny* (Toronto: University of Toronto Press, 2010).

2. See Braun, "A Great Break in the Common Course of Confession: Narrating Loss in Charlotte Brontë's *Villette*," *ELH* 78:1 (Spring 2011): 189–212; Mary Jacobus, "The Buried Letter: Feminism and Romanticism in *Villette*," in *Villette: Charlotte Brontë*, New Casebooks Series, edited by Pauline Nestor (New York: St. Martin's Press, 1992), 121–40.

3. Shuttlewoth, *Charlotte Brontë and Victorian Psychology*, 17.

4. Heather Glen, *Charlotte Brontë: The Imagination in History* (Oxford: Oxford University Press, 2002), 136.

5. Shuttleworth, *Charlotte Brontë and Victorian Psychology*, 141.

6. Shuttleworth puts more emphasis on the figure of monomania in Brontë's novels in this respect, showing how nineteenth-century psychiatry identified monomania as a form of partial insanity. While in *Villette*, Lucy on one occasion describes herself

as a monomaniac, both narrators diagnose themselves as hypochondriacal. I focus on hypochondria here too because its symptoms include clairvoyant foreboding. See Shuttleworth, *Charlotte Brontë*, esp. 51–56. On monomania, partial insanity, and the fragmented mind see also Simon During, "The Strange Case of Monomania: Patriarchy in Literature, Murder in *Middlemarch*, Drowning in *Daniel Deronda*," *Representations* 23 (Summer 1988): 86–104.

7. On Victorian medical accounts of hypochondriasis, see below. Gettelman has explored the tension in *Jane Eyre* between the pleasures of reverie (which are mimicked in readerly absorption) and a sense that daydreaming or overidentification may cause disruptive excess. See Gettelman, "'Making Out' Jane Eyre," *ELH* 74.3 (Fall 2007): 557–81.

8. Terry Eagleton, *Myths of Power: A Marxist Study of the Brontës*, 3rd ed. (Basingstoke, Hampshire: Palgrave Macmillan, 2005), 12.

9. Ibid., 4.

10. Ibid., 8–9.

11. Janna Henrichsen, "Choosing Servitude: The Influence of the Mosaic Law in *Jane Eyre*," *Brontë Studies* 29 (July 2004): 105–10 (107).

12. John G. Peters, "'We Stood at God's Feet, Equal': Equality, Subversion, and Religion in *Jane Eyre*," *Brontë Studies* 29 (March 2004): 53–64 (61).

13. Janet L. Larson, "'Who Is Speaking?' Charlotte Brontë's Voices of Prophecy," in *Victorian Sages and Cultural Discourse: Renegotiating Gender and Power*, edited by Thaïs E. Morgan (New Brunswick, NJ: Rutgers University Press, 1990), 66–86. Caldwell describes the tensions between spiritual and secular interpretation in *Jane Eyre* as an effect of the literalization of biblical images. See Caldwell, *Literature and Medicine*, 102.

14. Charlotte Brontë, *Villette* (Ware, Hertfordshire: Wordsworth Editions Ltd., 1999), all further references cited in the text.

15. Amariah Brigham, *Observations on the Influence of Religion upon the Health and Welfare of Mankind* (Boston: Marsh, Capen & Lyon, 1835), 299.

16. Charlotte Brontë, "When Thou Sleepest," *The Poems of Charlotte Brontë*, edited by Tom Winnifrith (Oxford: Basil Blackwell, 1984), 208.

17. Sandra M. Gilbert and Susan Gubar, *The Madwoman in the Attic: The Woman Writer and the Nineteenth-Century Literary Imagination*, 2nd ed. (New Haven, CT: Yale University Press, 2000).

18. Ibid., 430–33.

19. See Ivan Kreilkamp, *Voice and the Victorian Storyteller* (New York: Cambridge University Press, 2005), 122–54; Karen Lawrence, "The Cypher: Disclosure and Reticence in *Villette*," *Nineteenth-Century Literature* 42 (1988): 448–66; Helene Moglen, *Charlotte Brontë: The Self Conceived* (Madison: University of Wisconsin Press, 1984).

20. See, for example, Marie C. Hennedy, "Deceit with Benign Intent: Story-Telling in *Villette*," *Brontë Studies* 28 (March 2003): 1–14; John Kucich, "Passionate Reserve and Reserved Passion in the Works of Charlotte Brontë," *ELH* 52.4 (Winter 1985): 913–37.

21. Charlotte Brontë, *Jane Eyre* (London: Penguin, 2006), 187. All further references cited in the text.

22. "I will a round unvarnished tale deliver." William Shakespeare, *Othello, Riverside Shakespeare* (Boston: Houghton & Mifflin, 1974), 1.iii.144–45.

23. On the metaphorical cooption of colonial slavery to represent gender relations in *Jane Eyre*, see Susan Meyer, "Colonialism and the Figurative Strategy of *Jane Eyre*," in

Macropolitics of Nineteenth-Century Literature: Nationalism, Exoticism, Imperialism, ed. Jonathan Arac and Harriet Ritvo (Philadelphia: University of Pennsylvania Press, 1991), 159–83; Gayatri Chakravorty Spivak, "Three Women's Texts and a Critique of Imperialism," *Critical Inquiry* 12.1 (Autumn 1985): 243–61. See also Patrick Brantlinger, "Victorians and Africans: The Genealogy of the Myth of the Dark Continent," *Critical Inquiry* 12 (1985): 166–203.

24. Anne McClintock, *Imperial Leather: Race, Gender and Sexuality in the Imperial Contest* (New York: Routledge, 1995), 21–74 (40).

25. Sharon Marcus, "The Profession of the Author: Abstraction, Advertising and *Jane Eyre,*" *PMLA* 110.2 (March 1995): 206–19. In *Villette,* too, Lucy seems both abstracted and abstracting: She describes how "in my reverie, methought I saw the continent of Europe, like a wide dream-land" (49); and she ends her story with a vision of the "destroying angel of the tempest" that wrecks vessels across the entire distance of the Atlantic, thus bringing M. Paul's West Indian plantation into "imaginative proximity" (Marcus, 207) with European shores.

26. Ibid., 207

27. H. Hunt, "On Hypochondriasis and Other Forms of Nervous Disease," *Medical Times* 24 (1851): 150–53 (150).

28. Tougaw, *Strange Cases,* 102.

29. Janet Oppenheim, *Shattered Nerves: Doctors, Patients, and Depression in Victorian England* (New York: Oxford University Press, 1991), 96.

30. James Cowles Prichard, *A Treatise on Insanity,* 91.

31. Ibid., 91.

32. Ibid., 20–29.

33. John Conolly, *An Inquiry Concerning the Indications of Insanity,* edited by Richard Hunter and Ida Macalpine (London: Dawsons of Pall Mall, 1964), 103.

34. Ibid., 93–177.

35. John Barlow, *On Man's Power over Himself to Control Insanity,* 8.

36. Esquirol, *Mental Maladies,* 112.

37. Alison Byerly argues that even before reading *Modern Painters* in 1848, and certainly in *Villette,* Brontë illustrates Ruskin's assertion that visual art must be more than imitation, combining the depiction of material things with the representation of inner experience. See Byerly, *Realism, Representation, and the Arts in Nineteenth-Century Literature* (Cambridge: Cambridge University Press, 1997), 93.

38. William Buchan, *Domestic Medicine: or a Treatise on the Prevention and Cure of Diseases by Regimen and Simple Medicine,* 9th ed. (London: W. Strahan et al., 1784). On the Brontë family's reading see Clifford Whone, "Where the Brontës Borrowed Books," *Brontë Society Transactions* 11.2 (1950): 344–58; Sally Shuttleworth, *Charlotte Brontë and Victorian Psychology,* 40.

39. Shuttleworth, *Charlotte Brontë and Victorian Psychology,* 28.

40. Buchan, *Domestic Medicine,* 360.

41. Ibid., 362.

42. Buchan, *Advice to Mothers* (Boston: Joseph Bumstead, 1809), 45.

43. Ibid., 108.

44. *Mental Maladies,* 47.

45. John Reid, *Essays on Hypochondriacal and Other Nervous Affections* (Philadelphia: M. Carey, 1817), 23.

46. Ibid., 286.

47. Ibid., 9.

48. Ibid., 12.

49. James Frederick Ferrier, "An Introduction to the Philosophy of Consciousness," *Blackwood's Edinburgh Magazine* 43 (April 1838): 437–52 (447).

50. Ibid., 441.

51. Ibid. (June 1838): 784–91 (784).

52. "Vestiges of the Natural History of Creation," *Edinburgh Review* 82 (July 1845): 1–85 (12). The reviewer principally objected to Chambers's sloppy scientific method.

53. Chambers, *Vestiges of the Natural History of Creation*, 290.

54. Sally Shuttleworth, "Pyschological Definition and Social Power: Phrenology in the Novels of Charlotte Brontë," in *Nature Transfigured: Science and Literature 1700–1900*, edited by John Christie and Sally Shuttleworth (Manchester, UK: Manchester University Press, 1989), 121–51. Nathan Elliott recently argued that Brontë's novels in fact resist the interpretive influence of phrenology—frequently exposing faculty psychology as a false lead—and instead rely on the Gothic conventions of hidden motive and disguise. See Elliott, "Phrenology and the Visual Stereotype in Charlotte Brontë's *Villette*," *Nineteenth-Century Studies* 22 (2008): 41–55.

55. Shuttleworth, *Charlotte Brontë and Victorian Psychology*, 42.

56. Ibid., 44.

57. See Richardson, *British Romanticism and the Science of the Mind*, 1–38.

58. Darwin, *Zoonomia*, 1:394. See Richardson, *British Romanticism*, 46.

59. William Wordsworth, *The Prelude*, in *Wordsworth: Poetical Works*, edited by Thomas Hutchinson (Oxford: Oxford University Press, 1987), Bk. 7,11. 650–54.

60. Ibid., Bk. 2,1.56.

61. Richardson, *British Romanticism*, 66–74.

62. G. H. Lewes, "Recent Novels: French and English," *Fraser's Magazine* 36 (1847): 686.

63. Charlotte Brontë to George Smith, April 18, 1858, *The Brontës: Their Lives, Friendships, and Correspondence*, edited by Thomas James Wise, 4 vols. (Philadelphia: Porcupine Press, 1980), 3:101–2; further cited as *Correspondence*.

64. On the significance of the "unity of species" debate to racial theory in the early Victorian period, see Robert J. C. Young, *Colonial Desire: Hybridity in Theory, Culture, and Race* (London: Routledge, 1995), 6–19.

65. James Cowles Prichard, *Researches into the Physical History of Man*, edited by George W. Stocking (Chicago: University of Chicago Press, 1973), 33–35. Prichard shifted the emphasis from culture or "civilization" to climate in the second edition (1826). See George W. Stocking, "From Chronology to Ethnology: James Cowles Prichard and British Anthropology," *Researches*, ix–cx (lxviii).

66. Prichard, *Researches*, 172.

67. William Lawrence, *Lectures on Physiology, Zoology, and the Natural History of Man, Delivered at the Royal College of Surgeons* (London: J. Callow, 1819); Thomas Hodgkin, "On Inquiries into the Races of Man," *Reports of the British Association for the Advancement of Science* 11 (1842): 52–55. The polygenetic argument for multiple original human types is represented by Robert Knox, *The Races of Men: A Fragment* (Philadelphia: Lea and Blanchard, 1850); Josiah Nott and George Gidden, *Types of Mankind* (London: Trübner, 1854); Louis Agassiz, "The Geographical Distribution of Animals,"

Christian Examiner and Religious Miscellany 48.2 (1850): 181–204; Henry Holland, "The Natural History of Man," *Quarterly Review* 86 (1850): 1–40.

68. Patrick Matthew, *On Naval Timber and Arboriculture* (London: Longman, 1831), 370–71.

69. Ibid., 381. Matthew observes of the theory that all species descend from "one Proteus principle of life capable of gradual circumstance-suited modifications and aggregations": "There is more beauty and unity of design in this continual balancing of life to circumstance, and greater conformity to those dispositions of nature which are manifest to us, than in total destruction and new creation" (383–84). In turn of phrase as well as in meaning, this seems to anticipate Darwin's famous remark that "there is grandeur in this view of life, with its several powers having being breathed originally into a few forms or only one." Charles Darwin, *On the Origin of Species*, edited by Joseph Carroll (Peterborough, ON: Broadview, 2003), 398.

70. Matthew, *On Naval Timber*, 370.

71. Peter Bolt identifies how the imagery in Jane's symbolic paintings links them with her portraits. The portrait of Blanche Ingram, for example (painted before Jane actually meets her), associates her with the cormorant of the earlier painting because both are adorned with a gold bracelet. See Bolt, "Jane Eyre's Three Paintings: Biblical Warnings and Greek Legends," *Victorian Web*, http://victorianweb.org/authors/bronte/cbronte/bolt7.html (January 2012). Although nominally more realist, this portrait is also clearly drawn from the "spiritual eye."

72. Prichard, *A Treatise on Insanity*, 320.

73. Ibid., 303.

74. Ibid., 304.

75. Ibid., 320–22.

76. Ibid., 323.

77. Charlotte Brontë to James Taylor, January 15, 1851, *Correspondence*, III:200.

78. Charlotte Brontë to James Taylor, February 11, 1851, *Correspondence*, III:208.

79. Matthew, *On Naval Timber*, 375.

80. Charlotte Brontë to George Smith, October 30, 1852, *Correspondence*, IV:14.

81. Charlotte Brontë to G. H. Lewes, November 6, 1847, *Correspondence*, II:152–53.

82. Charlotte Brontë to W. S. Williams, November 6, 1852, *Correspondence* IV:17.

83. Charlotte Brontë to George Smith, [undated], 1852, *Correspondence* IV:17.

CHAPTER 2

1. "Doubtfully Divine Missions," *All the Year Round* 15 (May 1866): 404–8 (408); this journal is further cited as *AYR*.

2. "Well Authenticated Rappings," *Household Words* 17 (February 1858): 217–20.

3. "Wonders Will Never Cease," *AYR* 1 (September 1859): 497–500 (497).

4. Dickens, "The Haunted House," *AYR* Christmas Number (1859): 1–48 (5). See Louise Henson, "'In the Natural Course of Things': Ghosts and Science in Dickens's *All the Year Round*," in *Culture and Science in the Nineteenth-Century Media*, edited by Louise Henson, Geoffrey Cantor, Gowan Dawson, Richard Noakes, and Sally Shuttleworth (Aldershot, Hampshire: Ashgate Press, 2004), 113–23 (117–19). Robert Newsom also

describes Dickens's confidence in scientifically confirmed marvels like mesmeric clairvoyance and spontaneous combustion. See Newsom, *Dickens on the Romantic Side of Familiar Things* (New York: Columbia University Press, 1977), 8.

5. Dickens, "Strange and Yet True," *AYR* 7 (1862): 540–42 (540). Quoted in Henson, "In the Natural Course of Things," 114.

6. Charles Dickens, *Bleak House* (Oxford: Oxford University Press, 1996), 6. All further references cited in the text.

7. G. H. Lewes, "Dickens in Relation to Criticism," *Fortnightly Review* 17 (February 1872): 141–54 (144).

8. Ibid., 145.

9. Ibid., 144.

10. See Newsom, *Dickens on the Romantic Side of Familiar Things*, 1–9; Christopher Herbert, "The Occult in *Bleak House*," *Novel: A Forum on Fiction* 17.2 (Winter 1984): 101–15; Goldie Morgentaler, *Dickens and Heredity: When Like Begets Like* (Houndsmills, Basingstoke; Hampshire: Macmillan, 2000), 88–96; Harry Stone, *Dickens and the Invisible World: Fairy Tales, Fantasy and Novel-Making* (Bloomington: Indiana University Press, 1979), 39; Jonathan Arac, *Commissioned Spirits: The Shaping of Social Motion in Dickens, Carlyle, Melville and Hawthorne* (New Brunswick, NJ: Rutgers University Press, 1979), 114–38.

11. Arac, *Commissioned Sprits*, 164–85; Hilary Schor, *Dickens and the Daughter of the House* (Cambridge: Cambridge University Press, 1999), 178–207; John Romano, *Dickens and Reality* (New York: Columbia University Press, 1978), 8–82.

12. Audrey Jaffe, *Vanishing Points: Dickens, Narrative, and the Subject of Omniscience* (Berkeley: University of California Press, 1991).

13. See, for example, Newsom, *Dickens on the Romantic Side of Familiar Things*, 47–92; Herbert, "The Occult in *Bleak House*"; Michael Ginsberg, "Dickens and the Uncanny: Repression and Displacement in *Great Expectations*," *Dickens Studies Annual: Essays on Victorian Fiction* 13 (1984): 115–24.

14. Sara Thornton, "The Haunted House of Victorian Advertising: Hysteria, Paranoia, Perversion," *Anglophonia: French Journal of English Studies* 15 (2004): 59–73; Jen Cadwallader, "Spirits of the Age: Ghost Stories and the Victorian Psyche" (Ph.D. diss., University of North Carolina at Chapel Hill, 2009), 53–96. Cadwallader argues persuasively that ghost stories use contemporary psychology to reactivate human access to the divine. Louise Henson reads *A Christmas Carol*, *The Chimes*, and Dickens's shorter ghost stories alongside studies of the nervous origins of spectral illusions. See Henson, "Investigations and Fictions: Charles Dickens and Ghosts," in *The Victorian Supernatural*, 44–63. See also Hippolyte Taine, "Charles Dickens: son talent et ses œuvres," *Revue des deux mondes* (February 1, 1856): 618–47.

15. Peter Ackroyd, *Dickens* (London: Sinclair-Stevenson, 1990), 82; William Gordon Lennox and Margaret A. Lennox, *Epilepsy and Related Disorders*, 2 vols. (Boston: Little, Brown and Company, 1960), vol. 1, 704.

16. Fred Kaplan, *Dickens and Mesmerism: The Hidden Springs of Fiction* (Princeton, NJ: Princeton University Press, 1975), 38; Berg MS., Dickens to Emile de la Rue, January 1, 1845, quoted in Kaplan, *Dickens and Mesmerism*, 85; see Henson, "Investigations and Fictions," 46.

17. See, for example, Caroline Levine, "Narrative Networks: *Bleak House* and the

Affordances of Form," *Novel* 42.3 (Fall 2009): 517–23; Elizabeth Deeds Ermarth, *Realism and Consensus in the English Novel*, 181–221; Arac, *Commissioned Spirits*, 1–12.

18. Jill Matus has analyzed how Dickens uses the figure of recovered memory and trauma in her account of episodes of discontinuous consciousness and self-loss. See Matus, *Shock, Memory and the Unconscious in Victorian Fiction* (Cambridge: Cambridge University Press, 2009), 83–120.

19. Charles Dickens, *David Copperfield* (Hertfordshire: Wordsworth Classics, 1992), 482.

20. The passage is quoted in the following studies: John Hughlings Jackson, "On a Particular Variety of Epilepsy ('Intellectual Aura')," *Brain* 11 (1888): 179–207 (185); James Crichton-Browne, *Stray Leaves*, 2; John Pearce, "Dreamy States," 19.

21. Athena Vrettos identifies how fin-de-siècle accounts of the dreamy state recognize déjà vu as marking "the experiential borderland between science and faith." See Vrettos, "Dying Twice: Victorian Theories of Déjà Vu," in *Disciplinarity at the Fin de Siècle*, edited by Amanda Anderson and Joseph Valente (Princeton, NJ: Princeton University Press, 2002), 196–218 (200).

22. John Hughlings Jackson, "Intellectual Warnings of Epileptic Seizures," *Medical Times and Gazette* (December 23, 1876): 700–702 (702).

23. Ibid., 702.

24. Jackson, "Lectures on the Diagnosis of Epilepsy," 142.

25. Jackson, "On a Particular Variety of Epilepsy," 186.

26. Jackson, "Lectures on the Diagnosis of Epilepsy," 141.

27. Jackson, "On a Particular Variety of Epilepsy," 183.

28. Ibid., 181.

29. On Dickens's connections with the asylum physicians see Richard A. Hunter and Ida Macalpine, "Dickens and Conolly: An Embarrassed Editor's Disclaimer," *TLS* 11 (August 1961): 534–35, cited in Graeme Tytler, "Dickens's 'The Signalman,'" *The Explicator* 53.1 (Fall 1994): 26–29; David Oberhelman, *Dickens in Bedlam: Madness and Restraint in His Fiction* (Fredericton, New Brunswick, CA: York Press, 1995); Susan Shatto, "Miss Havisham and Mr. Hopes the Hermit: Dickens and the Mentally Ill," *Dickens Quarterly* 2.2 (June 1985): 43–49; and 2.3 (September 1985): 79–83.

30. See J. E. D. Esquirol, *Mental Maladies*, 151. Esquirol argues that hysteria, in particular, shares many of the symptoms of epilepsy, including precursory moodiness, convulsions, and often a permanent change in the psyche of its victim (151). See also Moritz Heinrich Romberg, *A Manual of the Nervous Diseases of Man*, 2 vols. (London: Sydenham Society, 1853), 2:202; Theodore Herpin, *Du pronostic et du traitement curatif de l'épilepsie* (Paris: Ballière, 1852), 459–65; S. A. Tissot, *Traité de l'épilepsie* (Lausanne: François Grasset, 1789). Owsei Temkin has a helpful summary of the nineteenth-century debate about the relationship between epilepsy and hysteria. See Temkin, *The Falling Sickness: A History of Epilepsy from the Greeks to the Beginnings of Modern Neurology*, 2nd ed. (Baltimore and London: The Johns Hopkins University Press, 1971), 351–59.

31. M. J. Eadie, and P. F. Bladin, *A Disease Once Sacred: A History of the Medical Understanding of Epilepsy* (Eastleigh, Southampton: John Libbey & Co., 2001), 46–47.

32. Herbert Mayo, *Popular Superstitons and the Truths Contained Therein; with an Account of Mesmerism*, 3rd ed. (Philadelphia: Lindsay and Blakiston, 1852), 96.

33. Esquirol, *Mental Maladies*, 146.

34. Eadie and Bladin, *A Disease Once Sacred,* 55–56. In *A Manual of the Nervous Diseases of Man* Romberg identified as "abortive fits" those symptoms of epilepsy in which there is only a momentary loss of consciousness and minor spasmodic activity. See Romberg, *Manual,* 2:200.

35. E. Fisher, "Remarks on Epilepsy," *Journal of Nervous and Mental Disorders* 13 (1886): 481–87; J. Corning, "Epilepsy: Its Clinical Manifestation, Pathology, and Treatment," *New York Medical Journal* 45 (1887): 685–89; both cited in Walter J. Friedlander, *The History of Modern Epilepsy: The Beginning, 1865–1914* (Westport, CT: Greenwood Press, 2001), 81.

36. John Hughlings Jackson, "On the Anatomical, Physiological, and Pathological Investigation of Epilepsies," *West Riding Lunatic Asylum Medical Reports* 3 (1873): 315–39 (323). Emphasis in original.

37. Jackson, "Variety of Epilepsy," 183.

38. Ibid., 181.

39. Jackson, "Remarks on the Evolution and Dissolution of the Nervous System," *Selected Writings* 2:100.

40. Ibid., 2:101

41. Ibid., 2:96 (emphasis in original).

42. Ibid.

43. Jackson, "Intellectual Warnings of Epileptic Seizures," 702.

44. Herbert Spencer, *The Principles of Psychology* (London: Longman, Brown, Green and Longmans, 1855), 550.

45. Ibid., 549.

46. Ibid., 548.

47. Ibid., 582

48. Ibid., 582, 610.

49. Ibid., 577.

50. Spencer, *Social Statics: or, The Conditions Essential to Human Happiness* (London: John Chapman, 1851), 435, 467.

51. Spencer, *First Principles,* 412–16.

52. Ibid., 531–50.

53. Ibid., 280.

54. Spencer, *The Principles of Psychology,* 2nd ed., 2 vols. (New York: D. Appleton & Co. 1873) 1:608.

55. Fred Kaplan, *Dickens and Mesmerism,* 19–20, 53–55; Martin Willis and Catherine Wynn, "Introduction," in Willis and Wynn, eds., *Victorian Literary Mesmerism* (Amsterdam: Rodopi B.V., 2006), 1–16 (2–3). Dickens's respect for Elliotson and Townshend was considerable. He dedicated *Great Expectations* to Townshend and edited Townshend's *Religious Opinions* (1869). In 1840 Elliotson invited Dickens to witness a demonstration of mesmerism, insisting, "I am anxious you should see human nature in a new state." John Elliotson to Charles Dickens, May 1841, *The Pilgrim Edition of the Letters of Charles Dickens,* 12 vols. (Oxford: Clarendon Press, 1965–2002), 2:148n1.

56. Spencer, "A Theory Concerning the Organ of Wonder," *The Zoist* 2 (1844–45): 316–25 (321).

57. Alison Winter describes the difficult career of therapeutic mesmerism in the 1830s. Notwithstanding that Thomas Wakely, editor of the influential *Lancet,* abandoned his unqualified contempt for mesmerism, Elliotson's experiments continued to

be associated with the sensational stuff of mass media like the weekly penny pamphlets. See Winter, *Mesmerized,* 30–46.

58. Elliotson, *Human Physiology* (London: Longman, Rees et al., 1835), 661–63.

59. Elliotson, "Reports of Various Trials of the Clairvoyance of Alexis Didier, Last Summer, in London, Collected by Dr. Elliotson," *The Zoist* 2 (1844–45): 477–529 (498).

60. Elliotson, "Instances of Double States of Consciousness Independent of Mesmerism," *The Zoist* 4 (1846–47): 157–87 (164).

61. Catalogue of the library of Charles Dickens from Gadshill and Catalogue of the library of W. M. Thackeray (London: Piccadilly Fountain Press, 1935).

62. Augustine Calmet, *The Phantom World, or the Philosophy of Spirits, Apparitions &c* (London: Richard Bentley, 1850), 252.

63. Robert Owen, *Footfalls on the Boundary of Another World* (Philadelphia: J. B. Lippincott & Co., 1860), 117.

64. Ibid., 209

65. Ibid., 170.

66. Alfred, Lord Tennyson, *The Princess: A Medley,* edited by Henry W. Boynton (New York: Leach, Shewell, & Co., 1896), 1:13–17.

67. Nancy Aycock Metz has described how self-annihilation in Dickens's writing registers the alienating force of a metropolitan landscape that betrays a vast history of decay and decline. See Metz, "*Little Dorrit*'s London: Babylon Revisited," *Victorian Studies* 33.3 (Spring 1990): 465–86.

68. George Levine, *Dying to Know,* 5.

69. Ibid., 149–55.

70. Catherine Gallagher, *The Body Economic: Life, Death, and Sensation in Political Economy and the Victorian Novel* (Princeton, NJ: Princeton University Press, 2006), 116. John Kucich's earlier study argues that the novel's preoccupation with death houses a longing for self-abnegation and that self-interest is a form of investment in selfhood which resists the pull to death. See Kucich, *Repression in Victorian Fiction: Charlotte Brontë, George Eliot, and Charles Dickens* (Berkeley: University of California Press, 1987), 201–13.

71. Timothy Peltason, "Esther's Will," *ELH* 59.3 (1992): 671–91 (698).

72. Peltason argues that the scene at the garden gate represents Esther's power to remove herself from desire. "Esther's Will," 672.

73. Dickens, "A Curious Dance around a Curious Tree," in Harry Stone, ed., *Uncollected Writings from Household Words, 1850–1859,* 2 vols. (Bloomington: Indiana University Press, 1968), 2:382–90; "Idiots," *Uncollected Writings,* 1:101–11.

74. *AYR* 2 (February 1860): 392–96 (393).

75. Ibid., 394.

76. Ibid., 392.

77. Charles Dickens, *Our Mutual Friend* (Harmondsworth, Middlesex: Penguin Books, 1971), 257. All further references cited in the text.

78. Elliotson, *Human Physiology,* 369.

79. Mary Poovey, *Making a Social Body: British Cultural Formation, 1830–1864* (Chicago: University of Chicago Press, 1995), 155–82.

80. Edumund Saul Dixon, "A Microscopic Dream," *Household Words* 17 (April 1858): 396–400 (396).

CHAPTER 3

1. George Eliot, "Review of *Modern Painters,* Vol. III," *Westminster Review* 65 (1856): 625–50 (626).

2. See George Levine, "George Eliot's Hypothesis of Reality," *Nineteenth-Century Fiction* 35.1 (1980): 1–28; Diana Postlethwaite, "George Eliot and Science," in *The Cambridge Companion to George Eliot,* edited by George Levine (Cambridge: Cambridge University Press, 2001), 98–118; Pamela Thurschwell, "George Eliot's Prophecies: Coercive Second Sight and Everyday Thought Reading," in *The Victorian Supernatural,* 87–108.

3. Sally Shuttleworth, *George Eliot and Nineteenth Century Science* (Cambridge: Cambridge University Press, 1984), 175–200.

4. Leona Toker, *Towards the Ethics of Form in Fiction: Narratives of Cultural Remission* (Columbus: The Ohio State University Press, 2010), 116–30 (118).

5. See Marc Redfield, *Phantom Formations: Aesthetic Ideology and the Bildungsroman* (Ithaca, NY: Cornell University Press, 1995), 134–70; Neil Hertz, *George Eliot's Pulse* (Stanford, CA: Stanford University Press, 2003), 1–19.

6. David Carroll, *George Eliot and the Conflict of Interpretations* (Cambridge: Cambridge University Press, 1992), 278–89.

7. George Levine, "George Eliot's Hypothesis of Reality," 3.

8. Ibid., 9.

9. Ramachandran and Blakeslee, *Phantoms in the Brain,* 174–98.

10. On Lewes's and Eliot's "quasi-religious" account of the work of the imagination in scientific inquiry, see Davis, *George Eliot and Nineteenth-Century Psychology,* 161–87 (180).

11. On this subject see Peter Alan Dale, *In Pursuit of a Scientific Culture: Science, Art, and Society in the Victorian Age* (Madison: University of Wisconsin Press, 1989), 111–26.

12. G. H. Lewes, *The Foundation of a Creed,* 2 vols. Problems of Life and Mind, 1st series (Boston: James R. Osgood & Co., 1875), 2:122.

13. Eliot, "Notes on Form in Art," in A. S. Byatt and Nicholas Warren, eds., *George Eliot: Selected Essays, Poems, and Other Writings* (London: Penguin Books, 1990), 231–36.

14. Ibid., 234.

15. Ibid., 235.

16. Eliot, "Silly Novels by Lady Novelists," *Westminster Review* 66 (October 1856): 442–61 (449).

17. Eliot, "Notes on Form in Art," 234, 232.

18. Ibid., 232.

19. Gillian Beer, *Darwin's Plots,* 137–95; Davis, *George Eliot,* 48–69.

20. Davis, *George Eliot,* 69–77. Although he objected both to Lamarck's progressivism and to the idea that an organism somehow wills its own development, Darwin himself continued to recognize the inheritance of acquired characteristics on evolution in combination with that of natural selection. See Joseph Carroll, "Introduction," *On the Origin of Species* (Peterborough, ON: Broadview Press, 2003), 30.

21. Eliot, "R. W. Mackay's *The Progress of the Intellect,*" *Westminster Review* 54 (January 1851): 353–68 (354).

22. Ibid., 179.

23. Ibid., 180.

24. Herbert Spencer, "The Development Hypothesis, in *Essays Scientific, Political and Speculative,* 3 vols. (New York: D. Appleton & Co., 1896), 1:1–7.

25. George Henry Lewes, "Mr. Darwin's Hypotheses," Part III, *Fortnightly Review* 4 (July 1, 1868): 61–80 (70–72).

26. Ibid., 78.

27. Royle, *Telepathy and Literature,* 107.

28. George Eliot, *Adam Bede* (Oxford: Oxford University Press, 1996), 178.

29. Ibid., 179.

30. Ibid., 177.

31. Ibid., 91.

32. Thurschwell, "George Eliot's Prophecies," 89.

33. See Saleel Nurbhai and K. M. Newton, *George Eliot, Judaism and the Novels: Jewish Myth and Mysticism* (Houndmills, Basingstoke; Hampshire: Palgrave Macmillan, 2002), 48–49.

34. On the link between Gwendolyn and Mordecai as subjects of heightened consciousness, see Thurschwell, "George Eliot's Prophecies," 92–102; Jill Matus, *Shock, Memory and the Unconscious,* 149–52.

35. On Eliot's use of the figure of Paracelsus and reanimation in *The Lifted Veil,* see Nurbhai and Newton, *Judaism and the Novels,* 6.

36. See Shuttleworth, *George Eliot and Nineteenth Century Science,* 175–76.

37. George Eliot, *The Lifted Veil* (London: Virago Press, 1985), 19.

38. Toker, *Towards the Ethics of Form,* 118.

39. See Vrettos, *Somatic Fictions;* Evelyn Ender, *Sexing the Mind: Nineteenth-Century Fictions of Hysteria* (Ithaca, NY: Cornell University Press, 1995), 229–72; Carole Stone, "George Eliot's *Daniel Deronda:* The Case History of Gwendolen H.," *Nineteenth-Century Studies* 7 (1993): 57–67.

40. Catalepsy was sometimes identified as a nervous disorder in its own right, alongside hysteria, epilepsy, and others (see, for example, Esquirol, *Mental Maladies,* 109), and sometimes as a symptom of hysteria or another condition: "Catalepsy is characterized by loss of will and muscular rigidity. It occurs in paroxysms with loss of consciousness, the limbs remaining in for long periods in any position in which they are placed. It occurs in hysteria, various psychoses, hypnotic states, and organic brain disease." Daniel E. Hughes, *Hughes' Practice of Medicine,* 12th ed. (Philadelphia: P. Blakiston's Son & Co., 1922), 552.

41. Eliot, *Silas Marner* (Ann Arbor, MI: Ann Arbor Media Group, 2004), 29. All further references cited in the text.

42. Eliot, "Evangelical Teaching: Dr. Cumming," *Westminster Review* 64 (October 1855): 436–62 (442).

43. George Eliot to John Blackwood, London, January 12, 1861. *The George Eliot Letters,* edited by Gordon S. Haight, 9 vols. (New Haven, CT: Yale University Press, 1954–78), 3:371.

44. Eliot, "Notes on Form in Art," 234.

45. Shuttleworth, *George Eliot and Nineteenth Century Science,* 95.

46. George Eliot, *Middlemarch* (London: Penguin, 1994), 838.

47. William Tennent, *Memoirs of the Life of Reverend William Tennent* (Poughkeepsie, NY: Paraclete and Sheldon Potter 1815), 17.

48. Sarah Alley, *Account of a Trance or Vision of Sarah Alley* (New York: Joseph Rakestraw 1807), 5–8. Other contemporary accounts of encounters with Christ during a state of suspended consciousness include George de Benneville, *The Life and Trance of Dr. George de Benneville* (Norristown, PA: printed by David Sower,1815); Samuel L. Mitchell, *Devotional Somnium, or, A Collection of Prayers and Exhortations Uttered by Miss Rachel Baker in the City of New York* (Sangerfield, NY: printed by Van Winkle and Wriley, 1816); and Charles William Twort, *The Vision of Judgment or the Return of Joanna from Her Trance* (London; printed by Charles W. Twort, 1829).

49. Isaiah Thomas, *The Prodigal Daughter, or, A Strange and Wonderful Relation* (Boston: Thomas's printing office, 1771).

50. Ann Taves, *Fits, Trances, and Visions: Experiencing Religion and Explaining Experience from Wesley to James* (Princeton, NJ: Princeton University Press, 1999), 25–46.

51. Taves, *Fits, Trances, and Visions,* 53.

52. Meric Casaubon, *A Treatise Concerning Enthusiasme,* ed. Paul J. Korshin (1656; repr., Gainsville, FL: Scholars' Facsimiles and Reprints, 1970), 82–83. All further references cited in the text.

53. James Braid, *Observations on Trance or Human Hibernation,* vi.

54. Ibid., 36.

55. Ibid., 43.

56. Ibid., 56.

57. William Tebb and Edward Perry Vollum, *Premature Burial and How it May Be Prevented with Special Reference to Trance, Catalepsy and Other Forms of Suspended Animation* (London: S. Sonnenschein & Co., 1896), 23.

58. Ibid., 25.

59. William Benjamin Carpenter, presidential address at the meeting of the British Association for the Advancement of Science, Brighton, 1872. Published as "Man the Interpreter of Nature," in *Nature and Man: Essays Scientific and Philosophical* (London; K. Paul, Trench & Co., 1888), 185–210 (187).

60. Carpenter, "Nature and Law," *The Modern Review* 1 (October 1880): 748–70 (753).

61. Carpenter, "Man the Interpreter of Nature," 194

62. Ibid., 197.

63. Carpenter, "On the Psychology of Belief," The Roscoe Lecture, delivered before the Literary and Philosophical Society of Liverpool, November 24, 1873. Published in *Nature and Man,* 211–38 (228).

64. Ibid., 223.

65. Carpenter, "On the Fallacies of Testimony in Relation to the Supernatural," *Contemporary Review* (January 1876): 279–95 (279).

66. Ibid., 285.

67. Ibid., 287.

68. Ibid., 282–83.

69. Patrick Winden, *Silas Marner: Memory and Salvation* (New York: Twayne Publishers, 1992), 31.

70. Richard Menke, "Fiction as Vivisection: G. H. Lewes and George Eliot," *ELH* 67 (2000): 617–53 (642).

71. Lewes, "On the Dread and Dislike of Science," *Fortnightly Review* 29 (June 1878): 805–15 (811).

72. Ibid., 811–12.

73. Eliot, "Evangelical Teaching," 442.

74. Lewes, "Dread and Dislike of Science," 815.

75. Lewes, *The Foundation of a Creed,* 2:121.

76. Ibid., 2:116.

77. Ibid., 2:116–19.

78. George Eliot, "Worldliness and Other-Worldliness: The Poet Young," *Westminster Review* 11, new series (January 1857): 1–42 (42).

CHAPTER 4

1. Such inquiry anticipates current research into the cognitive value of nondeliberate or intuitive thought in complex intellectual activity. See Ryan, "Fictions of Mind."

2. Daniel Pick, *Faces of Degeneration: A European Disorder, c. 1848–1918* (Cambridge: Cambridge University Press, 1989), 15.

3. B. A. Morel, *Traité des dégénérescences physiques, intellectuelles et morales de l'espèce humaine et des causes qui produisent ces variétés maladives* (Paris: J. B. Baillière, 1857).

4. See Nancy Stephan, "Biological Degeneration: Races and Proper Places," in *Degeneration: The Dark Side of Progress,* edited by J. Edward Chamberlain and Sander L. Gilman (New York: Columbia University Press, 1985), 97–120; Jenny Bourne Taylor, *In the Secret Theatre of Home: Wilkie Collins, Sensation Narrative, and Nineteenth-Century Psychology* (London: Routledge, 1988), 64–70.

5. Eugene S. Talbot, *Degeneracy: Its Causes, Signs, and Results* (London: Walter Scott Ltd., 1899), 63.

6. Max Nordau, *Degeneration,* 19. All further references cited in the text.

7. Henry Maudsley, *The Pathology of Mind* (New York: D. Appleton & Co., 1890), vi.

8. Ibid., 67, 52.

9. Ibid., 67.

10. Lankester, *Degeneration,* 62.

11. Dana Seitler has shown how corporeal atavism stamps ancestral history back onto the present, thus highlighting how reversal and retrogression structure the very modernist ethos that attempts a break from the past. See Seitler, *Atavistic Tendencies: The Culture of Science in American Modernity* (Minneapolis: University of Minnesota Press, 2008).

12. Winter, *Mesmerized,* 20; Janet Oppenheim, *The Other World: Spiritualism and Psychical Research in England, 1850–1914* (Cambridge: Cambridge University Press, 1985), 218–20.

13. W. B. Carpenter, *Mesmerism, Spiritualism, &c,* 6.

14. Ibid., 19.

15. Ibid., 15.

16. See Alan Gauld, *A History of Hypnotism* (Cambridge: Cambridge University Press, 1995), 204, 273–98.

17. Braid, *Neurypnology; or, the Rationale of Nervous Sleep* (London: John Churchill, 1843), 12.

18. Chauncy Hare Townshend, *Facts in Mesmerism* (London: Longman, 1840), 7.

19. Oppenheim, *The Other World*, 221–22.

20. Myers, *Human Personality and Its Survival of Bodily Death*, 1:217. All further references cited in the text.

21. See Oppenheim, *The Other World*, 207–49.

22. Winter, *Mesmerized*, 187–212.

23. James Esdaile, *Mesmerism in India and Its Practical Application in Surgery and Medicine* (Hartford, CT: Silus Andrews & Son, 1847), 37.

24. Ibid., 45.

25. John Campbell Colquhoun, *Isis Revelata: An Inquiry into the Origin, Progress and Present State of Animal Magnetism* (Edinburgh: Maclachlan and Stewart, 1836), 95.

26. Elliotson, *Human Physiology*, 667.

27. Kelly Hurley has argued that neo-Gothic forms respond to the theory of natural selection in combination with degenerationism. Darwinian evolution reduces humans to brute beasts and implies that they are as likely to retrogress as they are to progress to a higher intellectual and moral state. See Hurley, *The Gothic Body: Sexuality, Materialism and Degeneration at the Fin de Siècle* (Cambridge: Cambridge University Press, 1996).

28. George Du Maurier, *Trilby* (1895; reprint, London: facsimile reprint, Broadview Press, 2003), 416.

29. Ibid., 176.

30. Wilkie Collins, "Magnetic Evenings at Home: To G. H. Lewes," Letter I, *The Leader* (January 17, 1852), 64–65.

31. Taylor, *Secret Theatre*, 6, 8. See also Nicholas Rance, *Wilkie Collins and Other Sensation Novelists* (Rutherford, NJ: Fairleigh Dickinson University Press, 1991), 64–80.

32. Wilkie Collins, *The Woman in White* (London: Macmillan, 2005), 20.

33. Wilkie Collins, *The Haunted Hotel* (Phoenix Mill, Gloucestershire: Alan Sutton, 1990), 141,165.

34. On science and gender in Collins see Sharrona Pearl, "Dazed and Abused: Gender and Mesmerism in Wilkie Collins," in *Victorian Literary Mesmerism*, edited by Martin Willis and Catherine Wynne (New York: Rodopi, 2006), 163–82.

35. Compare Nicholas Dames's account of "the culture of forgetfulness" in Collins's novels from the 1860s. See Dames, *Amnesiac Selves: Nostalgia, Forgetting and British Fiction 1810–1870* (Oxford: Oxford University Press, 2001), 167–205 (180–81).

36. On this topic see Nicholas Saul, "Half a Gypsy: The Case of Ezra Jennings in Wilkie Collins's *The Moonstone*," in *The Role of the Romanies: Images and Counter-Images of 'Gypsies'/Romanies in European Cultures*, edited by Nicholas Saul and Susan Tebbutt (Liverpool: Liverpool University Press, 2005), 119–44.

37. Wilkie Collins, *The Moonstone* (Oxford: Oxford University Press, 1999), 319. All further references cited in the text.

38. Pearl, "Gender and Mesmerism," 167; A. D. Hutter, "Dreams, Transformations, and Literature: The Implications of Detective Fiction," in *New Casebooks: Wilkie Collins*, edited by Lyn Pykett (New York: St. Martin's Press, 1998), 181–209 (181).

39. See, for example, a report of a lecture at the Royal Institution, March 12, 1852, "On the Influence of Suggestion in Modifying and Directing Muscular Movement Independently of Volition," published in *Nature and Man*, 169–72; "Electro-Biology and Mesmerism," *Quarterly Review* 93 (September 1853): 501–57.

40. Arthur Conan Doyle, *A Study in Scarlet*, edited by Owen Dudley Edwards (Ox-

ford and New York: Oxford University Press, 1993), 6. All further references cited in the text.

41. Laura Otis describes how detection in Holmes's stories functions as "an imperial immune system" as it "identif[ies] and neutraliz[es] living threats to society" that invade from new regions of contact. Otis, *Membranes: Metaphors of Invasion in Nineteenth-Century Literature, Science, and Politics* (Baltimore: The Johns Hopkins University Press, 1999), 91.

42. Interestingly, Holmes's "methods"—including "retrospective narrative hypothesis, the importance of reading signs . . . the judicious use of tests, the preference for ruling out rather than ruling in, the use of maxims, and the claim to be engaged in a deductive science"—have been used to train medical students in diagnostic reasoning. See Kathryn Montgomery, "Sherlock Holmes and Clinical Reasoning," in *Teaching Literature and Medicine,* edited by Anne Hunsaker Hawkins and Marilyn Chandler McEntyre (New York: The Modern Language Association, 2000), 299–305, (299).

43. Smajic links ghost stories and detection through Victorian discoveries about the role of inference in vision. Smajic, *Ghost-Seers, Detectives, and Spiritualists: Theories of Vision in Victorian Literature and Science* (Cambridge: Cambridge University Press, 2010), 136.

44. In this way, as Nils Clausson has argued, the Gothic "questions and even subverts the aspirations of criminal science to subject crime and criminality to scientific analysis." See Clausson, "Degeneration, *Fin-de-Siècle* Gothic, and the Science of Detection: Arthur Conan Doyle's *The Hound of the Baskervilles* and the Emergence of the Modern Detective Story," *Journal of Narrative Theory* 35.1 (Winter 2005): 60–87 (63). This claim significantly revises Patrick Brantlinger's influential accounts both of sensation fiction as "a secularization and domestication of the mysteries of gothic romance" and of its maturation in the detective novel as the "transformation of metaphysical-religious knowledge into the solution of a crime puzzle." See Brantlinger, "What Is Sensational about the Sensational Novel?" *Nineteenth-Century Fiction* 37.1 (June 1982): 1–28 (8, 19).

45. J. Edward Chamberlin, "Images of Degeneration: Turnings and Transformations," in *Degeneration: The Myth of Progress,* edited by J. E. Chamberlin and S. L. Gilman (New York: Columbia University Press, 1985), 263–89.

46. Charles Darwin, *The Variation of Animals and Plants under Domestication,* 2 vols. (New York: D. Appleton & Co., 1887), 2:2.

47. Havelock Ellis, *The Criminal* (London: Walter Scott Publishing Co., 1913), 371.

48. Ibid., 252–53.

49. Henry Maudsley, *Body and Mind: An Inquiry into their Connection and Mutual Influence Especially in Reference to Mental Disorders* (New York: D. Appleton &Co., 1886), 57.

50. Ibid., 58.

51. Talbot, *Degeneracy,* 32

52. Ibid., 62.

53. Arthur Conan Doyle, "A Case of Identity," in *Sherlock Holmes: The Major Stories with Contemporary Critical Essay,* edited by John A. Hodgson (Boston: St. Martin's Press, 1994), 75. All further references cited in the text.

54. Brooks, *Realist Vision*, 3. On the panoramic vision "under the rooftops" see Jonathan Arac, *Commissioned Spirits*, 22–23.

55. Darwin, *Origin*, 397.

56. Smajic describes this scene as an enactment of the "disembodied panoptic eye" and evidence of Holmes's spiritualist powers—here levitation. Smajic, *Ghost-Seers, Detectives and Spiritualists*, 133.

57. Quoted from the original prospectus of the Society for Psychical Research. Published in Frank Podmore, *The Naturalization of the Supernatural* (New York: The Knickerbocker Press, 1908), 1.

58. See, for example, Podmore's conclusions about the physical phenomena of spiritualism: "the line between what was not possible to fraudulent ingenuity and what was not possible cannot be drawn with sufficient sharpness to arrant the invocation of any new agency." Podmore, *Apparitions and Thought-Transference: An Examination of the Evidence for Telepathy* (London: W. Scott Ltd., 1894), 37.

59. Oppenheim, *The Other World*, 111–58; Luckhurst, *Invention of Telepathy*, 56–58.

60. Arthur Conan Doyle, *The New Revelation* (London: Hodder and Stoughton, 1918), 39.

61. Arthur Conan Doyle, *The History of Spiritualism*, 2 vols. (New York: Arno Press, 1975), 1:181.

62. F. W. H. Myers "The Subliminal Self," *Proceedings of the Society for Psychical Research* 11 (1895), 334–593 (338).

63. Ibid., 338.

64. Arthur Pierce and Frank Podmore, "Subliminal Self or Unconscious Cerebration," *Proceedings of the Society for Psychical Research* 11 (1895): 317–32 (332).

65. Doyle, *History of Spiritualism*, 1: 38.

66. Ibid., 1: 42.

67. Alfred Russel Wallace, *Miracles and Modern Spiritualism* (London: George Redway, 1896), 216.

68. Cesare Lombroso, "Nordau's 'Degeneration': Its Value and Its Errors," *The Century Magazine* 50 (May–October 1895): 936–40.

69. Cesare Lombroso, *The Man of Genius*, edited by Havelock Ellis (New York: Walter Scott Publishing, 1901), 21.

70. Ibid., 63

71. Ibid., 170.

72. Ibid., 35.

73. Lombroso, "Nordau's 'Degeneration,'" 937.

74. Gina Lombroso-Ferrero, *Criminal Man According to the Classification of Cesare Lombroso* (New York: Putnam, 1911), xiv–xv.

75. Henry Maudsley, "Heredity in Health and Disease," *Fortnightly Review* 39 (January–June 1886): 648–59 (656).

76. Ibid., 651.

77. Ibid., 652.

78. Darwin, *On the Origin of Species*, 110.

79. Quoted in Ellis, *The Criminal*, 253.

80. Darwin, *The Voyage of the Beagle* (London: J. M. Dent & Sons Ltd., 1959), 195.

81. Cannon Schmitt, *Darwin and the Memory of the Human: Evolution, Savages and South America* (Cambridge: Cambridge University Press, 2009), 32–56.

82. Pick, *Faces of Degeneration*, 109–52; David G. Horn, *The Criminal Body: Lombroso and the Anatomy of Deviance* (New York: Routledge, 2003), 43–51.

83. See Ronald R. Thomas, *Detective Fiction and the Rise of Forensic Science* (Cambridge: Cambridge University Press, 1999), 75–90.

84. Arthur Conan Doyle, *The Hound of the Baskervilles* (New York: The Modern Library, 2002), 42. All further references cited in the text.

85. Doyle, "A Scandal in Bohemia," *Sherlock Holmes*, 32.

86. Doyle, "The Speckled Band," *Sherlock Holmes*, 153.

87. Carpenter, *Principles*, 640.

88. For an 1890s account of the cranial morphology of prehistoric man, see J. G. Garson, "Remarks on Skulls Dredged from the Thames in the Neighbourhood of Kew," *The Journal of the Anthropological Institute of Great Britain and Ireland* 20 (1891): 20–25.

89. Doyle, *History of Spiritualism*, 1:181.

90. Doyle, "When the World Screamed," in *The Complete Professor Challenger Stories* (London: John Murray, 1976), 548.

91. Ibid., 548.

92. Doyle, *The Lost World and Other Stories*, edited by Philip Gooden (London: Penguin, 2001), 158.

93. Doyle, "The Land of Mist," *Complete Professor Challenger*, 501.

94. Doyle, "The Final Problem," *Sherlock Holmes*, 218.

CHAPTER 5

1. Thomas Hardy, *The Life and Work of Thomas Hardy*, edited by Michael Millgate (London: Macmillan, 1984), 256.

2. Ibid., 214.

3. Gowan Dawson has shown how Victorians associated mid-century evolutionism with "the notoriously dissipated ethics of the pagan world." See Dawson, *Darwin, Literature and Victorian Respectability* (Cambridge: Cambridge University Press, 2007), 92.

4. "The Science of Fiction," *Thomas Hardy's Personal Writings*, edited by Harold Orel (New York: St. Martin's Press, 1990), 134–38 (137).

5. John Glendening, *The Evolutionary Imagination*, 69–106.

6. The now commonplace emphasis on Darwinian determinism in Hardy's novels has been challenged in recent years. Gillian Beer argues that his characters find a consoling sense of continuity with nature, despite being sidelined by its non-human-centered plot. In *Dying to Know*, George Levine points out that Hardy's naturalistic pessimism is offset by his emphasis on human consciousness as the source of meaning, "although with no sense that such power can transform the material world." See Beer, *Darwin's Plots*, 220–41; Levine, *Dying to Know*, 200–219 (202).

7. See Glendening, *Evolutionary Imagination*, 70.

8. McKeon, *The Origins of the English Novel*, 225–72.

9. Hardy, "Candour in English Fiction, *Personal Writings,* 125–33 (127–28).

10. Ibid., 127.

11. See David. J. de Laura, "'The Ache of Modernism' in Hardy's Later Novels," *ELH* 34.3 (September 1967): 380–99.

12. J. Hillis Miller, *Thomas Hardy: Distance and Desire* (Cambridge, MA: Harvard University Press, 1970), 17.

13. Bruno Latour, *We Have Never Been Modern,* translated by Catherine Porter (Cambridge, MA: Harvard University Press, 1993), 36–37.

14. Ibid., 37.

15. See Kevin Padian, "'A Daughter of the Soil': Themes of Deep Time and Evolution in Thomas Hardy's *Tess of the d'Urbervilles,*" *Thomas Hardy Journal* 13.3 (1997): 65–81.

16. Kay Young describes such episodes in *Tess* as "dissociative," where dissociation means limiting self-reflection to that which is necessary for survival. Young suggests that these dissociative, automatic states precipitate tragic events in the novel but also represent a form of defense against their psychic consequences. See Young, *Imagining Minds: The Neuro-Aesthetics of Austen, Eliot, and Hardy* (Columbus: The Ohio State University Press, 2010), 157–84.

17. Thomas Hardy, *The Return of the Native,* edited by Phillip Mallett, 2nd ed. (New York: W. W. Norton and Co., 2006), 8. All further references cited in the text.

18. Jules Law links the conflation of prehistoric, medieval, and modern in the landscapes of *The Return of the Native* and *Tess* to the depiction of the female body as a site of conflicting attitudes toward historical change. See Law, "Sleeping Figures: Hardy, History, and the Gendered Body," *ELH* 65.1 (1998): 223–57.

19. Elaine Scarry points out the difference between Hardy's depictions of the deep embodiment of work in contrast to the half-absorption in one's activity of "play" (working the land as opposed to walking through it). See Scarry, *Resisting Representation* (New York: Oxford University Press, 1994), 49–90 (52).

20. In an interview with William Archer, Hardy explained, "my pessimism, if pessimism it be, does not involve the assumption that the world is going to the dogs. . . . On the contrary, my practical philosophy is distinctly meliorist." "Real Conversations II—With Mr. Thomas Hardy," *Critic* 38 (April 1901): 309–18 (317).

21. Hardy, *The Dynasts* (London: Macmillan, 1978), 21.

22. Ibid, 22.

23. Ibid, 702.

24. Ibid., 705.

25. Ibid., 8.

26. Henry Lyman, *Insomnia and Other Disorders of Sleep* (Chicago: W. T. Keener, 1885), 168.

27. Hack Tuke, *Sleep Walking and Hypnotism,* 37–40, 101.

28. Ibid., 5

29. Ibid., 40.

30. Ibid., 44.

31. Lyman, *Insomnia and Other Disorders,* 161–62.

32. Hamilton, *Lectures on Metaphysics,* 1:236.

33. Ibid., 1:235.

34. Esquirol, *Mental Maladies,* 93.

35. Maudsley, *Pathology of Mind*, 112, 404.

36. See Tony James, *Dream, Creativity, and Madness in Nineteenth-Century France* (Oxford: Clarendon Press, 1995), 145–51; Ivan Leudar and Philip Thomas, *Voices of Reason, Voices of Insanity: Studies of Verbal Hallucinations* (London: Routledge, 2002), 8–14.

37. Alexandre Brière de Boismont, *Hallucinations, or the Rational History of Apparitions, Dreams, Ecstasy, Magnetism, and Somnambulism* (Philadelphia: Lindsay and Blakiston, 1853), xi. All further references cited in the text.

38. See Frank Podmore, *Studies in Psychical Research* (London: Routledge and Kegan Paul, Trench Trübner & Co., 1897), 9.

39. Frank Podmore, *Modern Spiritualism: A History and a Criticism*, 2 vols. (London: Metheun, 1902), 2: 76.

40. Ibid., 2: 76–77.

41. Alfred Russell Wallace, *Miracles and Modern Spiritualism*, 43.

42. F. W. H. Myers, "Science and a Future Life," in *Science and a Future Life with Other Essays* (London: Macmillan, 1901), 1–50.

43. Myers, "Tennyson as Prophet," in *Science and a Future Life*, 127–65 (128). All further references cited in the text.

44. *The Literary Notebooks of Thomas Hardy*, edited by Lennart A. Björk, 2 vols. (London: Macmillan, 1985), 2:865n1.

45. Ibid., 2:1907n

46. Hardy, "Letter to Dr. C. W. Saleeby," quoted in Hardy, *Life and Work*, 400.

47. See Willburn, *Possessed Victorians*, 115–40.

48. Marie Corelli, *A Romance of Two Worlds* (London, 1896), 176. See Willburn's discussion of "Victorian Women in Outer Space," in *Possessed Victorians*, 134–40.

49. Alisha Siebers, "Marie Corelli's Magnetic Revitalizing Power," in *Victorian Literary Mesmerism*, edited by Martin Willis and Catherine Wynne (Amsterdam: Rodopi B.V., 2006), 183–202.

50. Théordore Flournoy, *From India to the Planet Mars: A Study of a Case of Somnambulism*, translated by Daniel B. Vermilye (New York and London: Harper Brothers Publishers, 1900), 140.

51. Ibid., 26.

52. "To William Archer," November 24, 1898, in *Thomas Hardy: Selected Letters*, edited by Michael Millgate (Oxford: Clarendon Press, 1990), 125.

53. "To H. W. Massingham," July 7, 1907, in *Selected Letters*, 194.

54. Hardy, *Life and Works*, 309.

55. See "To Sir George Douglas," December 21, 1888; "To Amy Lowell," January 26, 1919, *Selected Letters*, 51, 329.

56. "As I am old-fashioned, and think lucidity a virtue in poetry, as in prose, I am at a disadvantage in criticizing recent poets who apparently aim at obscurity." "To Ezra Pound," March 18, 1921, *Selected Letters*, 357.

57. Susan M. Miller, "Thomas Hardy and the Impersonal Lyric," *Journal of Modern Literature* 30.3 (2007): 94–115.

58. Thomas Hardy, *Collected Poems of Thomas Hardy* (New York: Macmillan, 1958).

59. Ibid., 98.

60. This point is made by Marjorie Levinson. See Levinson, "Object-Loss and Object-Bondage: The Economics of Representation in Hardy's Poetry," *ELH* 73 (2006): 549–80.

61. *Daily Chronicle,* December 28, 1899. Reprinted in *Thomas Hardy's Public Voice: The Essays, Speeches, and Miscellaneous Prose,* edited by Michael Millgate (Oxford: Clarendon Press, 2001), 156–58 (157).

62. Ibid., 158.

63. Hardy, *Life and Works,* 323.

64. Ibid., 123.

65. Ibid., 227.

CONCLUSION

1. Antonio Damasio, *Self Comes to Mind: Constructing the Conscious Brain* (New York: Pantheon Books, 2010), 13.

2. Damasio, *The Feeling of What Happens: Body and Emotion in the Making of Consciousness* (New York: Harcourt Brace & Co., 1999), 26.

3. Ibid, 195–98.

4. Ibid., 4.

5. Ibid, 8.

6. Young, *Imagining Minds,* 1–28.

7. William James, *The Principles of Psychology,* 3 vols. (Cambridge, MA: Harvard University Press, 1981), 1:284.

8. Ibid., 354.

9. Ibid., 223.

10. Ibid., 286.

11. Ibid., 291.

WORKS CITED

Ackroyd, Peter. *Dickens.* London: Sinclair-Stevenson, 1990.

Alley, Sarah. *Account of a Trance or Vision of Sarah Alley.* New York: Joseph Rakestraw, 1807.

Agassiz, Louis. "The Geographical Distribution of Animals." *Christian Examiner and Religious Miscellany* 48.2 (1850): 181–204.

Amundson, Ron. Introduction to *On the Nature of Limbs,* by Richard Owen. Chicago: University of Chicago Press, 2007.

Anderson, Amanda. *Powers of Distance: Cosmopolitanism and the Cultivation of Detachment.* Princeton, NJ: Princeton University Press, 2001.

Arac, Jonathan. *Commissioned Spirits: The Shaping of Social Motion in Dickens, Carlyle, Melville, and Hawthorne.* New Brunswick, NJ: Rutgers University Press, 1979.

Atkinson, Henry G., and Harriet Martineau. *Letters on the Laws of Man's Nature and Development.* Boston: Josiah P. Mendum, 1851.

Bain, Alexander. *The Emotions and the Will.* 2nd ed. London: Longmans Green & Co., 1865.
———. *The Senses and the Intellect.* London: Longman, Green & Co., 1873.

Barlow, John. *On Man's Power over Himself to Prevent or Control Insanity.* 2nd ed. London: William Pickering, 1843.

Beer, Gillian. *Darwin's Plots: Evolutionary Narrative in Darwin, George Eliot, and Nineteenth-Century Fiction.* 2nd ed. Cambridge: Cambridge University Press, 2000.

Bender, John. "Enlightenment and the Scientific Hypothesis." *Representations* 60 (Winter 1997): 1–23.

Benneville, George de. *The Life and Trance of Dr. George de Benneville.* Norristown, PA: David Sower, 1815.

Boismont, Alexandre Brière de. *Hallucinations, or the Rational History of Apparitions, Dreams, Ecstasy, Magnetism, and Somnambulism*. Philadelphia: Lindsay and Blakiston, 1853.

Bolt, Peter. "Jane Eyre's Three Paintings: Biblical Warnings and Greek Legends." *Victorian Web*, http://victorianweb.org/authors/bronte/cbronte/bolt7.html (January 2012).

Bowler, Peter J. *The Eclipse of Darwinism: Anti-Darwinian Evolution Theories in the Decade around 1900*. Baltimore: The Johns Hopkins University Press, 1983.

———. *The Non-Darwinian Revolution: Reinterpretation of a Historical Myth*. Baltimore: The Johns Hopkins University Press, 1992.

———. *Reconciling Science and Religion: The Debate in Early Twentieth-Century Britain*. Chicago: University of Chicago Press, 2001.

Bown, Nicola. "What Is the Stuff That Dreams Are Made Of?" In *The Victorian Supernatural*, edited by Nicola Bown, Carolyn Burdett, and Pamela Thurschwell, 151–72. Cambridge: Cambridge University Press, 2004.

Braid, James. *Neurypnology; or, the Rationale of Nervous Sleep*. London: John Churchill, 1843.

———. *Observations on Trance and Human Hibernation*. London: John Churchill, 1850.

Bramwell, J. Milne. "Hypnotism: A Reply to Recent Critics." *Brain* 22.1 (1899): 141–56.

Brantlinger, Patrick. "What Is Sensational about the Sensational Novel?" *Nineteenth-Century Fiction* 37.1 (June 1982): 1–28.

———. "Victorians and Africans: The Genealogy of the Myth of the Dark Continent." *Critical Inquiry* 12 (1985): 166–203.

Braun, Gretchen. "A Great Break in the Common Course of Confession: Narrating Loss in Charlotte Brontë's *Villette*." *ELH* 78.1 (Spring 2011): 189–212.

Brigham, Amariah. *Observations on the Influence of Religion upon the Health and Welfare of Mankind*. Boston: Marsh, Capen & Lyon, 1835.

Brontë, Charlotte. *The Poems of Charlotte Brontë*, edited by Tom Winnifrith. Oxford: Basil Blackwell, 1984.

———. *Villette*. Ware, Hertfordshire: Wordsworth Editions Ltd., 1999.

———. *Jane Eyre*. London: Penguin, 2006.

Brooks, Peter. *Realist Vision*. New Haven, CT: Yale University Press, 2005.

Buchan, William. *Domestic Medicine: or a Treatise on the Prevention and Cure of Diseases by Regimen and Simple Medicine*. 9th ed. London: W. Strahan et al., 1784.

———. *Advice to Mothers*. Boston: Joseph Bumstead, 1809.

Byerly, Alison. *Realism, Representation, and the Arts in Nineteenth-Century Literature*. Cambridge: Cambridge University Press, 1997.

Cadwallader, Jen. "Spirits of the Age: Ghost Stories and the Victorian Psyche." Ph.D. diss., University of North Carolina at Chapel Hill, 2009.

Caldwell, Janis McLarren. *Literature and Medicine in Nineteenth-Century Britain*. Cambridge: Cambridge University Press, 2004.

Calmet, Augustine. *The Phantom World, or the Philosophy of Spirits, Apparitions &c*. London: Richard Bentley, 1850.

Carpenter, William B. "Physiology an Inductive Science." *British and Foreign Medical Review* 5 (April 1838): 317–42.

———. "Electro-Biology and Mesmerism." *Quarterly Review* 93 (September 1853): 501–57.

———. "Spiritualism and Its Recent Converts." *Quarterly Review* 131 (October 1871): 301–53.

———. "On the Fallacies of Testimony in Relation to the Supernatural." *Contemporary Review* (January 1876): 279–95.

———. *Mesmerism, Spiritualism &c. Historically and Scientifically Considered*. New York: D. Appleton & Co., 1877.

———. "Nature and Law," *The Modern Review* 1 (October 1880): 748–70.

———. *Nature and Man: Essays Scientific and Philosophical.* London; K. Paul, Trench & Co., 1888.

———. *Principles of Mental Physiology.* 4th ed. New York: D. Appleton & Co., 1894.

Carroll, David. *George Eliot and the Conflict of Interpretations.* Cambridge: Cambridge University Press, 1992.

Carroll, Joseph. "Introduction." *On the Origin of Species by Means of Natural Selection,* edited by Charles Darwin. Peterborough, ON: Broadview Press, 2003.

Casaubon, Meric. *A Treatise Concerning Enthusiasme,* edited by Paul J. Korshin. 1656; reprint Gainesville, FL: Scholars' Facsimiles and Reprints, 1970.

Catalogue of the Library of Charles Dickens from Gadshill and Catalogue of the Library of W. M. Thackeray. London: Piccadilly Fountain Press, 1935.

Chamberlin, J. Edward. "Images of Degeneration: Turnings and Transformations." In *Degeneration: The Myth of Progress,* edited by J. E. Chamberlin and S. L. Gilman, 263–89. New York: Columbia Press, 1985.

Chambers, Robert. *Vestiges of the History of Natural Creation.* 10th ed. London: John Churchill, 1853.

Chan D. et al. "The Clinical Profile of Right Temporal Lobe Atrophy." *Brain* 132.5 (2009): 1287–98.

Charet, F. X. *Spiritualism and the Foundations of C. G. Jung's Psychology.* Albany, NY: SUNY Press, 1993.

Clarke, J. Mitchell Clarke. "Hysteria and Neurasthenia: Papers on Hypnotism, Hysterical Somnambulism, and Double Consciousness." *Brain* 17.2 (1894): 272–80.

Clausson, Nils. "Degeneration, *Fin-de-Siècle* Gothic, and the Science of Detection: Arthur Conan Doyle's *The Hound of the Baskervilles* and the Emergence of the Modern Detective Story." *Journal of Narrative Theory* 35.1 (Winter 2005): 60–87.

Collins, Wilkie. "Magnetic Evenings at Home: To G. H. Lewes." *The Leader,* January 17, 1852.

———. *The Haunted Hotel.* Phoenix Mill, Gloucestershire: Alan Sutton Publishing, 1990.

———. *Heart and Science.* Peterborough, ON: Broadview Press, 1997.

———. *The Moonstone.* Oxford: Oxford University Press, 1999.

———. *The Woman in White.* London: Macmillan, 2005.

Colquhoun, John Campbell. *Isis Revelata: An Inquiry into the Origin, Progress, and Present State of Animal Magnetism.* Edinburgh: Maclachlan and Stewart, 1836.

Comte, Auguste. *A General View of Positivism.* Translated by J. H. Bridges. London: Trübner & Co., 1865.

Conolly, John. *An Inquiry Concerning the Indications of Insanity,* edited by Richard Hunter and Ida Macalpine. London: Dawsons of Pall Mall, 1964.

Corelli, Marie. *A Romance of Two Worlds.* London, 1896.

Corning, J. "Epilepsy: Its Clinical Manifestation, Pathology, and Treatment." *New York Medical Journal* 45 (1887): 685–89.

Crichton-Browne, James. *Stray Leaves from a Physician's Portfolio.* London: Hodder and Stoughton, 1927.

Dale, Peter Alan. *In Pursuit of a Scientific Culture: Science, Art, and Society in the Victorian Age.* Madison: University of Wisconsin Press, 1989.

Dallas, E. S. *The Gay Science.* 2 vols. London: Chapman & Hall, 1866.

Damasio, Antonio. *The Feeling of What Happens: Body and Emotion in the Making of Consciousness.* New York: Harcourt Brace & Co., 1999.

———. *Self Comes to Mind: Constructing the Conscious Brain.* New York: Pantheon Books, 2010.

Dames, Nicholas. *Amnesiac Selves: Nostalgia, Forgetting, and British Fiction 1810–1870*. Oxford: Oxford University Press, 2001.

———. *The Physiology of the Novel: Reading, Neural Science, and the Form of Victorian Fiction*. Oxford: Oxford University Press, 2007.

Darwin, Charles. *The Variation of Animals and Plants under Domestication*. 2 vols. New York: D. Appleton & Co., 1887.

———. *The Voyage of the Beagle*. London: J. M. Dent & Sons Ltd., 1959.

———. *On the Origin of Species*, edited by Joseph Carroll. Peterborough, ON: Broadview, 2003.

———. *The Descent of Man, and Selection in Relation to Sex*. London: Penguin, 2004.

———. *Evolutionary Writings*, edited by James A. Secord. Oxford: Oxford University Press, 2008.

Darwin, Erasmus. *Zoonomia, or the Laws of Organic Life*. 2 vols. Dublin: P. Byrne, 1796–1800.

Daston, Lorraine J. "British Reponses to Psycho-Physiology, 1860–1900." *Isis* 69 (1978): 192–208.

———. "Objectivity and the Escape from Perspective." In *The Science Studies Reader*, edited by Mario Biagiolli, 110–23. New York: Routledge, 1999.

Davis, Lennard J. *Factual Fictions: The Origins of the English Novel*. New York: Columbia University Press, 1983.

Davis, Michael. *George Eliot and Nineteenth-Century Psychology*. Aldershot, Hampshire: Ashgate Press, 2006.

Dawson, Gowan. *Darwin, Literature and Victorian Respectability*. Cambridge: Cambridge University Press, 2007.

Dennsky, O., and G. Lai. "Spiritualists and Religion in Epilepsy." *Epilepsy Behavior* 12.4 (May 2008): 636–43.

Dickens, Charles. "Well Authenticated Rappings." *Household Words* 17 (February1858): 217–20.

———. "Wonders Will Never Cease." *All the Year Round* 1 (September 1859): 497–500.

———. "The Haunted House." *All the Year Round*. Christmas Number (1859): 1–48.

———. "The Uncommercial Traveller." *All the Year Round* 2 (February1860): 392–96.

———. "Strange and Yet True." *All the Year Round* 7 (1862): 540–42.

———. "Doubtfully Divine Missions." *All the Year Round* 15 (May 1866): 404–8.

———. *The Pilgrim Edition of the Letters of Charles Dickens*. 12 vols. Oxford: Clarendon Press, 1965–2002.

———. *Uncollected Writings from Household Words, 1850–1859*, edited by Harry Stone. 2 vols. Bloomington: Indiana University Press, 1968.

———. *Our Mutual Friend*. Harmondsworth, Middlesex: Penguin Books, 1971.

———. *David Copperfield*. Hertfordshire: Wordsworth Classics, 1992.

———. *Bleak House*. Oxford: Oxford University Press, 1996.

———. *A Christmas Carol and Two Other Christmas Books*. London: Collector's Library, 2004.

Dixon, Edmund Saul. "A Microscopic Dream." *Household Words* 17 (April 1858): 396–400.

Dixon, Thomas M. *From Passions to Emotions: The Creation of a Secular Psychological Category*. Cambridge: Cambridge University Press, 2003.

Doyle, Arthur Conan Doyle. *The New Revelation*. London: Hodder and Stoughton, 1918.

———. *The History of Spiritualism*. 2 vols. New York: Arno Press, 1975.

———. *The Complete Professor Challenger Stories*. London: John Murray, 1976.

———. *A Study in Scarlet.* Oxford and New York: Oxford University Press, 1993.

———. *Sherlock Holmes: The Major Stories with Contemporary Critical Essays,* edited by John A. Hodgson. Boston: St. Martin's Press, 1994.

———. *The Lost World and Other Stories.* Edited by Philip Gooden. London: Penguin, 2001.

———. *The Hound of the Baskervilles.* New York: The Modern Library, 2002.

Du Maurier, George. *Trilby.* 1895. Reprint, London: Broadview Press, 2003.

During, Simon. "The Strange Case of Monomania: Patriarchy in Literature, Murder in *Middlemarch,* Drowning in *Daniel Deronda.*" *Representations* 23 (Summer 1988): 86–104.

Eadie, M. J., and P. F. Bladin. *A Disease Once Sacred: A History of the Medical Understanding of Epilepsy.* Eastleigh, South Hampton: John Libbey & Co., 2001.

Eagleton, Terry. *Myths of Power: A Marxist Study of the Brontës.* 3rd ed. Basingstoke, Hampshire: Palgrave Macmillan, 2005.

Eliot, George. "R. W. Mackay's *The Progress of the Intellect.*" *Westminster Review* 54 (1851): 353–68.

———. "Evangelical Teaching: Dr. Cumming," *Westminster Review* 64 (1855): 436–62.

———. "Review of *Modern Painters* Vol. III," *Westminster Review* 65 (1856): 625–50.

———. "Silly Novels by Lady Novelists." *Westminster Review.* 66 (1856): 442–61.

———. "Worldliness and Other-Worldliness: The Poet Young." *Westminster Review* 11. New series (1857), 1–42.

———. *The George Eliot Letters,* edited by Gordon S. Haight. 9 vols. New Haven, CT: Yale University Press, 1954–78.

———. *The Lifted Veil.* London: Virago Press, 1985.

———. "Notes on Form in Art." In *George Eliot: Selected Essays, Poems, and Other Writings,* edited by A. S. Byatt and Nicholas Warren, 231–36. London: Penguin Books, 1990.

———. *Middlemarch.* London: Penguin, 1994,

———. *Daniel Deronda.* London: Penguin Books, 1995.

———. *Adam Bede.* Oxford: Oxford University Press, 1996.

———. *Silas Marner.* Ann Arbor: Ann Arbor Media Group, 2004.

Elliotson, John. *Human Physiology.* London: Longman, Rees et al., 1835.

———. "Reports of Various Trials of the Clairvoyance of Alexis Didier, Last Summer, in London, Collected by Dr. Elliotson." *The Zoist* 2 (1844–45): 477–529.

———. "Instances of Double States of Consciousness Independent of Mesmerism." *The Zoist* 4 (1846–47): 157–87.

Elliott, Nathan. "Phrenology and the Visual Stereotype in Charlotte Brontë's *Villette.*" *Nineteenth-Century Studies* 22 (2008): 41–55.

Ellis, Havelock. *The Criminal.* London: Walter Scott Publishing Co., 1913.

Ender, Evelyn. *Sexing the Mind: Nineteenth-Century Fictions of Hysteria.* Ithaca, NY: Cornell University Press, 1995.

Ermath, Elizabeth Deeds. *Realism and Consensus in the English Novel.* Princeton, NJ: Princeton University Press, 1983.

Erwin, Edward, ed. *The Freud Encyclopedia: Theory, Therapy, and Culture.* New York: Routledge, 2001.

Esdaile, James. *Mesmerism in India and Its Practical Application in Surgery and Medicine.* Hartford, CT: Silus Andrews & Son, 1847.

Esquirol, Jean-Étienne. *Mental Maladies: A Treatise on Insanity.* Translated by E. K Hunt. Philadelphia: Lea and Blanchard, 1845.

Ferrier, James Frederick. "An Introduction to the Philosophy of Consciousness." *Blackwood's Edinburgh Magazine* 43 (April, June 1838): 437–52, 784–91.

Fisher, E. "Remarks on Epilepsy." *Journal of Nervous and Mental Disorders* 13 (1886): 481–87.

Fleck, J. I., D. L. Green, J. L. Stevenson et al. "The Transliminal Brain at Rest: Baseline EEG, Unusual Experiences, and Access to Unconscious Mental Activity." *Cortex* 44.10 (November–December 2008): 1353–63.

Flournoy, Théodore. *From India to the Planet Mars: A Study of a Case of Somnambulism.* Translated by Daniel B. Vermilye. New York and London: Harper Brothers Publishers, 1900.

Friedlander, Walter J. *The History of Modern Epilepsy: The Beginning, 1865–1914.* Westport, CT: Greenwood Press, 2001.

Gallagher, Catherine. *The Body Economic: Life, Death, and Sensation in Political Economy and the Victorian Novel.* Princeton, NJ: Princeton University Press, 2006.

Galvan, Jill. *The Sympathetic Medium: Feminine Channeling, the Occult, and Communication Technologies.* Ithaca, NY: Cornell University Press, 2010.

Garson, J. G. "Remarks on Skulls Dredged from the Thames in the Neighbourhood of Kew." *The Journal of the Anthropological Institute of Great Britain and Ireland* 20 (1891): 2–25.

Gauld, Alan. *A History of Hypnotism.* Cambridge: Cambridge University Press, 1995.

Gettelman, Debra. "Reverie, Reading, and the Victorian Novel." Ph.D. diss., Harvard University, 2005.

———. "'Making Out' Jane Eyre." *ELH* 74.3 (Fall 2007): 557–81.

Gilbert, Sandra M., and Susan Gubar. *The Madwoman in the Attic: The Woman Writer and the Nineteenth-Century Literary Imagination.* 2nd ed. New Haven, CT: Yale University Press, 2000.

Ginsberg, Michael. "Dickens and the Uncanny: Repression and Displacement in *Great Expectations.*" *Dickens Studies Annual: Essays on Victorian Fiction* 13 (1984): 115–24.

Glen, Heather. *Charlotte Brontë: The Imagination in History.* New York: Oxford University Press, 2002.

Glendening, John. *The Evolutionary Imagination in Late-Victorian Novels: An Entangled Bank.* Aldershot, Hampshire: Ashgate Publishing, 2007.

Gould, Stephen J. *The Structure of Evolutionary Theory.* Cambridge, MA: Belknap Press of Harvard University Press, 2002.

Granville, J. Mortimer. "Hypnotism." *British Medical Journal* (August 1881): 305.

Haeckel, Ernst. *Generelle Morphologie der Organismen.* 2 vols. Berlin: G. Reiner, 1866.

Hamilton, William. *Lectures on Metaphysics and Logic,* edited by H. L. Mansel and J. Veitch. 4 vols. Boston: Gould and Lincoln, 1859.

Hardy, Thomas. *A Pair of Blue Eyes.* New York: Henry, Holt & Co., 1874.

———. *Collected Poems of Thomas Hardy.* New York: Macmillan, 1958.

———. *The Dynasts.* London: Macmillan, 1978.

———. *The Life and Work of Thomas Hardy,* edited by Michael Millgate. London: Macmillan, 1984.

———. *The Literary Notebooks of Thomas Hardy,* edited by Lennart A. Björk. 2 vols. London: Macmillan, 1985.

———. *Thomas Hardy's Personal Writings.* edited by Harold Orel. New York: St. Martin's Press, 1990.

———. *Thomas Hardy: Selected Letters,* edited by Michael Millgate. Oxford: Clarendon Press, 1990.

———. *Thomas Hardy's Public Voice: The Essays, Speeches, and Miscellaneous Prose,* edited by Michael Millgate. Oxford: Clarendon Press, 2001.

————. *Tess of the d'Urbervilles*. London: Penguin Books, 2003.

————. *The Return of the Native*, edited by Phillip Mallett. 2nd ed. New York: W. W. Norton and Co., 2006.

Hardy, Thomas, and William Archer. "Real Conversations II—With Mr. Thomas Hardy." *Critic* 38 (April 1901): 309–18.

Hayles, N. Katherine. "Constrained Constructivism: Locating Scientific Inquiry in the Theater of Representation." In *Realism and Representation: Essays on the Problem of Realism in Relation to Science, Literature, and Culture,* edited by George Levine, 27–43. Madison: University of Wisconsin Press, 1993.

Heady, Emily W. "Must I Render an Account? Genre and Self-Narration in Charlotte Brontë's *Villette*." *Journal of Narrative Theory* 36.3 (2006): 341–64.

Hennedy, Marie C. "Deceit with Benign Intent: Story-Telling in *Villette*." *Brontë Studies* 28 (March 2003): 1–14.

Henrichsen, Janna. "Choosing Servitude: The Influence of the Mosaic Law in *Jane Eyre*." *Brontë Studies* 29 (July 2004): 105–10.

Henson, Louise. "'In the Natural Course of Things': Ghosts and Science in Dickens's *All the Year Round*." In *Culture and Science in the Nineteenth-Century Media,* edited by Louise Henson, Geoffrey Cantor, Gowan Dawson, Richard Noakes, and Sally Shuttleworth, 113–23. Aldershot, Hampshire: Ashgate Press, 2004.

————. "Investigations and Fictions: Charles Dickens and Ghosts." In *The Victorian Supernatural,* edited by Nicola Bown, Carolyn Burdett, and Pamela Thurschwell, 44–63. Cambridge: Cambridge University Press, 2004.

Herbert, Christopher. "The Occult in *Bleak House*." *Novel: A Forum on Fiction* 17.2 (Winter 1984): 101–15.

Herpin, Theodore. *Du pronostic et du traitement curative de l'épilepsie.* Paris: Ballière, 1852.

Hertz, Neil. *George Eliot's Pulse.* Stanford, CA: Stanford University Press, 2003.

Hodgkin, Thomas. "On Inquiries into the Races of Man." *Reports of the British Association for the Advancement of Science* 11 (1842): 52–55.

Holland, Henry. "The Natural History of Man." *Quarterly Review* 86 (1850): 1–40.

Holmes, Oliver Wendell. *The Autocrat of the Breakfast Table.* Boston: Houghton, Mifflin & Co., 1894.

Horn, David G. *The Criminal Body: Lombroso and the Anatomy of Deviance.* New York: Routledge, 2003.

Hughes, Daniel E. *Hughes' Practice of Medicine.* 12th ed. Philadelphia: P. Blakiston's Son & Co., 1922.

Hughes, Linda K., and Michael Lund. *The Victorian Serial.* Charlottesville: University Press of Virginia, 1991.

Hunt, H. "On Hypochondriasis and Other Forms of Nervous Disease." *Medical Times* 24 (1851): 150–53.

Hunter, J. Paul. *Before Novels: The Cultural Contexts of Eighteenth-Century English Fiction.* New York: W. W. Norton & Co., 1992.

Hunter, Richard A., and Ida Macalpine. "Dickens and Conolly: An Embarrassed Editor's Disclaimer." *TLS* 11 (August 1961): 534–35.

Hurley, Kelly. *The Gothic Body: Sexuality, Materialism and Degeneration at the Fin de Siècle.* Cambridge: Cambridge University Press, 1996.

Hutter, A. D. "Dreams, Transformations, and Literature: The Implications of Detective Fiction." In *New Casebooks: Wilkie Collins,* edited by Lyn Pykett, 181–209. New York: St. Martin's Press, 1998.

Huxley, Thomas Henry. "On the Physical Basis of Life," *Fortnightly Review* 11 (February 1868): 129–45.

———. *Evidence as to Man's Place in Nature*. New York: D. Appleton & Co., 1873.

———. *Evolution and Ethics*. London: Macmillan & Co., 1893.

———. *Lessons in Elementary Physiology*, edited by Frederic S. Lee, 545. New York: The Macmillan Company, 1900.

Jackson, John Hughlings. "On the Anatomical, Physiological, and Pathological Investigation of Epilepsies." *West Riding Lunatic Asylum Medical Reports* 3 (1873): 315–39.

———. "Intellectual Warnings of Epileptic Seizures." *Medical Times and Gazette* (December 23, 1876). 700–702.

———. "Lectures on the Diagnosis of Epilepsy." *The Medical Times and Gazette*. January 11, 1879, 29–33; January 25, 1879, 85–88; February 8, 1879, 141–43; March 7, 1879, 223–26.

———. "Evolution and Dissolution in the Nervous System." *British Medical Journal* 1 (1884): 591, 660, 703.

———. "Remarks on the Evolution and Dissolution of the Nervous System." *Journal of Mental Science* 33 (1887): 25–48.

———. "On a Particular Variety of Epilepsy ('Intellectual Aura')." *Brain* 11 (1888): 179–207.

———. *Selected Writings of John Hughlings Jackson*, edited by James Taylor, 2 vols., 45–118 (New York: Basic Books, 1958).

Jacobus, Mary. "The Buried Letter: Feminism and Romanticism in *Villette*." In *Villette: Charlotte Brontë*. New Casebooks Series, edited by Pauline Nestor, 121–40. New York: St. Martin's Press, 1992.

Jaffe, Audrey. *Vanishing Points: Dickens, Narrative, and the Subject of Omniscience*. Berkeley: University of California Press, 1991.

James, Tony. *Dream, Creativity, and Madness in Nineteenth-Century France*. Oxford: Clarendon Press, 1995.

James, William. *The Principles of Psychology*. 3 vols. Cambridge, MA: Harvard University Press, 1981.

———. *The Varieties of Religious Experience: A Study in Human Nature*. Scotts Valley, CA: IAP, 2009.

Kaplan, Fred. *Dickens and Mesmerism: The Hidden Springs of Fiction*. Princeton, NJ: Princeton University Press, 1975.

Kapogiannis, D., A. K. Barbey, M. Su et al. "Neuroanatomical Variability of Religiosity." *PLoS One* 4.9 (September 28, 2009): e7180.

Knox, Robert. *The Races of Men: A Fragment*. Philadelphia: Lea and Blanchard, 1850.

Kreilkamp, Ivan. *Voice and the Victorian Storyteller*. New York: Cambridge University Press, 2005.

Kucich, John. "Passionate Reserve and Reserved Passion in the Works of Charlotte Brontë." *ELH* 52.4 (Winter 1985): 913–37.

———. *Repression in Victorian Fiction: Charlotte Brontë, George Eliot, and Charles Dickens*. Berkeley: University of California Press, 1987.

Lamarck, Jean Baptiste. *Zoological Philosophy: An Exposition with Regard to the Natural History of Animals*. Translated by Hugh Elliot. London: Hafner Publishing, 1963.

Landau, Misia. *Narratives of Human Evolution*. New Haven, CT: Yale University Press, 1982.

Lankester, Edwin Ray. *Degeneration: A Chapter in Darwinism*. London: Macmillan & Co., 1880.

Larson, Janet L. "'Who Is Speaking?' Charlotte Brontë's Voices of Prophecy." In *Victorian Sages and Cultural Discourse: Renegotiating Gender and Power,* edited by Thaïs E. Morgan, 66–86. New Brunswick, NJ: Rutgers University Press, 1990.

Latour, Bruno. *We Have Never Been Modern.* Translated by Catherine Porter. Cambridge, MA: Harvard University Press, 1993.

Laura, David J. de. "'The Ache of Modernism' in Hardy's Later Novels." *ELH* 34.3 (September 1967): 380–99.

Law, Graham. *Serializing Fiction in the Victorian Press.* New York: Palgrave, 2000.

Law, Jules. "Sleeping Figures: Hardy, History, and the Gendered Body." *ELH* 65.1 (1998): 223–57.

Lawrence, Karen. "The Cypher: Disclosure and Reticence in *Villette.*" *Nineteenth-Century Literature* 42 (1988): 448–66.

Lawrence, William. *Lectures on Physiology, Zoology, and the Natural History of Man, Delivered at the Royal College of Surgeons.* London: J. Callow, 1819.

Laycock, Thomas. "On the Reflex Function of the Brain." *British and Foreign Medical Review* 19 (1845): 298–311.

———. *Mind and Brain; or, the Correlations of Consciousness and Organization.* 2 vols. Edinburgh: Sutherland and Knox, 1860.

Lennox, William Gordon, and Margaret A. Lennox. *Epilepsy and Related Disorders.* 2 vols. Boston: Little, Brown and Company, 1960.

Leudar, Ivan, and Philip Thomas. *Voices of Reason, Voices of Insanity: Studies of Verbal Hallucinations.* London: Routledge, 2002.

Levine, Caroline. *The Serious Pleasures of Suspense: Victorian Realism and Narrative Doubt.* Charlottesville: University of Virginia Press, 2003.

———. "Narrative Networks: *Bleak House* and the Affordances of Form." *Novel* 42.3 (Fall 2009): 517–23.

Levine, George. "George Eliot's Hypothesis of Reality." *Nineteenth-Century Fiction* 35.1 (1980): 1–28.

———. *The Realistic Imagination: English Fiction from Frankenstein to Lady Chatterley.* Chicago: University of Chicago Press, 1981.

———. *Darwin and the Novelists: Patterns of Science in Victorian Fiction.* Cambridge, MA: Harvard University Press, 1988.

———. *Dying to Know: Scientific Epistemology and Narrative in Victorian England.* Chicago: University of Chicago Press, 2002.

Levinson, Marjorie. "Object-Loss and Object-Bondage: The Economics of Representation in Hardy's Poetry." *ELH* 73 (2006): 549–80.

Lewes, George Henry. "Recent Novels: French and English." *Fraser's Magazine* 36 (1847): 686.

———. "Of Vision in Art." *Fortnightly Review* 1 (July 15, 1865): 572–89.

———. "Mr. Darwin's Hypotheses." Part III. *Fortnightly Review* 4 (July 1, 1868): 61–80.

———. "Dickens in Relation to Criticism." *Fortnightly Review* 17 (February 1872): 141–54.

———. *The Foundation of a Creed.* 2 vols. Problems of Life and Mind. First series. Boston: James R. Osgood & Co., 1875.

———. *The Physical Basis of Mind.* Problems of Life and Mind. 2nd series. London: Trübner & Co., 1877.

———. "On the Dread and Dislike of Science." *Fortnightly Review* 29 (June 1878): 805–15.

———. *The Study of Psychology.* Problems of Life and Mind. Third series. London: Trübner & Co., 1879.

Lindquist, Jason. "'The Mightiest Instrument of the Physical Discoverer': The Visual 'Imagination' and the Victorian Observer." *Journal of Victorian Culture* 13.2 (2008): 171–99.

Livingston, Paisley. "Why Realism Matters: Literary Knowledge and the Philosophy of Science." In *Realism and Representation: Essays on the Problem of Realism in Relation to Science, Literature, and Culture,* edited by George Levine, 134–54. Madison: University of Wisconsin Press, 1993.

Logan, Peter Melville. *Nerves and Narratives: A Cultural History of Hysteria in Nineteenth-Century British Prose.* Berkeley: University of California Press, 1997.

Lombroso, Cesare. "Nordau's 'Degeneration': Its Value and Its Errors." *The Century Magazine* 50 (May–October 1895): 936–40.

———. *The Man of Genius,* edited by Havelock Ellis. New York: Walter Scott Publishing, 1901.

Lombroso-Ferrero, Gina. *Criminal Man According to the Classification of Cesare Lombroso.* New York: Putnam, 1911.

Luckhurst, Roger. *The Invention of Telepathy.* Oxford and New York: Oxford University Press, 2002.

———. "Passages in the Invention of the Psyche: Mind-Reading in London, 1881–84." In *Transactions and Encounters: Science and Culture in the Nineteenth Century,* edited by Roger Luckhurst and Josephine McDonagh, 117–50. Manchester: Manchester University Press, 2002.

Lukács, György. "Realism in the Balance." In *Aesthetics and Politics,* edited by Ernst Bloch, 28–59. London: Verso, 1977.

Lyman, Henry. *Insomnia and Other Disorders of Sleep.* Chicago: W. T. Keener, 1885.

Macnish, Robert. *The Philosophy of Sleep.* New York: D. Appleton & Co., 1834.

Marcus, Sharon. "The Profession of the Author: Abstraction, Advertising and *Jane Eyre.*" *PMLA* 110.2 (March 1995): 206–19.

Matthew, Patrick. *On Naval Timber and Arboriculture.* London: Longman, 1831.

Matus, Jill. *Shock, Memory and the Unconscious in Victorian Fiction.* Cambridge: Cambridge University Press, 2009.

Maudsley, Henry. *The Physiology of Mind; Being the First Part of a 3rd Ed. Revised, Enlarged, and in Great Part Rewritten of "The Physiology and Pathology of Mind."* London: Macmillan & Co., 1876.

———. "Heredity in Health and Disease." *Fortnightly Review* 39 (January–June 1886): 648–59.

———. *Body and Mind: An Inquiry into Their Connection and Mutual Influence Especially in Reference to Mental Disorders.* New York: D. Appleton &Co., 1886.

———. *Natural Causes and Supernatural Seemings.* 2nd ed. London: Kegan Paul, Trench & Co., 1887.

———. *The Pathology of Mind.* New York: D. Appleton & Co., 1890.

Mayo, Herbert. *Popular Superstitions and the Truths Contained Therein; with an Account of Mesmerism.* 3rd ed. Philadelphia: Lindsay and Blakiston, 1852.

McClintock, Anne. *Imperial Leather: Race, Gender and Sexuality in the Imperial Contest.* New York: Routledge, 1995.

McKeon, Michael. *The Origins of the English Novel 1600–1740.* Baltimore: The Johns Hopkins University Press, 1987.

Menke, Richard. "Fiction as Vivisection: G. H. Lewes and George Eliot." *ELH* 67 (2000): 617–53.

Metz, Nancy Aycock. "*Little Dorrit's* London: Babylon Revisited." *Victorian Studies* 33.3 (Spring 1990): 465–86.

Meyer, Susan. "Colonialism and the Figurative Strategy of *Jane Eyre.*" In *Macropolitics of Nineteenth-Century Literature: Nationalism, Exoticism, Imperialism,* edited by Jonathan Arac and Harriet Ritvo, 159–83. Philadelphia: University of Pennsylvania Press, 1991.

Miller, J. Hillis. *Thomas Hardy: Distance and Desire.* Cambridge, MA: Harvard University Press, 1970.

Miller, Susan M. "Thomas Hardy and the Impersonal Lyric." *Journal of Modern Literature* 30.3 (2007): 94–115.

Mitchell, Samuel L. *Devotional Somnium or a Collection of Prayers and Exhortations Uttered by Miss Rachel Baker in The City of New York.* Sangerfield, NY: Van Winkle and Wriley, 1816.

Moglen, Helene. *Charlotte Brontë: The Self Conceived.* Madison: University of Wisconsin Press, 1984.

Moll, Albert. *Hypnotism.* 2nd ed. London: Walter Scott, 1890.

Montgomery, Kathryn. "Sherlock Holmes and Clinical Reasoning." *Teaching Literature and Medicine,* edited by Anne Hunsaker Hawkins and Marilyn Chandler McEntyre, 299–305. New York: The Modern Language Association, 2000.

Moore, James R. *The Post-Darwinian Controversies: A Study of the Protestant Struggle to Come to Terms with Darwin in Great Britain and America 1870–1900.* Cambridge: Cambridge University Press, 1979.

Morel, B.A. *Traité des dégénérescences physiques, intellectuelles et morales de l'espèce humaine: et des causes qui produient ces variétiés maladives.* Paris: J. B. Baillière, 1857.

Morgentaler, Goldie. *Dickens and Heredity: When Like Begets Like.* Houndsmills, Basingstoke: Macmillan, 2000.

Myers, F. W. H. "The Subliminal Self." *Proceedings of the Society for Psychical Research* 11 (1895): 334–593.

———. *Science and a Future Life with Other Essays.* London: Macmillan, 1901.

———. *Human Personality and Its Survival of Bodily Death.* 2 vols. New York: Longmans, Green & Co., 1903.

Nagel, Thomas. *The View from Nowhere.* Oxford: Oxford University Press, 1986.

Newsom, Robert. *Dickens on the Romantic Side of Familiar Things.* New York: Columbia University Press, 1977.

Ng, F. "The Interface between Religion and Psychosis." *Australian and New Zealand Journal of Psychiatry* 15.1 (February 2007): 62–66.

Noakes, Richard. "Spiritualism, Science and the Supernatural in Mid-Victorian Britain." In *The Victorian Supernatural,* 23–43. Cambridge: Cambridge University Press, 2004.

Nordau, Max. *Degeneration.* 1895. Reprint, New York: Howard Fertig, 1968.

Nott, Josiah, and George Gidden. *Types of Mankind.* London: Trübner, 1854.

Nurbhai, Saleel, and K. M. Newton. *George Eliot, Judaism and the Novels: Jewish Myth and Mysticism.* Houndmills, Basingstoke: Palgrave, 2002.

Oberhelman, David. *Dickens in Bedlam: Madness and Restraint in His Fiction.* Fredericton, New Brunswick: York Press, 1995.

Oppenheim, Janet. *The Other World: Spiritualism and Psychical Research in England, 1850–1914.* Cambridge: Cambridge University Press, 1985.

———. *Shattered Nerves: Doctors, Patients, and Depression in Victorian England.* New York: Oxford University Press, 1991.

Otis, Laura. *Membranes: Metaphors of Invasion in Nineteenth-Century Literature, Science, and Politics.* Baltimore: The Johns Hopkins University Press, 1999.

———. *Networking: Communicating with Bodies and Machines in the Nineteenth Century.* Ann Arbor: University of Michigan Press, 2001.

Owen, Robert. *Footfalls on the Boundary of Another World*. Philadelphia: J. B. Lippincott & Co., 1860.

Padian, Kevin. "'A Daughter of the Soil': Themes of Deep Time and Evolution in Thomas Hardy's *Tess of the d'Urbervilles*." *Thomas Hardy Journal* 13.3 (1997): 65–81.

Pearce, John. "Dreamy States." *ACNR* 3.2 (May–June 2003): 17–20.

Pearl, Sharrona. "Dazed and Abused: Gender and Mesmerism in Wilkie Collins." In *Victorian Literary Mesmerism*, edited by Martin Willis and Catherine Wynne, 163–82. New York: Rodopi, 2006.Peltason, Timothy. "Esther's Will." *ELH* 59.3 (1992): 671–91.

Penfield, Wilder, and Herbert Henri Jasper. *Epilepsy and the Functional Anatomy of the Brain*. Boston: Little, Brown and Co., 1954.

Persinger, M. A. "Religious and Mystical Experiences as Artifacts of Temporal Lobe Function." *Perception Motor Skills* 53.3 (Part 2) (December 1983): 1255–62.

Peters, John G. "'We Stood at God's Feet, Equal': Equality, Subversion, and Religion in *Jane Eyre*." *Brontë Studies* 29 (March 2004): 53–64.

Pick, Daniel. *Faces of Degeneration: A European Disorder, c. 1848–1918*. Cambridge: Cambridge University Press, 1989.

———. *Svengali's Web: The Alien Enchanter in Modern Culture* (New Haven, CT: Yale University Press, 2000).

Pierce, Arthur, and Frank Podmore. "Subliminal Self or Unconscious Cerebration." *Proceedings of the Society for Psychical Research* 11 (1895): 317–32.

Podmore, Frank. *Apparitions and Thought-Transference: An Examination of the Evidence for Telepathy*. London: W. Scott Ltd., 1894.

———. *Studies in Psychical Research*. London: Kegan Paul, Trench, Trübner & Co., 1897.

———. *Modern Spiritualism: A History and a Criticism*. 2 vols. London: Metheun, 1902.

———. *The Naturalization of the Supernatural*. New York: The Knickerbocker Press, 1908.

Poovey, Mary. *Making a Social Body: British Cultural Formation, 1830–1864*. Chicago: University of Chicago Press, 1995.

———. *A History of the Modern Fact: Problems of Knowledge in the Sciences of Wealth and Society*. Chicago: University of Chicago Press, 1998.

Postlethwaite, Diana. "George Eliot and Science." In *The Cambridge Companion to George Eliot*, edited by George Levine, 98–118. Cambridge: Cambridge University Press, 2001.

Prichard, James Cowles. *Researches into the Physical History of Man*, edited by George W. Stocking. Chicago: University of Chicago Press, 1973.

———. *A Treatise on Insanity and Other Disorders Affecting the Mind*. 1837 reprint. New York: Arno Press, 1973.

Pyrohönen, Heta. *Bluebeard Gothic: Jane Eyre and Its Progeny*. Toronto: University of Toronto Press, 2010.

Ramachandran, V. S., and Sandra Blakeslee. *Phantoms in the Brain: Probing the Mysteries of the Human Mind*. New York: HarperCollins, 1998.

Rance, Nicholas. *Wilkie Collins and Other Sensation Novelists*. Rutherford, NJ: Fairleigh Dickinson University Press, 1991.

Redfield, Marc. *Phantom Formations: Aesthetic Ideology and the Bildungsroman*. Ithaca, NY: Cornell University Press, 1995.

Reed, Edward S. *From Soul to Mind: The Emergence of Psychology from Erasmus Darwin to William James*. New Haven, CT: Yale University Press, 1997.

Reid, John. *Essays on Hypochondriacal and Other Nervous Affections*. Philadelphia: M. Carey, 1817.

Richardson, Alan. *British Romanticism and the Science of the Mind*. Cambridge: Cambridge University Press, 2001.

Robertson, George Croom. "Prefatory Words." *Mind* 1.1 (January 1876): 1–6.

Robinson, Marilynne. *Absence of Mind: The Dispelling of Inwardness from the Modern Myth of the Self.* New Haven, CT: Yale University Press, 2010.

Romano, John. *Dickens and Reality.* New York: Columbia University Press, 1978.

Romberg, Moritz Heinrich. *A Manual of the Nervous Diseases of Man.* 2 vols. London: Sydenham Society, 1853.

Royle, Nicholas. *Telepathy and Literature.* Oxford: Basil Blackwell, 1990.

Ryan, Vanessa. "Fictions of Medical Minds: Victorian Novels and Medical Epistemology." *Literature and Medicine* 25 (Fall 2006): 277–97.

———. "Reading the Mind: From George Eliot's Fiction to James Sully's Psychology." *Journal of the History of Ideas* 70.4 (October 2009): 615–35.

Rylance, Rick. *Victorian Psychology and British Culture 1850–1880.* Oxford: Oxford University Press, 2000.

Sandby, George. *Mesmerism and its Opponents.* London: Longman, Brown, Green, and Longmans, 1848.

Saul, Nicholas. "Half a Gypsy: The Case of Ezra Jennings in Wilkie Collins's *The Moonstone.*" In *The Role of the Romanies: Images and Counter-Images of 'Gypsies'/Romanies in European Cultures,* edited by Nicholas Saul and Susan Tebbutt, 119–44. Liverpool: Liverpool University Press, 2005.

Saver, Jeffrey L., and John Rabin. "The Neural Substrate of Religious Experience." *Journal of Neuropsychiatry* 9.3 (Summer 1997): 498–510.

Scarry, Elaine. *Resisting Representation.* New York: Oxford University Press, 1994.

Schiller, J. "Physiology's Struggle for Independence in the First Half of the Nineteenth Century." *History of Science* 7 (1968): 64–89.

Schmitt, Cannon. *Darwin and the Memory of the Human: Evolution, Savages, and South America.* Cambridge: Cambridge University Press, 2009.

Schor, Hilary. *Dickens and the Daughter of the House.* Cambridge: Cambridge University Press, 1999.

Scott, Walter. *Guy Mannering.* Edinburgh: T & A Constable, 1901.

Seitler, Dana. *Atavistic Tendencies: The Culture of Science in American Modernity.* Minneapolis: University of Minnesota Press, 2008.

Shakespeare, William. *Riverside Shakespeare.* Boston: Houghton & Mifflin, 1974.

Shatto, Susan. "Miss Havisham and Mr. Hopes the Hermit: Dickens and the Mentally Ill." *Dickens Quarterly* 2.2 (June 1985): 43–49; and 2.3 (September 1985): 79–83.

Shaw, Harry E. *Narrating Reality: Austen, Scott, Eliot.* Ithaca, NY: Cornell University Press, 1999.

Shuttleworth, Sally. *George Eliot and Victorian Science.* Cambridge: Cambridge University Press, 1984.

———. "Psychological Definition and Social Power: Phrenology in the Novels of Charlotte Brontë." In *Nature Transfigured: Science and Literature 1700–1900,* edited by John Christie and Sally Shuttleworth, 121–51. Manchester: Manchester University Press.

———. *Charlotte Brontë and Victorian Psychology.* Cambridge: Cambridge University Press, 1996.

Shuttleworth, Sally, and Jenny Bourne Taylor, eds. *Embodied Selves: An Anthology of Psychological Texts 1830–1890.* Oxford: Clarendon Press, 1998.

Siebers, Alisha. "Marie Corelli's Magnetic Revitalizing Power." In *Victorian Literary Mesmerism,* edited by Martin Willis and Catherine Wynne, 183–202. Amsterdam: Rodopi B.V., 2006.

Smajic, Srdjan. *Ghost-Seers, Detectives, and Spiritualists: Theories of Vision in Victorian Literature and Science*. Cambridge: Cambridge University Press, 2010.

Smith, C. U. M. "Evolution and the Problem of Mind: Part II. John Hughlings Jackson." *Journal of the History of Biology* 15.2 (Summer 1982): 241–62.

Spencer, Herbert. "A Theory Concerning the Organ of Wonder." *The Zoist* 2 (1844–45): 316–25.

———. *Social Statics: or, the Conditions Essential to Human Happiness*. London: John Chapman, 1851.

———. "The Development Hypothesis," *The Leader*, March 20, 1852; reprinted in *Essays Scientific, Political and Speculative*, 3 vols. (New York: D. Appleton & Co., 1896), 1:1–7.

———. *The Principles of Psychology*. London: Longman, Brown, Green and Longmans, 1855.

———. *First Principles*. London: Williams and Norgate, 1862.

———. *The Principles of Psychology*. 2nd ed. 2 vols. New York: D. Appleton & Co. 1873.

———. *The Principles of Psychology*. 3rd ed. 2 vols. New York: D. Appleton & Co., 1883.

———. *Essays: Scientific, Political, and Speculative*. 3 vols. London: Williams and Norgate, 1891.

Spivak, Gayatri Chakravorty. "Three Women's Texts and a Critique of Imperialism." *Critical Inquiry* 12.1 (Autumn 1985): 243–61.

Stephan, Nancy Stephan. "Biological Degeneration: Races and Proper Places." In *Degeneration: The Dark Side of Progress*, edited by J. Edward Chamberlain and Sander L. Gilman, 97–120. New York: Columbia University Press, 1985.

Stone, Carole. "George Eliot's *Daniel Deronda*: The Case History of Gwendolen H." *Nineteenth-Century Studies* 7 (1993): 57–67.

Stone, Harry. *Dickens and the Invisible World: Fairy Tales, Fantasy, and Novel-Making*. Bloomington: Indiana University Press, 1979.

Sully, James. "The Dream as a Revelation." *Fortnightly Review* 59 (March 1893): 354–65.

Symonds, John Addington. *The Memoirs of John Addington Symonds*, edited by Phyllis Grosskurth. Chicago: University of Chicago Press, 1986.

Symonds, John Addington Sr. *Miscellanies by John Addington Symonds, M.D.*, edited by his son, John Addington Symonds. London: Macmillan and Co., 1873.

Taine, Hippolyte. "Charles Dickens: son talent et ses oeuvres." *Revue des deux mondes*. (February 1, 1856). 618–47.

Talbot, Eugene S. *Degeneracy: Its Causes, Signs, and Results*. London: Walter Scott Ltd., 1899.

Taves, Ann. *Fits, Trances, and Visions: Experiencing Religion and Explaining Experience from Wesley to James*. Princeton, NJ: Princeton University Press, 1999.

Taylor, Jenny Bourne. *In the Secret Theatre of Home: Wilkie Collins, Sensation Narrative, and Nineteenth-Century Psychology*. London: Routledge, 1988.

———. "Obscure Recesses: Locating the Victorian Unconscious." In *Writing and Victorianism*, edited by J. B. Bullen, 137–79. London: Longman, 1997.

Tebb, William, and Edward Perry Vollum. *Premature Burial and How It May Be Prevented with Special Reference to Trance, Catalepsy and Other Forms of Suspended Animation*. London: S. Sonnenschein & Co., 1896.

Temkin, Owsei. *The Falling Sickness: A History of Epilepsy from the Greeks to the Beginnings of Modern Neurology*. 2nd ed. Baltimore and London: The Johns Hopkins University Press, 1971.

Tennent, William. *Memoirs of the Life of Reverend William Tennent*. Poughkeepsie, NY: Paraclete and Sheldon Potter 1815.

Tennyson, Alfred. *The Princess: A Medley*, edited by Henry W. Boynton. New York: Leach, Shewell, & Co., 1896.

Tennyson, Hallam. *Alfred, Lord Tennyson: A Memoir by His Son.* 4 vols. Leipzig: Bernhard Tauchnitz, 1899.

Thomas, Isaiah. *The Prodigal Daughter, or, a Strange and Wonderful Relation.* Boston: Thomas's printing office, 1771.

Thomas, Ronald R. *Detective Fiction and the Rise of Forensic Science.* Cambridge: Cambridge University Press, 1999.

Thornton, Sara. "The Haunted House of Victorian Advertising: Hysteria, Paranoia, Perversion." *Anglophonia: French Journal of English Studies* 15 (2004): 59–73.

Thurschwell, Pamela. *Literature, Technology, and Magical Thinking.* Cambridge: Cambridge University Press, 2001.

———. "George Eliot's Prophecies: Coercive Second Sight and Everyday Thought Reading." In *The Victorian Supernatural*, 87–108.

———. "Forecasting Falls: Icarus from Freud to Auden to 9/11." *Oxford Literary Review* 30.2 (2008): 301–22.

Tissot, S. A. *Traité de l'épilepsie.* Lausanne: François Grasset, 1789.

Toker, Leona. *Towards the Ethics of Form in Fiction: Narratives of Cultural Remission.* Columbus: The Ohio State University Press, 2010.

Tougaw, Jason Daniel. *Strange Cases: The Medical Case History and the British Novel.* New York: Routledge, 2006.

Townshend, Chauncy Hare. *Facts in Mesmerism.* London: Longman, 1840.

Tromp, Marlene. *Altered States: Sex, Nation, Drugs, and Self-Transformation in Victorian Spiritualism.* Albany, NY: SUNY Press, 2006.

Tuke, Daniel Hack. "On the Mental Condition in Hypnosis." *The Journal of Mental Science* (April 1883): 55–80.

———. *Sleepwalking and Hypnotism.* London: J. & A. Churchill, 1884.

Twort, Charles William. *The Vision of Judgment or the Return of Joanna from Her Trance.* London: Charles W. Twort, 1829.

Tyndall, John. "'Materialism' and Its Opponents." *Fortnightly Review* 18 (1875): 579–99.

———. "Address Delivered Before the British Association Assembled at Belfast." In *Victorian Science: A Self-Portrait from the Presidential Addresses to the British Association for the Advancement of Science*, edited by George Basalla, William Coleman, and Robert H. Kargon, 436–78. New York: Anchor Books, 1970.

Tytler, Graeme. "Dickens's 'The Signalman.'" *The Explicator* 53.1 (Fall 1994): 26–29.

"Vestiges of the Natural History of Creation." *Edinburgh Review* 82 (July 1845): 1–85.

Vrettos, Athena. *Somatic Fictions: Imagining Illness in Victorian Culture.* Stanford, CA: Stanford University Press, 1995.

———. "Dying Twice: Victorian Theories of Déjà Vu." In *Disciplinarity at the Fin de Siècle*, edited by Amanda Anderson and Joseph Valente, 196–218. Princeton, NJ: Princeton University Press, 2002.

Wallace, Alfred Russel Wallace. *Miracles and Modern Spiritualism.* London: George Redway, 1896.

Waller N. G., B. A. Kojetin, T. J. Bouchard et al. "Genetic and Environmental Influences on Religious Interests, Attitudes, and Values: A Study of Twins Reared Apart and Together." *Psychological Science* 1 (1990): 138–42.

Warhol, Robyn R. "Double Gender, Double Genre in *Jane Eyre* and *Villette.*" *Studies in English Literature* 36.4 (1996): 857–75.

Watt, Ian. *The Rise of the Novel: Studies in Defoe, Richardson and Fielding.* Berkeley: University of California Press, 1957.

Wein, Toni. "Gothic Desire in Charlotte Brontë's *Villette.*" *Studies in English Literature* 39.4 (1999): 733–46.

Whone, Clifford. "Where the Brontës Borrowed Books." *Brontë Society Transactions* 11.2 (1950): 344–58.

Willburn, Sarah. *Possessed Victorians: Extra Spheres in Nineteenth-Century Mystical Writings.* Aldershot, Hampshire: Ashgate, 2006.

Willis, Martin, and Catherine Wynn, eds. *Victorian Literary Mesmerism.* Amsterdam: Rodopi B.V., 2006.

Wilson, Edward. O. *Consilience: The Unity of Knowledge.* New York: Alfred A. Knopf, 1998.

Winden, Patrick. *Silas Marner: Memory and Salvation.* New York: Twayne Publishers, 1992.

Winter, Alison. *Mesmerized: Powers of Mind in Victorian Britain.* Chicago: University of Chicago Press, 1998.

Wise, Thomas James, ed. *The Brontës: Their Lives, Friendships, and Correspondence.* 4 vols. Philadelphia: Porcupine Press, 1980.

Wood, Jane. *Passion and Pathology in Victorian Fiction.* Oxford: Oxford University Press, 2001.

Wordsworth, William. *Wordsworth: Poetical Works,* edited by Thomas Hutchinson. Oxford: Oxford University Press, 1987.

Wynne, Deborah. *The Sensation Novel and the Victorian Family Magazine.* Basingstoke, Hampshire: Palgrave, 2001.

Young, Kay. *Imagining Minds: The Neuro-Aesthetics of Austen, Eliot, and Hardy.* Columbus: The Ohio State University Press, 2010.

Young, R. M. *Mind, Brain and Adaptation in the Nineteenth Century: Cerebral Localization and Its Biological Context from Gall to Ferrier.* Oxford: Clarendon Press, 1970.

Young, Robert J. C. *Colonial Desire: Hybridity in Theory, Culture, and Race.* London: Routledge, 1995.

CPSIA information can be obtained
at www.ICGtesting.com
Printed in the USA
FFOW02n1902240317
33695FF